Rich and
Poor Countries

Rich and Poor Countries

Consequences of International Economic Disorder

4th edition

Hans W. Singer
Institute of Development Studies
University of Sussex

Javed A. Ansari
The City University

London
UNWIN HYMAN
Boston   Sydney   Wellington

Published by the academic division of
Unwin Hyman Ltd
15/17 Broadwick Street, London W1V 1FP

Allen & Unwin Inc.,
8 Winchester Place, Winchester, Mass. 01890, USA

Allen & Unwin (Australia) Ltd,
8 Napier Street, North Sydney, NSW 2060, Australia

Allen & Unwin (New Zealand) Ltd
in association with the Port Nicholson Press Ltd,
60 Cambridge Terrace, Wellington, New Zealand

First published in 1977
Second edition 1978
Third edition 1982
Fourth edition 1988

British Library Cataloguing in Publication Data

Singer, H. W.
   Rich and poor countries: consequences
   of international economic disorder. – 4th ed.
1. International economic relations
2. Developing countries – Foreign economic relations
I. Title   II. Ansari, Javed A.
337'.09172'4   HF1413
ISBN 0–04–445044–3

Library of Congress Cataloging-in-Publication Data

Singer, Hans Wolfgang, 1910–
   Rich and poor countries.
Includes bibliographies and index.
1. Developing countries – Economic conditions.
2. Economic history – 1971–   3. Developing countries
– Dependency on foreign countries.   I. Ansari, Javed A.
II. Title.
HC59.7.S467   1988   337'.09'048   87–30632
ISBN 0–04–445044–3 (pbk.: alk. paper)

Set in 10 on 12 point Bembo by Nene Phototypesetters Ltd
and printed in Great Britain by Billing & Sons Ltd, London and
Worcester.

Contents

Contents

vii

List of Abbreviations

ACP	African, Caribbean and Pacific countries associated with the EEC
BIS	Bank for International Settlements
CAP	Common Agricultural Policy (EEC)
CES	constant elasticity of substitution
CFF	Compensatory Financing Facility (IMF)
CFS	compensatory financing scheme
Comecon	Council for Mutual Economic Assistance
DAC	Development Assistance Committee (OECD)
EAF	Enlarged Access Facility
ECU	European currency unit
EDF	European Development Fund
EEC	European Economic Community
EMS	European Monetary System
EO	export-oriented/orientation
EOI	export-oriented industrialization
ERP	effective rate of protection
FAO	Food and Agriculture Organization (UN)
GAB	General Agreement to Borrow
GATT	General Agreement on Tariffs and Trade
GDP	gross domestic product
GNP	gross national product
GSP	General System of Preferences (UNCTAD)
GTSP	Global System of Trade Preferences (UNCTAD)
IBRD	International Bank for Reconstruction and Development
ICU	international clearing union
IDA	International Development Association (UN)
IMF	International Monetary Fund
IPC	International Commodity Programme
IS	import-substituting/substitution
ISI	import-substituting industrialization
ITC	International Tin Council
IWC	International Wheat Council
LAFTA	Latin American Free Trade Association

LAIA	Latin American Integration Association
LDC	less developed country
MFA	Multi-Fibre Agreement
MFN	most favoured nation
MIGA	Multilateral Investment Guarantee Agency
MNC	multinational corporation
MTN	multilateral trade negotiation
NIC	newly industrializing country
NIEO	New International Economic Order
NTB	non-tariff barrier
NTM	non-tariff measure
ODA	official development assistance
OECD	Organization for Economic Co-operation and Development
OIEO	Old International Economic Order
OMA	orderly marketing arrangements
OPEC	Organization of Petroleum Exporting Countries
RCA	relative comparative advantage
SAF	Structural Adjustment Facility
SDR	Special Drawing Rights (IMF)
SFS	supplementary financing scheme
STABEX	Export Stabilization Programme (EEC)
STYMIN	Mineral Exports Stabilization Programme
TNC	transnational corporation
UN	United Nations
UNCTAD	United Nations Conference on Trade and Development
UNDP	United Nations Development Programme
UNIDO	United Nations Industrial Development Organization
VER	voluntary export restraint

A Note on Terminology

The terminology used in this book is derived from Table 1.1 (p. 4). By 'poor countries' is meant the thirty-six low-income countries in the world that had a per capita income of less than US$ 400 in 1984. The terms 'developing countries' and 'Third World', used interchangeably, apply to three country groups: low-income countries, middle-income countries, and high-income oil exporters – also referred to as the Organization of Petroleum Exporting Countries (OPEC). Two sub-categories have been identified within the 'developing countries'. These are the thirty-nine African countries south of the Sahara, excluding South Africa, and the newly industrializing countries (NICs). The term 'developed countries' includes the industrial market economies of the western world, including Japan, and the East European non-market economies. The book is primarily concerned with the relationship between the 'developing poor countries' and the 'developed rich western countries'.

To our parents
Dr Henrick and Antonia Singer
and
Humayun and Tahera Ansari
and to
Raul Prebisch
intellectual, statesman and campaigner
for
Third World development

Preface

The 1980s have been a very difficult period for the developing countries, especially the poorest among them. Most of these have experienced negative income growth and sub-Saharan Africa has been the scene of widespread famine, malnutrition and acute poverty. Meanwhile the international economic system has become less and less responsive to the needs of the developing countries and, as the recently concluded UNCTAD VII deliberations illustrate, there is very little hope for revitalizing the 'North–South' dialogue.

Despite these setbacks, the Third World remains of interest to the peoples of the West. Ordinary men and women have shown massive support for non-governmental initiatives – such as those of Bob Geldof – for providing aid to Africa. The citizens of the western countries continue to be concerned about the injustices that the existing international economic order justifies and the inequalities that it promotes.

While no book on this subject can be up to date in the light of a rapidly changing situation, this book deals with some of the fundamental aspects of the relationship between rich and poor countries as they will continue to govern economic relations with the poorer countries, which contain a very high proportion of the people of the Third World and, indeed, of mankind as a whole.

This book has been written specifically to be useful to the general reader as well as to second- and third-year undergraduates. For that reason no highly technical or theoretical discussions should be expected. We have tried to combine a certain modest measure of theory with some discussion of policy problems which are of importance in the actual empirical relations between rich and poor countries. This fourth edition has been extensively rewritten to take account of the changed international environment, and there are new chapters on debt and aid and a new Statistical Appendix.

There are many people to whom we owe thanks for their advice and comments on various sections and drafts. Above all, we thank Professor Sir Charles Carter, the editor of the original series in which this book first appeared, and the then economics editor Mr C. Furth of Allen & Unwin for the patience with which they acted as midwives when this book was originally born. Our thanks are also due to the Editor of the *Journal of Modern African Studies* for letting us use in Chapter 1 material which first appeared in that publication, and to Professor H. C. H. Rao and P. C. Joshi who allowed us to draw upon H. W. Singer's contribution to V. K. R. V. Rao's *Festschrift* for the final chapter. We are also grateful to Hugh Corbet of the Trade Policy Research Centre and to the staff of the United Nations Conference on Trade and Development and the Overseas Development Institute in London for providing access to statistical sources. V. Jabamalai Arachi of the Centre for Research on the New International Economic Order, Madras (India), kindly provided a section on regional economic integration, in which field his knowledge is well known. We would also like to thank Frank Ellis and Lyn Reynolds of the Institute of Development Studies, University of Sussex, John Salter of Queen Mary College, University of London, and Robert Ballance of UNIDO for valuable comments, and Margot Cameron, Jennifer Kearns and Marlene Cassell for invaluable assistance with the preparation of the fourth edition.

Hans W. Singer
Javed A. Ansari

PART I

Perspectives

1 Introduction: The Current Economic Crisis and the Developing World

The current world economic crisis is a central concern of all students of economics today, and especially of those studying development problems. Theorists investigate the flaws in our approaches and institutions that gave birth to this present crisis. Policy-makers query the institutions and the rules that governed and shaped economic life in the post-Second World War era. The man in the street seeks an insight into the working of the national and the international economy in order to understand the implications of this chaos.

An alarming aspect of this concern is the introversion and short-sightedness of many of the solutions and schemes that are now put forward to overcome the impending catastrophe. The crisis is conceived of as being precipitated by events regarded as external to the western economic system – the instability and recent fall in primary commodities, the ups and downs of oil prices and the gyrations of OPEC politics, wars in the Middle East and elsewhere, droughts and famines in Africa exacerbated by civil wars, continuing debt crises, etc. – and *ad hoc* and piecemeal solutions are devised that seek to insulate the western world from such developments in the future. International economic organizations create elaborate mechanisms for coping with the balance of payments and debt problems arising, not only in the developing countries but also within the western world.

Table 1.1 describes the structure of the world economy in 1984. From this table we see that the global pattern of production and consumption is marked by a high degree of inequality. 50 per cent of

the world's population has a per capita gross national product (GNP)
that is less than 3 per cent of the per capita GNP of the 15 per cent of
the world's population living in the industrialized western nations.
Taking the world as a whole, the developing countries, which have
approximately 75 per cent of the world's population, have a GNP of
less than 20 per cent of the world's total. The vision of economic
inequality conjured up by these figures is staggering (this point is
developed in greater detail in Chapter 2). As the average annual
growth rate of GNP per capita since the mid-1960s has been virtually
the same for both the developed and the developing countries, as a
whole, there is clear evidence that the actual distance between the
rich and the poor countries has further widened during a period
when the world community had implicitly undertaken the responsibility of bridging the economic gap between the nations.

The difference in the material condition of people living in various

Table 1.1   *World economic structure, 1984*

Country groups[a]	No. of countries	Population (millions)	As % total	Total GNP (US$ billion)	As % total	Per capita GNP Average annual growth rate 1965–84
Low income	36	2,389.5	50.6	621.2	5.2	2.8
Middle income	60	1,187.6	25.2	1,484.5	12.6	3.1
High-income oil exporters	5	18.6	0.39	209.2	1.7	3.2
Industrial market economies	19	733.4	15.5	8,382.7	71.1	2.4
East European non-market economies	8	389.3	8.2	1,081.8[b]	9.1	n.a.
Newly industrializing countries[c]	7	299.4	6.3	626.5	5.3	5.4[d]
Sub-Saharan Africa	39	406.1	8.6	155.0	1.3	1.1

Notes
[a] For countries in each group refer to *World Development Report 1986*.
[b] Net Material Product. Derived by applying the 1983/4 growth rates to NMP 1982 for Eastern Europe.
[c] NICs: Yugoslavia, Mexico, Brazil, Singapore, South Korea, Taiwan, Hong Kong (*OECD Economic Outlook 1986*, Paris).
[d] Data for Taiwan from Economic Intelligence Unit, *Annual Report 1985* (London).

Source: World Bank, *World Development Report 1986* (Washington DC).

parts of the world is reflected most graphically in two socio-economic indicators: the literacy rates and infant mortality rates (see Table S.1 in the Statistical Appendix, p. 304). Together these two indices provide a telling measure of the development of human resources and standard of living of a country, and they are more significant than indicators based on GDP. (Developed countries exhibit varying rates of production of heavy manufactured goods, but they all have high literacy and infant mortality rates.) Literacy in developing countries is considerably lower than in the rich nations, and the infant mortality rate is about seven times higher in the former. This structural characteristic of the economy reflects the inability of the poorer countries to exploit their economic potential. Whereas the rich countries are capable of using their economic resources in a way that maximizes productivity in the long run, the developing countries are forced to tolerate the existence of disguised unemployment of labour and under-utilization of capital. They are faced with the challenge of devising or adapting a technology that can lead them to the realization of their economic potential. Their basic motivation as participants in the international economy is reflected in their desire to obtain support for development policies that aim at bridging the technological gap – as measured by the differences in literacy and infant mortality rates – between the 'have' and 'have not' nations of the world.

To be sure, the developing world is not without cleavages. As Table 1.1 illustrates, there are significant differences in the economic structure of the various segments of the Third World. At one extreme are the thirty-nine countries of sub-Saharan Africa with incomes per capita under the $400 benchmark and imperceptible or negative growth rates. At the other extreme are the oil-exporting countries, which continue to reflect the impact of the 1970s oil price rises with per capita incomes of over $11,000. An emerging group of developing countries exhibiting high growth rates are the newly industrializing countries (NICs). Their per capita income is approximately $2,000, while their average annual rate of growth since the mid-1960s is more than double that of the rich countries.

Despite this structural difference, and despite the consequent differences in the requirements and needs of the various countries, the Third World has maintained a broadly united posture in international economic negotiations. This unity reflects the essen-

5

tially unchanged nature of the relationship between the rich and the poor countries, despite the events of the past decade. The dramatic increase in oil prices in 1973/4 and the similar rise in the price of some primary commodities led a number of analysts to believe that the resource-rich developing countries had succeeded in achieving a breakthrough that would permanently and irrevocably alter their position within international commodity, factor and money markets. This belief was reflected in the call for the implementation of a New International Economic Order, in a resolution adopted by a special session of the UN General Assembly in 1974. However, though the oil crisis as well as other shortages emphasized the importance of a group of the poor countries in the international economy, it failed to bring about a restructuring of the world economy. Instead, the move towards alternative sources of energy, the evolution of the food crisis, the failure of the international community to bring about commodity price stabilization, the growth of protectionism and the newly emerging debt crisis depict a protracted conflict between the rich and the poor countries. Moreover, the unity of the Third World (as also that of developed countries) is itself threatened by these events, for despite the public statements and resolutions in the United Nations the fact is that the position of the oil-exporting developing countries and the NICs is today vastly different from the rest of the Third World, particularly from the countries of sub-Saharan Africa. Hence there exists the potential for conflict of interest within the hitherto ostensibly united Third World. The oil crisis in particular provided an apt illustration of the difference in approach and in objectives pursued by a group of formerly poor countries that suddenly found themselves in the unique (if temporary) position of having the rest of the world at their mercy.

The New International Economic Order

The term 'New International Economic Order', often referred to as NIEO, suggests two immediate thoughts: the first is related to 'new' and the second emphasizes 'order'.

The new versus the old

If there is to be a *new* order, then presumably it must be contrasted with an *old* order, an OIEO, namely the Bretton Woods system, which was established at the end of the Second World War as a result of Anglo-American negotiations, with an absorbing interplay between the intellect of Keynes, subtly representing British interests, coming up against the hard facts of US power and economic supremacy.

The Bretton Woods system certainly served the western industrial countries extremely well during the twenty-five years 1946–71, an era of unprecedented progress and full employment without inflation. Here, in what may be called the 'First World', severe poverty almost disappeared. The tremendous increase in GNP and technological power was accompanied by more equal internal income distribution, symbolized by the term 'welfare state'. Furthermore, the growth of the various countries concerned was convergent – that is to say, those that were the richest at the beginning of the period, including the United States, Canada, the United Kingdom, Sweden, and Switzerland, showed relatively slow growth, whereas the poorest, and specifically those defeated and devastated during the war, such as West Germany and Japan, showed the most rapid growth. It is a debatable point to what extent the big success story of these twenty-five years was due to the Bretton Woods system as such, or perhaps to an extremely farsighted and generous US policy embodied in the Marshall Plan. Probably it was a combination of the two that produced the end result.

Even for the Third World the Bretton Woods era was, in some ways, not a bad period, since many countries – and South Korea is an outstanding example – then laid the foundations of their economic growth. The GNP of the Third World as a whole increased by 5–6 per cent per annum, a growth rate very similar to that of the industrial countries – although, of course, a much higher percentage of this aggregate growth was swallowed up by population growth, so that growth per capita was less. The 'trickle-down' effect of growth from the industrial countries to the Third World was unmistakable and the flow of aid was considerable, particularly during the earlier part of this period, even if at no time comparable to the Marshall Plan. A number of developing countries clearly achieved the situation described by Walt W. Rostow in his famous image – so typical of the technological aura of the 1950s and early 1960s – of the 'take-off into self-sustained growth'.

However, there were great sources of weakness in the progress made by many Third World countries during the Bretton Woods era. Above all – in sharp contrast to the industrial countries – their growth was divergent, that is to say, the better-off tended to grow faster, leaving the poorer countries far behind. Thus the Third World began to split during this period. A group of what are now called the newly industrializing countries (typified by Brazil and Mexico in one hemisphere and by Korea, Taiwan, Singapore and Hong Kong in another) left behind a group of poorest countries, a 'Fourth World' (typified by India, Bangladesh, Indonesia and most of Africa).

The growth was also divergent in the internal sense, because contrary to what happened elsewhere it was accompanied by increased inequalities in income distribution. Thus, because of divergence both between and within countries, Third World poverty did not show any signs of disappearing or even diminishing. Further intensified by the speeding-up of population growth due to the reduction in death rates – in itself a sign of the progress achieved – the absolute volume of world poverty was thus increasing quite rapidly during the Bretton Woods era.

Another source of weakness for the Third World countries was the tendency for their terms of trade to deteriorate in the course of the Bretton Woods era. This had in fact been forecast initially, although it remained a contested view; but certainly, with the exception of the temporary boom during the 1950/1 Korean War, the prices of primary commodities showed a distinct tendency to sag in relation to those of manufactured goods, to the great disadvantage of the Third World.

Fundamentally and perhaps even more important, was the rapid development of technology in the direction of greater sophistication and capital requirements, making the technological gap progressively more unbridgeable (see Chapter 2).

There were thus plenty of reasons for Third World countries to be dissatisfied with the Bretton Woods order. As regards the deteriorating terms of trade, it is of special interest to note that, in the original Keynesian conception, the system was to rest on three pillars: a world central bank (realized in the attenuated form of the International Monetary Fund, IMF), a world development agency (realized in the attenuated form of the World Bank) and an international trade organization. The charter of the latter was negotiated in Havana during 1947 but was never implemented owing to the failure of the US Congress to ratify the proposals. The gap left was partly filled by the General Agreement on Tariffs and Trade (GATT) with much more limited provisions. It was, therefore, a case of retributive justice that the complaints of the Third World about the inefficiency of the Bretton Woods system should have been so strongly concentrated on the problems of commodity trade (see Chapter 5). This dissatisfaction encouraged the formation of the United Nations Conference on Trade and Development (UNCTAD). But its effective working in the interests of the poor countries has been affected by its lack of support from the developed world.

Order versus disorder

There is another way of reading the demands for a New International Economic Order, with the accent on the last word. The Bretton Woods system has been dated above as ruling for twenty-five years, from 1946 to 1971. Since then, however, it has visibly disintegrated, and only remnants now remain.

This collapse is often associated with the oil embargo by the Organization of Petroleum Exporting Countries (OPEC) and the quadrupling of oil prices in late 1973. However, while that action may well be considered as the last nail in its coffin, one of the chief elements of Bretton Woods – the free convertibility of the US dollar as the world's main reserve currency into gold at a fixed low price – was suspended as early as 1971. That was already a clear signal that the system was no longer working. This was followed in 1972 by the world food crisis resulting from simultaneous crop failures in the Soviet Union, India and Sahelian Africa, and poor or moderate production elsewhere. This meant that the large surplus stocks of food, which had been an essential part of the Bretton Woods system, dwindled away rapidly, and the prices of cereals quadrupled like those of oil. Recovery from the shock to the world economy in the mid-1970s was slow, highlighting the growing obsolescence of the old order.

So the demand for an NIEO must be contrasted not with an

OIEO, but with the subsequent state of disorder. A slowing-down of growth and rising unemployment combined with speeded-up inflation expressed itself in a major recession in the industrialized countries. 'Stagflation' was an entirely new experience because the foundation of the Bretton Woods system was a trade-off between unemployment and inflation. The recession had the effect of slowing down growth rates world-wide, the hardest hit being the oil-importing poor countries. The early impact of the recession was contained by the commercial banks, which recycled oil revenue in the form of loans to many developing countries. The unforeseen consequence of this action was to be felt at a later stage. But at the time, these developments created a fresh situation, namely a mutual interest in the re-establishment of economic order. Whether this was defined as something really 'new' or a return to the kind of economic order that existed previously was perhaps more a matter of semantics and political preference than of reality.

It was initially felt that the cost to the industrial countries as a result of stagflation (that is, the difference between what would have been produced each year if the steady growth of the Bretton Woods era had continued compared with what in fact was produced) would be an impetus to them to agree to the concessions that were demanded as part of the NIEO. The expectation was that measures taken to aid the economic recovery of the developing countries would, in the long term, be beneficial to the world economic order by acting as the 'engine of growth' for the world as a whole. The NIEO negotiations thus evolved around the financing of the Common Fund, the reduction of trade barriers, stabilization of commodity prices, tighter control of the activities of multinational corporations, improved representation for the poor countries in international agencies like the IMF, IBRD (International Bank for Reconstruction and Development) and the GATT, the strengthening of UNCTAD and the adoption of a 0.7 per cent target for official development assistance.

Unfortunately, the early stages of the negotiations proved that the clear existence of a major mutual interest was not sufficient to guarantee the successful adoption of the NIEO proposals. This was partially owing to a lack of consensus on the main symptoms of what was actually wrong and to the fact that the Third World countries gave prominence to the need to eliminate or reduce perceived inequalities and inequities in the system. In addition, the slow recovery of the economics of the industrialized countries, the negative effects of the prolonged recession on world trade combined with the second oil price rise in 1979–80 and rising interest rates created an international environment that was hostile to the concept of mutual cooperation (see Chapter 3). The global recession that followed the second oil crisis resulted in a further deterioration in international trade and in the growth of industrial protectionism in the industrialized countries. Those developing countries that had borrowed heavily in the mid-1970s were now facing the prospect of economic collapse, owing to their inability to service their external debt, and the lending institutions in the industrialized countries had to contend with the possibility of default on the part of some of their major debtors. Thus the world economy fell into further disarray with the debt crisis in 1982. The two solutions of debt restructuring and national adjustment strategies were implemented in order to avert an international financial crisis (see Chapter 9).

In the 1980s, therefore, the polarization in the world economic order has continued to grow, with the industrialized countries pursuing strategies that aid their own growth, whereas within the developing countries a group, including the NICs, India and China, have been able to achieve rapid growth, while in the disaster-beset countries of sub-Saharan Africa, growth has been halting (see Table 1.2).Therefore the experiences of the last decade have shown, more than ever, the need for a NIEO, in order to escape from the harsh consequences of remaining in a state of 'disorder'.

Inequities and Inequalities between Countries

For many of the poorer countries, political independence is a relatively recent phenomenon. Memories of colonial relationships

Table 1.2 *Average annual growth rates in GNP 1965–85*

	1965–73	*1973–80*	*1981–4*	*1985*
Industrial market economies	3.7	2.1	1.3	2.4
Developing countries	4.1	3.2	0.9	2.4
Sub-Saharan Africa	2.0	0.5	–2.8	–0.6

Source: World Bank, World Development Report 1986 (Washington DC).

and a desire for real independence have prompted the emphasis upon the major inequalities, inherent in a system that in most cases is older than they are. The continuing economic dependence of the poor countries upon the rich countries is often described as neo-colonialism and, in the sense of a highly unequal distribution of wealth and power between countries, is a continuing fact of life. The industrial nations, with just 15 per cent of the world's population, have over 70 per cent of its income and wealth. This tremendous imbalance has come to be termed the 'North–South' divide, where 'North' and 'South' are broadly synonymous with 'rich' and 'poor'.

This unequal relationship is true as regards:

- military power and the concentration of armaments production;
- financial and economic power, notably if measured by GNP per capita;
- technological power, symbolized by the fact that 98 per cent of all R&D expenditures in this field are in the developed countries;
- industrial power, with 90 per cent of industries in the North;
- commercial power, with the bulk of trade taking place among the industrial countries;
- the power of the multinational corporations radiating from the western nations; and even
- food power, with the United States, Europe and Canada emerging as the granaries of the world.

There is one great exception, and it is perhaps for this reason that the assertion of oil power by OPEC initially found such strong and enthusiastic support in the Third World, although many low-income oil importers were perhaps even more severely affected by the higher prices than the industrial North. For the first time a group of countries from the 'South' had been able to exert considerable pressure upon the international community. Despite the power wielded by OPEC on behalf of the rest of the South (and themselves) they were unable to bring about the restructuring of the world economy. This can be partially attributed to their dependence upon the multinational corporations and financial institutions of the North to develop their oil industry and invest their surplus.

A second group of poor countries – the NICs – geared their economics towards the export of manufactured goods and experienced high growth rates in the 1970s. Many other poor countries attempted to follow this strategy of export-led economic growth, but as the effects of the competition with 'cheap' imports were felt in the economies of the industrialized nations they began to reduce access to their markets by raising trade barriers. The Multi-Fibre Agreement (MFA) restricts the import of textiles by developed countries. In this instance the contradictory role played by the institutions of the old order such as the IMF and the World Bank is highlighted: they espouse the concept of 'free trade' and yet remain silent when rich countries impose restrictions upon free trade.

It is therefore understandable that the Third World also feels strongly about the power inequalities that exist in the control of the major international organizations, especially the World Bank and the IMF, arising mainly from their dependence on voluntary contributions or on permission to use the capital markets of the rich countries, and embodied in the voting system of, roughly, one dollar one vote. The Third World is in favour of 'one country one vote', such as obtains in the UN General Assembly – albeit not in the Security Council, with its veto. There are those who wonder whether the right system might not be 'one person one vote', although this would also give the developing countries a built-in majority, as well as a very strong position to China and India.

It is true that some 'dependent' relationships are not always as clear-cut as might appear at first sight. Thus, the growing indebtedness of many of the poor countries may look like a clear expression of dependence, but it also gives the debtors some leverage over the creditors, as in the cases of Mexico in 1982 and 1986 and Peru in 1985. While creditors have been forced to renegotiate debts in order to avoid further disorder in the world economy, the situation in the debtor countries has not altered significantly as a result of this action. Ironically, some of the largest debtor nations are to be found amongst the NICs, for their policies of industrialization led the lending institutions to consider them 'good risks'. Despite the sheer size of the debt of the seventeen largest debtor nations,[1] particularly those in Latin America, the crisis facing the countries of sub-Saharan Africa is more acute, for their per capita debt is extremely high. The servicing of this debt combined with the famine resulting from long-term drought has created a bleak prospect for their economic recovery. The case of the poorer countries of sub-Saharan Africa has intensified the moral obligation of the rich nations towards its weaker dependents. Similarly the large transnational corporations may dominate the industrial scene in many developing countries, but their dependence upon this new international division of labour in order to remain competitive makes them vulnerable to the uncertainties of local politics in the host country, with the threat of nationalization without compensation providing some leverage for the host government.

As already mentioned, in the current discussion it is not so much a workable new order, or the question of internal national differences, that is emphasized, but rather inequalities between countries, and these often appear to be a 'zero-sum game'. You cannot give the Third World greater weight in the IMF without reducing the voting power of the industrial countries. You cannot increase the terms of trade of primary commodities relative to manufactures without lowering them in the opposite direction. It is for this reason that the emphasis on inequality between countries gives the NIEO debate its note of acerbity, and presents a formidable obstacle to making progress in the negotiations.

However, it does not follow that *all* the specific demands made to reduce inequalities between countries represent a real zero-sum game. On the contrary, it becomes more and more apparent that a wide range of issues could actually be settled to the advantage of both the industrial as well as the developing countries. For example, better terms of trade for primary commodities can be in the interest of the industrial countries if they lead to greater investment in creating more sources and security of supply. The removal of instability in the prices of primary commodities is as much in the interest of consumers as of producers. Better access for manufactured imports from the Third World is in the interest not only of the consumers in industrialized countries, but also of their governments struggling to control inflation. If the developing countries acquired greater technological capacity to solve their own problems by methods more appropriate to their factor endowment, for example by more labour-intensive or smaller-scale technologies, this could be of considerable beneficial application in the industrial countries themselves. Or again, if the developing countries increased their trade with each other to remove the present anomaly whereby one-third of mankind in the industrial countries does 80 per cent of

14

world trade with itself, it is difficult to see how the major interests of
the industrialized countries could be hurt by such a natural development. Moreover, the long-term position of the richer countries is
best safeguarded in a world in which the poorer feel that they have a
real opportunity of improving their situation. The alternative is a
sharply divided world of seething discontent among the majority of
countries, especially as many of them are today pursuing the
objective of the development of nuclear power.

Inequities and Inequalities within Countries

On the whole, the empirical evidence suggests that the development
of the Third World under the Bretton Woods system tended to be
divergent within countries. In India, for example, the emphasis on
industrialization, with strict regulation of foreign investment,
caused the rate of growth of the economy to rise significantly, but
the inequality of the income distribution has increased both in the
rural areas and in the urban areas, and between the two sectors. This
is primarily owing to the fact that the majority of India's labour force
is engaged in agriculture. In Latin America, the high growth rates
experienced by some countries hide the layer of acute poverty that
continues to exist. Amongst the oil-exporting countries, those with
small populations are exceptional in the equitable income distribution they have managed to achieve. In the poorer countries of
sub-Saharan Africa, where low levels of national income are the
norm, distribution has little impact.

The reason for this tendency towards internal inequality within
Third World countries has been analysed elsewhere, and helps to
explain the continuing revisions in development thinking. Here we
are concerned with the problem of internal income distribution, and
the resulting failure of poverty to diminish in line with economic
growth, as an element in the NIEO debate. In this debate, issue has
been taken up more passionately by the industrial countries, who
seem to prefer to discuss the relief of world poverty to the removal of
inequalities between countries. For obvious reasons, humanitarian
sentiments in the industrial countries create a public opinion more
favourable to the relief of unmistakable poverty and distress abroad,
rather than the removal of structural imbalances in the world trading
or financial system now operating against the Third World.

The developing countries tend to be deeply suspicious of the tendency of western governments to talk about poverty and human needs instead of, say, a Common Fund or voting rights in the IMF. They consider this preference of the West partly as an intervention in their own internal affairs, and partly as a device to avoid the discussion of really important questions, which are much more awkward for the industrial countries. The concern with basic needs has, for this reason, been described as 'NIEO neo-colonialism'.

The industrial countries, on their part, criticize the reluctance and unwillingness of Third World countries to discuss the issue of poverty within their borders, and consider this as a device by their governments to avoid the discussion of issues of domestic policies that are awkward for *them*. They suspect many regimes of seeking external scapegoats in order to divert attention away from their own domestic inefficiencies, elitism and lack of concern for their own poor.

There is thus plenty of room for misunderstanding and friction on both sides. This is further intensified by a tendency on the part of industrial countries to broaden the discussion further by including human rights and democratic participation in decision-making as part of basic needs. The Third World countries cannot avoid discussion of world poverty as an immediate issue, but they certainly seem entitled to insist that this should not be the only issue on the agenda of the NIEO negotiations.

Fortunately, the concern for inequities both among and within countries tends to overlap more and more as we move down the development ladder towards those who comprise the Fourth World – the low-income economies, where mass poverty would still be prevalent even with perfectly equal internal income distribution. Hence, there is relatively easy agreement in the NIEO debate on the need for special action on behalf of the so-called 'least-developed countries'. Compensatory finance enables these poorest countries to stabilize their financial situation when their export earnings are fluctuating. The IMF's Compensatory Financing Facility provides assistance to those facing balance of payments difficulties, and the EEC's Export Stabilization scheme (STABEX) in the Lomé Agreement is a commodity-specific agreement that provides compensation to individual African, Caribbean and Pacific countries that are associated with the European Community. These two schemes, effective as they are, are examples of the way in which the rich countries choose to address the symptoms of poverty rather than to probe deeper into its causes.

Summary and Conclusions

So, with goodwill, packages could be prepared that allow for simultaneous discussion and action in relation to the three broad areas distinguished above:

1 the restoration of international order after the collapse of the Bretton Woods system;
2 the removal of inequalities between countries;
3 the reduction of world poverty.

However, the fact that all these issues, and possibly others, are at present simultaneously discussed and subsumed under the title of NIEO is a source of considerable confusion and a great obstacle to productive agreement. It is all too easy for misunderstandings to arise, because governments talk about different things when they meet, and give different priorities to them in debate.

The first requirement would be to bring out more clearly the various issues at stake and the mutuality of interests involved. Such has been the purpose of this chapter. It should then be possible, as the next step, to draw up priorities for different groups of countries in relation to the three areas already mentioned, and any others that it is agreed require action. In the case of the industrial countries, which have benefited so conspicuously and one-sidedly in the past, there would also be a need to define their own interests in a broader and longer-term sense.

After nearly a decade of discussion there has been only a degree of progress on the original NIEO demands. The Agreement for the Common Fund awaits ratification by the USA and a few other countries prior to its becoming operational. The inability of debtor countries to meet their repayments has necessitated action from the international financial community on the question of debt. But, as identified earlier, rescheduling debt only turns short-term debt into long-term debt and hardly contributes to the alleviation of the problem.

The LDC Group of 77 (now numbering over 100 members), which acts as a group within most UN organizations, consistently and constantly repeats the call for a reform of the international monetary, financial and trading system. Despite the diversity of the group, they have maintained their solidarity by presenting a long shopping list of demands in which the interests of all the countries on the group are represented. The issues raised for negotiation ten years ago remain as the issues of today.

The industrial countries, on the other hand, have adopted the opposite strategy of never yet putting forward their own full version of a NIEO. Instead, they confine themselves to the rejection or amendment of specific points in the shopping list of the Group of 77. Also, by failing quite often to agree amongst themselves, they make discussion and progress more difficult. Thanks to the efforts of the OECD (Organization for Economic Co-operation and Development) and the EEC, there has been some progress towards formulating common positions; but much still remains to be done.

It is in all our interests that a satisfactory wide agreement should be reached so that the world economy can enter into an era of practical and orderly progress.

Note

1 Argentina, Bolivia, Brazil, Chile, Colombia, Costa Rica, Cote d'Ivoire, Ecuador, Jamaica, Mexico, Morocco, Nigeria, Peru, the Philippines, Uruguay, Venezuela, Yugoslavia (World Bank, *World Development Report 1986*, Washington DC).

2　The International Economy

A World View of the Development Process

The problem of economic development[1] cannot be adequately analysed in the context of a closed economy model. This becomes clear if an examination is made of the structure of an economy that is in a process of development in the world of today. Typically, such an economy is an importer of both capital and technology (as well as consumption goods) from 'the rest of the world'. This imported capital and technology play a crucially important part in its development. Domestic substitution for foreign capital and foreign technical know-how is a very costly affair, often indeed impossible. This is true whether we think of replication or genuine substitution allowing for the different needs of a poorer country. For most African, Asian and Latin American countries (especially the smaller and poorer ones) the external (export) sector is the leading sector – the sector that sets the pace of development and shapes for the rest of the economy both the pattern and pace of growth. Typically, size by size, the poorer a country, the more dependent it is on foreign markets and foreign sources of supply. If the external sector stagnates, so that the inflow of resources from abroad is constrained, the pace of growth and rate of structural change are likely to be highly sensitive to such a decline. However, there have been situations where the resulting shock and enforced readjustment have been beneficial; the forces involved are political and social, not only economic. Economic planners are thus compelled to give due weight to the problem of foreign resource inflows, in the form of export earnings, aid and foreign investment, along with the problems of domestic resources mobilization.

　　The terms on which the developing countries can obtain foreign exchange, capital and technology reflect the relationship between the rich and poor countries in the world economy. There are exceptions, where the poorer countries command a strategic material or strategic bases, or where they effectively cooperate with each other; the oil-producing countries are a relatively recent example. Generally, however, in the face of the existing distribution of economic power it is the rich countries that determine the terms, because in the short run the developing countries need the products and services of the developed countries much more than the latter need the output of the former. This imbalance of need is evident from the striking fact that the poor countries trade mainly with the rich countries, whereas the rich countries mainly trade among themselves. Over the period 1982–4 the rich OECD countries, with less than one-fifth of the world's population, accounted for about 57 per cent of world exports, and as much as 65 per cent of these exports represented trade within the OECD bloc. As against this, the share of the developing countries in world exports was roughly 35 per cent (22 per cent of this total being exports from the rich oil exporters) during this period. Intra Third World exports accounted for about 30 per cent of total Third World exports during 1982–4.[2] Moreover, the annual average rate of growth of developing country exports was substantially lower than that of the rich nations in every year during 1980–5.[3] Thus the gain in world export shares achieved by the developing countries during 1973–80 was to some extent offset by substantial losses incurred during the recession that began in 1982. The greater negative impact of this recession on the export performance of the poor countries reflects their relatively weaker bargaining position in the world commodity and factor markets, in which they are mainly price takers. They are also 'takers' in trade negotiations and trade policy formulation.

This dependence of the developing countries on the industrial countries has far-reaching consequences for the development prospects of the Third World. It also poses a challenge to the rich nations in that, although such dependence may be a short-run advantage to them, western statesmen such as Willy Brandt and Edward Heath have stressed that the long-term economic interests of the West lie in the strengthening of the economies of the Third World and in accelerating their pace of development. The second Brandt Report[4] develops the theme of 'mutual benefits and interests' and asserts that it should provide both a moral and economic basis for cooperation between the West and the developing countries. The existence of large disparities in the international distribution of income and wealth is both unjustifiable on moral grounds and inefficient in economic terms. The Brandt Report makes a strong plea for bridging the enormous resource and entitlements gap that separates the rich and poor countries. It argues that the mitigation of economic inequalities between the citizens of different countries should, surely, rank high on any action agenda drawn up by the international community. On economic grounds, too, there exist strong arguments for undertaking a comprehensive international programme for a broad preferential treatment of the less developed countries (LDCs). In the long run, the world economy cannot expand rapidly if over two-thirds of the world's population live in abject poverty and misery (and four-fifths of the world's children – the citizens and producers of tomorrow!). The long-term prosperity of the rich 'North' depends to a great extent on its own ability and willingness to share its advantages with the deprived 'South'. If this does not happen, the economic, political and social tensions that are building up in the poorer parts of the world threaten the stability, indeed the very existence, of the world order that has made the progress and prosperity of the richer countries possible. It is imperative, therefore, that we think and plan for development in an international perspective, and that we realize the interdependence of the world's constituent units.

Structural Change in the World Economy

The lopsided interdependence of nations is of comparatively recent origin. The fact that it has gained such importance is due to a number of technological as well as social factors. As long as the economic structure and economic performance of different countries (or groups of countries) were not too dissimilar, a situation could be visualized where economic independence was a meaningful concept. It was only when the gap between the rich and poor countries widened significantly and progressively that the external sector gained the importance pointed out in the previous section, deriving from the fact that the rich countries are in a position to export goods and factors (especially technology) that are vitally necessary for the economic development of the poor countries and that are not substitutable by their domestic production. It is this wide gap between the two types of countries that determines their relations and that makes the system so interdependent that it is unrealistic, even impossible, to consider the development of the poorer and more dependent units separately from the effects of their coexistence with the richer and more powerful countries.

It is worth looking a little more closely at the more important structural changes that have taken place in the international economy. This can serve a dual purpose. On the one hand, it can provide us with a better perspective for analysing the impact of various policy measures on the development of the world economy; on the other, it can help us to understand the *nature* of the dependence of the different economic units on each other. We will then be in a position to identify the important areas of action and cooperation between the rich and poor countries and to focus attention on those policies that could bring about a significant reduction of international economic inequalities. It will then become clear that it is not merely the *quantum* of resource flows from the developed to the underdeveloped countries that is important. The *type* of resources that are transferred, as well as the *terms* on which they are transferred, are of equal importance.

The resources and needs of the poor countries are determined essentially by the structural imbalances of the world economy. Up to about 1850, the world economy could be described as largely stationary or stagnant, by almost any standards. Real elements of growth could be discerned only in Britain, and a few rudiments elsewhere. It has been estimated that, in the period AD 1 to AD 1850, total output grew at about 0.1 per cent per annum and per capita output at about 0.09 per cent per annum.[5] The level and process of growth were by no means stable – there were wide fluctuations over different periods – but a consistent upward trend could just be discerned.

In the last 135 years the situation has changed radically for those countries that today are classified as rich. Their population has increased about three times, whereas their total output has increased almost twenty-five times; their rate of growth of output has risen to about 5 per cent per annum; and their average level of per capita income has increased more than ten fold. It is important to note that the growth of population absorbs only a minor share of the increase in the production of the rich countries.

The structure of the economies of the rich countries has also changed significantly over the last 135 years. Before, nearly all countries produced more than half of their total output in the form of agricultural goods; now the share of agriculture in the total product of the rich countries is typically less than 5 per cent – although this has been consistent with big, indeed unprecedented, absolute increases in agricultural output. Whereas agricultural output has grown four or five times over this period in these countries, industrial output has grown to almost fifty times its original level. Within industrial output, the rate of growth of capital goods (as distinct from consumer goods) industries is even more spectacular; consumer goods production has grown twenty times over the last century, but capital goods production has grown phenomenally to more than 100 times its original level.

This big change in economic structure reflects a tremendous increase in the technological sophistication of the production mechanism in the rich countries. This becomes clear if their trade patterns are examined. When a rich country of today started its process of development it was an exporter of an agriculture-based product that had been processed, if at all, by simple and crude techniques; e.g. Britain exported textiles, Sweden exported timber and Canada exported wheat. As the process of development continued, export lines, like product lines, were shifted; e.g. Britain changed from exporting wool and cloth to exporting transport equipment, mechanical goods, electrical supplies, etc. In other words, the change in the technology of production manifested itself in the foreign trade structure of the countries concerned.

The then late-developer countries, e.g. Germany, Japan and Russia, found it possible to adopt and adapt the technology that had been developed by the countries that preceded them. Indeed, the fact that the latecomers could leap over the intermediate stages and adopt the most efficient (existing) technology made their rate of growth higher than the rate of growth of the older rich countries. No wonder economists firmly believed that the accumulation of scientific and technological knowledge would make development progressively easier and ultimately bring a golden age of worldwide development.

The transfer of technology from the old to the new growing countries in the nineteenth century – both groups now included in the rich countries – took place through the agency of a local entrepreneurial class, which borrowed both capital and technology from the established industrial and financial centres but which by and large confined its production activities to one national state (and sometimes its colonies). Today's giant production unit, the multinational corporation, has attained its predominant position comparatively recently. Each national entrepreneurial class found it fairly easy to learn the production techniques from elsewhere and to adapt them to its own environment. This was so for three reasons: (1) entrepreneurial ability existed in similar degrees in the new-rich countries; (2) the technology was not too different from the familiar traditional one; and (3) the environment to which the technologies had to be adapted was also only moderately different. These new entrepreneurial classes were usually nationalist in their interests and outlook.[6]

In sharp contrast to the experience of the rich countries, the countries now euphemistically classified as 'developing' – OPEC apart – have not grown at a significant rate during the same period of 150 years, except during 1950–78. Aggregate output has no doubt risen, but this has been largely matched by the increased rate of growth in the population, so that output, and income, per capita have remained little changed. Whereas the rich countries had a standard-of-living explosion, the poor countries had a population explosion. There have of course been exceptional years and countries where growth has been high, but even where per capita growth has been substantial it has often been of an unbalanced nature and has not really reduced the incidence and extent of poverty – for reasons that are by no means accidental. Even if the post-war period should represent a turning point – and it is too early yet to say – the growth in standards of living has remained modest, and the number of the poor and unemployed has increased rather than diminished (as was the case in the long-run development of the richer countries).

The rise in the income of the OPEC countries during 1973–83 clearly cannot be compared with the rise that resulted from the early industrialization of Germany or Japan. This increase in income has not been occasioned by the emergence of a private or state entrepreneurial class that has enhanced productivity levels. Quite the contrary, the ruling elite of the OPEC countries tried to use the opportunity offered by rising oil prices to raise aggregate productivity. In other words, the increase in income *preceded* the increase in factor productivity, and whether or not self-sustaining development occurs in even these economies of the Third World is still open to question, to be determined by the terms on which the West will permit them to transfer technology and by the degree to which the higher productivity is fed back into the various sectors of the economy and spreads among the general population.

The extent to which the gap between rich and poor countries has widened can be realized from the following figures. In 1850, today's rich countries accounted for 26 per cent of the total population of the world and for about 35 per cent of its total income. In the 1980s the rich countries accounted for 25 per cent of the population (not much changed from 1850) but 68 per cent of the total income.[7] The difference between the per capita incomes of the poor and rich countries increased from 70 per cent in 1850 to more than 1,000 per cent by the early 1980s.[8]

Moreover, the *pattern* of inequality is more important than its *quantum*. US production in agriculture (taken per capita of the whole population) is twice as high as that of India, but US per capita output in industry is twenty-five to thirty times as high, and US per capita output of services is thirteen times as high. This brings to light two important facts. First of all, the absolute level of *present* inequality between the rich and poor countries is certainly not of unmanageable proportions, at least if we can afford to take a philosophical long-run view. If the poor countries were to grow at an average yearly rate of 5 per cent per capita for the next half-century, they could statistically attain the *present* output and income level of the rich countries.[9] Of course, to grow by 5 per cent per capita yearly for fifty years would be by no means an easy task if only because of population expansion, especially in the large poor countries such as India, Bangladesh and Indonesia. However, it is in no sense an inconceivable task, given the resources of the international economy and provided the full power of science and technology and other efforts are concentrated on this as a world priority objective.

The second important fact is that the poverty of the Third World countries reflects essentially the technological[10] gap between them and the rich countries. The developing countries are unable to produce by themselves goods that require modern technical know-how as an important input, let alone to develop an autonomous alternative technology to substitute. The trade patterns of the developing countries show that they usually export crude or processed, agriculture- or mineral-based products. These countries have not succeeded in adapting or replicating for their own conditions the technological developments that have occurred in the rich countries. Although this monopoly of new knowledge cannot be strictly measured, since the *output* cannot be directly measured, the *input* – research and development expenditures – can be measured, and by that measure the rich countries account for 98–99 per cent of the world figure.

We may thus conclude that, though the international economy has evolved at a rapid rate over the course of the last century and a half, this accelerated expansion has been limited to certain regions of the world. This limitation has given rise to an imbalance in the standard of living of the different regions. The rest of this book aims at discussing some ways in which we should move if the worst effects of this imbalance are to be corrected.

The Core of The Problem: Technology

It is the central thesis of this book that the imbalance between the rich and poor countries cannot be corrected by means of an automatic, self-operating market mechanism. Specific policy measures will have to be adopted by both the rich and developing countries if the latter are to experience the structural changes that are necessary for sustained economic growth. The cliché that 'each country has the primary responsibility for its own development' is a half-truth. The statement that we are 'all members one of another' comes nearer the truth, since the world economy forms an interdependent system.

Economic interdependence is inescapable in the modern world. Such interdependence can be of mutual benefit to both rich and poor countries since both possess essential resources that the other group needs. However, it has been maintained by a number of economists since the late 1940s that there is a tendency for the rich countries to gain from *any* economic dealings (whether in the form of trade, transfer of technology, or investment) that they have with the poor countries.[11] Already in 1949 and 1950 the view was being put forward that the gains from international trade and investment accrued mainly to the rich countries,[12] the reason being that the rich countries produced and exported industrial commodities, whereas the poor countries specialized in primary goods. The terms of trade tended to move against the primary goods producers, and technological progress also tended to work to their disadvantage. Hence industrialization was seen as the great panacea. The dynamic effects of industrialization, it was maintained, would overcome any 'enclave' associated with foreign investment. Today it has to be admitted that industrialization, even import-substituting industrialization specifically geared to the home market, has not generated self-perpetuating growth in the poor countries. It does not lead by itself to a full transplantation and subsequent indigenous development of an effective technology, as happened for example when Japan first adopted and adapted the technology of Western Europe. Industrialization, *per se*, does not reduce the dependence of the poor countries on the rich – in some ways it adds to it – and hence does not bridge the fundamental gap between the two.

As industrialization proceeds in a typical 'poor country', import substitution becomes more and more difficult, for the import-substituting industries are themselves import-dependent. Hence the essential difference between the rich and poor countries is not that they produce different types of commodities, as both Prebisch and Singer initially assumed. The fact that they do, in general, produce a different 'mix' of goods is merely an indicator of a more fundamental difference in the structure of these two types of economies. Indeed, it has been shown that the deterioration of the terms of trade of primary products in relation to manufactured commodities during the 1950s and 1960s really concealed a deterioration of the terms of trade of the poor countries in all their dealings with the rich countries (see Chapter 6).

Clearly, the relationship between types of *countries* is more significant than the relationship between types of *products*. The fundamental advantage of the rich countries is not that they produce certain *types* of commodities, but rather that they are the home of modern technology and the seats of the multinational corporations. Any increase in the price of the exports of the developing countries that does not translate itself into an increase in the average labour

27

productivity of the developing country (i.e. an increase in the technological sophistication of its production structure) will inevitably be eroded by the greater adaptability of the rich countries, which by developing substitutes for the scarce or expensive Third World exports reassert their position of strength in the world economy.

The rich industrial countries will therefore tend to be the chief gainers from any type of commercial relationship with the Third World – be it in the form of trade or investment. Over the long run, the LDC, irrespective of the commodity it produces, will not share the gains fairly, except in the case of those groups or sectors that become integrated into the economy of the rich country. These will become oases of growth surrounded by a desert of stagnation, thus reinforcing other elements of dualism already present in the poorer countries. The way leads to polarization within the poor country, clashing with the objectives of national planning and national integration. This polarization expresses itself in widening internal income disparities, larger numbers exposed to extreme poverty, and rising unemployment.

The real source of the maldistribution of the gains from trade and investment lies in the nature of modern technology and the process of its development. Modern technology, as already mentioned, is concentrated in the rich countries and is oriented towards *their* conditions, problems and factor endowments. This goes much deeper than just the development of substitutes for primary commodities. By rendering obsolete the older, simpler, more labour-intensive existing technology, this process creates a condition of continued and sharpening technological dependence and continued and sharpening lack of productive employment within the LDCs. It is this technological dependence that has to be corrected if the poor countries are to emerge from the depths of poverty. Salvation lies in the development of indigenous scientific and technological capacities within the developing countries and in a reorientation of the present system of research and development, which by and large ignores their needs.

The traditional view, of course, is that the factor endowment of a country determines the production mix and at the same time the technology. For a poor country, this means that the abundant labour and scarce capital should lead to: (1) concentration and specialization on labour-intensive products, and (2) choice of a labour-intensive technology within the available spectrum of technologies for each product. This situation is assumed to have the happy result for poor countries of producing a tendency towards full employment, saving of scarce capital, fruitful international trade and gradual factor price equalization.

It is, of course, recognized that the present trade restrictions concerning labour-intensive manufactured products, the agricultural protectionism by rich countries, and the heavy effective tariff barriers against the processing of crude commodities in the developing countries prevent this advantageous process from operating in so far as it depends on the international division of labour. However, there is something much more fundamentally wrong with the idea that trade and investment benefit poor countries (as well as rich countries) by bringing into play their different factor endowments. The logic of the preceding argument is that, in fact, it should be looked at the other way round: it is the *technology* that is given that determines the production mix and factor endowment, at least in the sense of factor *use*. And since the given technology is the 'modern' technology of the developed countries (capital-intensive, skill-intensive, labour-saving, raw material-saving, and raw material-substituting), neither the technology used nor the production mix corresponds to the factor endowment of the developing countries. Unemployment of labour and extreme shortage of capital outside the small modern sector are the natural outcome of this situation. In a sense, they act as equilibriating factors that reconcile the given technology (that of the richer countries) with the factor proportions of the poorer countries.

Another way of explaining the same situation is to pay more attention to factor *use*. As the unemployment situation and absence of new labour-intensive technologies in developing countries indicate, recent investments have not been guided in their factor use by the existing factor endowment. So, analytically, it would be more realistic to substitute for the old sequence (factor endowment—product mix—technology—factor use) the following sequence: new technology—factor use—dualism—unemployment – factor endowment. This sequence, centred upon technology, explains more of the maldistribution of benefits from trade and investment than does the previous emphasis on deteriorating terms of trade and foreign trade restrictions.

The point previously made, that more emphasis should be placed upon the characteristics of *countries* than upon the characteristics of specific *commodities*, can now be further elaborated. The superior technology and monopoly of technological improvement possessed by the rich countries are but one aspect of their superiority of access to the relevant information necessary for policy-making and bargaining. Here we clearly have a cumulative process at work, for information, like technology, feeds upon itself. If at the beginning there is not enough information on where to look for the information needed or on what new information should be assembled, initial inferiority is bound to be sharpened and perpetuated. This unequal bargaining situation will affect *all* relations between the developed and developing countries, whether labelled aid, trade, investment, transfer of technology, technical assistance or any other.

The realization that the concentration of technical progress of a specific kind within richer countries is *the* basic determinant of the uneven distribution of gains from trade and investment, leads to the further realization that simple manufactured products of the type capable of production in developing countries share many of the characteristics that were attributed to primary commodities ('unwrought commodities') as against manufactured goods ('wrought commodities'). The real line of division in the present day seems to lie, not between primary commodities and manufactured goods, but between primary commodities *plus* simple manufactured goods on the one hand, and the sophisticated new products – especially (but not exclusively) intermediate goods, including new equipment, as well as know-how and management – on the other hand. Import substitution shifts the geographical location of manufacturing plants, but continued technological dependence will ensure that the real terms of trade continue to go against the poor countries – except for short-run periods where effective producer cartels raise the prices of scarce commodities – and in favour of the rich countries from which the required intermediate inputs flow. Where the relationship is between a multinational corporation and its subsidiary in a developing country, the case is particularly obvious. The sort of technology transfer that usually takes place through the agency of multinational corporations is based upon the needs and experience of the multinational, which is primarily concerned with its own comparative advantages, which include the application of a sophisticated technology developed by itself. It will tend to create an industrial structure based on neither the real resource potential of the poor country nor the real needs of its low-income majority, and which is hence incapable of generating self-sustained growth. If the developing country believes that it is developing because of a geographical shift in the location of plants to within its own boundaries, this merely shows that the planners and politicians, no less than the economists, have become the slaves of geography. It has often been pointed out that, when all the dynamic effects are taken into account, the net marginal social productivity of much import-substituting production may well be zero or negative, especially where the import substitute is produced by a foreign investor. This is but another way of expressing the idea that import-substituting industrialization becomes a part of the deteriorating terms-of-trade syndrome, rather than an escape route from it.[13]

Effective import substitution, on the other hand, increases a developing country's technological capacity – as has been the case in many industrial branches in both China and India since the mid-1950s. The Third World countries cannot overcome the problem of underdevelopment as long as efforts are not made to bridge the technological gap that separates them from the richer countries. The poor countries must somehow obtain and apply a technology that takes into account their factor endowment and fits their needs and requirements. The key to the whole issue is to reorient the system of trade, aid and other forms of resource flows and transfer that characterizes the relationship of the rich and poor countries. If a method can be devised and built into the various transfer mechanisms that ensures that the poor countries successfully adapt technological developments to their own requirements and also create their own indigenous technology based on their own resource potential, every form of association and contact between the rich and poor countries will be of much enhanced use to the latter. If the technological gap is not overcome, no form of assistance, trade concessions, aid, grants, technical assistance or fortuitous price rises will prove to be of lasting value. International cooperation policies must be devised that serve to remove this fundamental obstacle in the path of development.

The evolution of such policies cannot take place in a political vacuum. All international trade and monetary reforms have occurred as a consequence of protracted bargaining in which political factors have played an important role. The view that such reforms are mere institutional rationalizations of change, occasioned by developments in the international environment and by automatic self-equilibriating market forces, is based on an entirely unjustified belief in economic determinism. In particular, the distribution of gains between different groups must be determined by a set of political and social criteria that finds expression in specific policies. If the rich countries seek today to retain the existing international economic structure, it is primarily because they lack the political will to make sacrifices that can permit both rich and poor countries to take better advantage of the potential for world economic growth. Policies aimed at creating a new international division of labour have been in short supply since the early 1980s, due – at least in part – to the triumph of the advocates of monetarist doctrines in key western economies. One of the consequences of this has been the emergence of a stalemate in negotiations between North and South for an orderly reform of the international trade and financial system. However, since 1982 the United States has effectively abandoned monetarist policies, seeking deliberately to stimulate domestic demand and maintain it at a high level. There is also some renewed interest in restructuring the dialogue between North and South so as to discover areas in which cooperation can lead to discovering the real and concrete mutual interests that link progress in the Third World with the economic wellbeing of the West. Cooperation between North and South is essential because the South cannot of itself bridge the technological gap that divides it from the North and because the North cannot in the long run sustain its economic recovery without supporting genuine economic progress in the Third World.

Notes

1   By 'economic development' is meant not simply an increase in the GNP of a country, but rather a decrease in poverty at an individual level. Probably the best indicators of poverty are low food consumption and high unemployment. If these problems are effectively dealt with along with growth of GNP and with a reasonably equitable income distribution, then and only then can genuine economic development be thought to have occurred.

2 Calculated from World Bank, *World Development Report 1985* (Washington DC). and UNCTAD, *Trade and Development Report 1985* (New York 1986).

3 UNCTAD (n.2).

4 W. Brandt, *Common Crisis* (London: Fontana, 1983).

5 Surendra Patel, 'World economy in transition 1850–2060', in R. Feinstein (ed.), *Capitalism, Socialism and Economic Growth* (London: CUP, 1967).

6 No exception, but on the contrary an extreme example of this, was the entrepreneurial (managerial) class of Soviet Russia, which was inspired by Stalin's philosophy of 'building socialism in one country'.

7 In these calculations we include both OECD and Soviet bloc East European countries in order to make the figures comparable with those provided by Patel (n.5).

8 This estimate expresses the average per capita income of the industrial country group as a percentage of the average per capita income of the developing countries. Estimates for 1850 are taken from Patel (n.5), p. 123. Estimates for the 1980s are very approximate as they are taken from a wide variety of sources.

9 This would not, of course, necessarily reduce the gap between the rich and poor countries, because the rich would be growing too. However, any country that attains the income level of a rich country of 1987 (in real terms) would no doubt have escaped the vicious circle of stagnation or downward cumulative causation.

10 'Technology is the employed or operative knowledge of the means of production of a particular group of goods or services' (D. Yudelman, C. Butler and R. Banerji, *Technological Change in Agriculture and Employment in Developing Countries*, Paris: OECD Development Centre, 1971).

11 The term 'economic dealings' does not cover grants and untied aid, which may not be of economic benefit to the rich countries in a short-run sense.

12 H. W. Singer, 'The distribution of gains between investing and borrowing countries', Paper presented at the 1949 meeting of the American Economic Association, *American Economic Review*, May 1950. Also R. Prebisch, *Economic Development of Latin America and the Principal Problems* (New York: UN Economic Commission for Latin America, 1950). Recent evidence on the continuing decline in the terms of trade of developing countries is provided by A. Thirlwall and B. Trevithick, 'Trend, cycles and asymmetries in terms of trade', *World Development*, July 1985.

13 This argument is developed at greater length in H. W. Singer, 'Dualism revisited', *Journal of Development Studies*, 7(1), 1970.

3   *The Poor Countries*

Chapter 2 has attempted to focus attention on the nature of the imbalances that characterize the international economy today. It has been maintained that the technological gap between the rich and poor countries is the main cause of this imbalance. The fact that the rich countries are the natural home of multinational investment and of scientific and technological research and development conforming to their factor endowment goes a long way to explaining why – relatively speaking – it is easier for these countries to make rapid economic progress and to maintain high levels of output, employment, investment and consumption. The poor countries, on the other hand, cannot initiate or sustain high levels or rapid growth, precisely because they do not possess those institutions that can create and foster a technology based on their own resource endowments. In all the late-starters of the rich world the initial days of rapid development were characterized by the mushrooming of numerous business groups, research institutions, etc., which learnt the techniques then in vogue from the older countries and then adapted these techniques for their own use. This allowed countries like Japan and West Germany to take innumerable short-cuts and to profit from the experiences of the Anglo-Saxon countries. Hence the pace of development of the late-starters has been much more rapid than that of the older industrialized countries.

Why is the performance of the poor countries of today so different from that of some of the poor countries of, say, 100 years ago? The answer to this question lies in the much greater *relative* strength of the countries that are rich now, and the much greater *relative* weakness of the poor countries of today. The gap between the rich and poor countries has widened to such an extent that it is no longer possible for the poor countries to make good their deficiency in the way in which a number of the then poor countries did in the last century.

This is demonstrated most strikingly when we examine the impact of the world recession during 1979–83 on the developing countries.

The Impact of the Recession

During 1979–83, there were sharp reductions in the rates of growth of output in almost all the developed economies of the world. Unemployment rates rose to levels higher than at any time since the Great Depression of the 1930s. Developing countries' economies contracted as well, particularly those dependent upon the industrial countries through trade in primary commodities and finance.

Sharp rises in the price of oil and grain, lower growth and generally high rates of inflation had already been experienced in the 1970s and imposed considerable hardships on people in almost all countries. Yet, except in Africa, the overall rates of growth of output over the 1970s remained high enough in both the developed and developing market economies to prevent actual decline in per capita output and real income. Moreover, some of the poorer oil exporters (like Indonesia and Nigeria) gained significantly from oil price increases. Others, adversely affected by the oil price hike, avoided retrenchment and decline by securing loans from various sources. This was particularly true of the newly industrializing countries such as Brazil and South Korea.

All this changed in the early 1980s. Not only did rates of growth of output turn negative in many LDCs, but the terms of trade also moved sharply against the developing world, hitting particularly those dependent on exports of primary products. Countries that had earlier borrowed heavily were now burdened with debt-servicing problems on an unprecedented scale, especially on account of higher interest rates and the shorter periods for which the loans were being extended. Many were also constrained by contractionary policies often put in place as part of a package of 'adjustment measures' required to meet the conditions for obtaining balance of payments assistance. What was in the beginning seen as only a temporary dislocation had turned into a crisis of very serious proportions for the developing countries.

Another feature that is revealing of the gravity of the recession was

35

the widespread loss of employment in the manufacturing sector mostly urban-based, of many developing countries. Such loss, the first since the early 1960s, provoked a significant fall in the income of the industrial workforce. The gravity of the situation was compounded in most developing countries by the sharp decline of imports, which fell well below the 1980 level. Unlike on the occasion of the previous downturn of the world economy – when several poor countries were able to maintain their imports and growth through massive borrowing – this resulted in lower imports of food, drugs and other basic items.

This adverse turn reduced the rate of growth of output most seriously in Africa and Latin America (including the Caribbean). South Asia and East Asia were less seriously affected, partly because China and India were much less vulnerable to external pressures exerted through international trade and finance and continued to grow at about the same rate as earlier. Many countries in East and South-east Asia also showed greater resilience, partly on account of the stimulus and support received from their close relations with the dynamic Japanese economy.

A disaggregation of the rates of growth of output in developing countries makes clear the widening impact of world recession. In at least thirty-four countries per capita output appears to have fallen between 1979 and 1985; the number in which per capita *income* fell must be presumed to have been still larger. And in most cases the extent of the decline was very much greater than in the industrialized countries.

It is not only countries whose output has fallen that have been adversely affected by the deepening of economic disorder in the world over the last few years. Other countries (such as the Philippines) have managed to prevent noticeable declines in the rates of growth of output but have suffered substantial deterioration in terms of trade, particularly on account of the rise in oil prices and continuing upward movement in the price of machinery and other capital equipment. Their national incomes adjusted for the terms of trade have been negatively affected far more than GDP figures would suggest. Still others have had to bear rapidly growing debt-service burdens arising from the loans secured to tide over their adjustment problems in the course of the last decade. Lower growth and the adjustments to balance-of-payments problems have created

36

the prospects of long-term stagnation in these countries as well as leading to growing unemployment and substantial cuts in various social service programmes, usually with serious repercussions on the poorest and most vulnerable sections of society. In short, the momentum of development in the less advanced countries of all shades (including those that were doing well until 1980) has been severely reduced. The spectre of a world depression that might, in certain parts of the world last several years, possibly the rest of this decade, can no longer be dismissed as a mere figment of pessimistic imagination.

It is widely recognized that world economic recovery in the West, though necessary for the rekindling of economic growth in the poor countries, cannot of itself – through a 'trickle-down' effect – stimulate economic expansion in the Third World. Thus Third World economies have continued to lag behind and have hardly benefited at all from the western economic recovery of 1984–6. That is why the second Brandt Report[1] puts special emphasis on highlighting the ways in which the rich countries could stimulate economic recovery of the South. Effective stimulus can be provided only by taking into consideration the needs and capabilities of the countries of the Third World.

In this chapter a little time will be spent discussing the structure of the economy of a 'typical' poor country. This will enable us to understand (1) the ways in which the rich countries can help the poor countries, and (2) the extent to which the poor countries can, and must, help themselves. The fact that a country is poor reflects the existence of a set of structural relationships, between sectors and between factors of production, that impede development. It is often forgotten that development means growth *plus* change. To initiate a process of sustained development it is therefore necessary:

- to alter the existing pattern of economic relationships in such a way that the released dynamism of the economic structure induces growth in production,
- to make this growth in production self-sustaining, and
- to spread it through the different sectors and groups of the population, especially those below the poverty line.

Development of a country thus requires the formulation and

implementation of a specific strategy that identifies both the bottlenecks and the methods by which they are to be overcome. Such a strategy will, of course, vary from country to country, and over time.

The development strategy that is adopted must take into account the interrelationship of the different economic sectors within the country. Policy-makers should concentrate on fostering development in the sectors that, if developed, promise to propel the rest of the economy into a process of rapid growth or that, if left underdeveloped, would crucially constrain the development of the economy. The foreign trade sector, for example, deserves attention in a country where industrial development depends crucially on the availability of certain inputs that cannot be domestically produced.

The extent to which the rich countries can help (or hinder) the poor countries in their development depends critically on the role and importance of the foreign sector in the latter, which is best estimated by the substitutability of domestic resources for foreign resources. Countries that do not have a high ratio of foreign trade and investment to GNP may yet be dependent on the supply of crucial imports that cannot be substituted by domestic resources and that have considerable forward and backward linkage effects. Trade may also be important because it leads to an expansion of employment or a desired change in the pattern of income distribution, even if this does not mean a rapid increase in GNP per capita. On the other hand, certain sectors of the economy may be entirely uninfluenced by foreign resource flows. Thus the balance between the use of domestic and foreign resources will depend on the extent to which the growing sectors of the economy need these resources. The structural relationships, including specifically income distribution, within the economy will determine the proportion in which domestic and foreign resources are required. Preliminary to an analysis of trade and aid, therefore, is a discussion of the structure of the economies of the underdeveloped countries and a look at the major structural changes that are needed for sustaining a process of self-perpetuating development.

The Economic Structure of the Poor Countries: Unity in Diversity

The poorer countries of the world include the whole of Asia with the exception of Japan, the whole of Africa with the exception of South Africa, and the whole of the western hemisphere except for the United States and Canada (i.e. Latin America and the Carribean area). Thus defined, the developing countries include about two-thirds of the world's population – approximately 2,500 million people. Much of what will be said also applies to the poorer countries on the southern fringe of Europe (e.g. Portugal, Spain, Albania, Greece, Yugoslavia and southern Italy). The mention of southern Italy is a reminder of the oversimplification involved in speaking of the poorer 'countries'. Many or all of the richer countries (e.g. the United Kingdom and United States) include regions of groups that have low incomes and share many of the characteristics of the poorer or less developed countries. On the other hand, many of the poorer countries have areas or enclaves of glittering modernity, and their higher-income groups may live at levels of affluence greatly exceeding the average affluence of the so-called richer countries. Regional differences (e.g. those between southern and north-eastern Brazil) may span a range similar to that between rich and poor countries. This oversimplication need not worry us too much, however, as long as we take due account of the diversity of situations within the poorer countries and remember that 'development' must mean bringing forward their poorer groups and regions.

More serious is another oversimplification. The 'Third World' includes about 150 independent countries and dependent territories, which differ from each other in practically every imaginable respect except that, on average, they are to a greater or lesser extent dependent on the rich countries as a source of technology and information. Some of the poorer countries are very large and populous (e.g. India and China), while others are tiny mini-states. Some have good and stable governments; others are extremely badly governed. Some have oil or other valuable resources; others have little or nothing (presently known). Some represent natural arteries of world trade (e.g. Singapore); others are remote and landlocked (e.g. Nepal, Bolivia, Chad and Afghanistan). Some are extremely primitive and have very little beyond traditional subsistence agriculture; others have sophisticated industrial, urban and social patterns (e.g. India, Brazil and Egypt). Some have shown rapid economic growth in the recent past; others have been stagnant. Some have experienced sharp social and political changes; others have remained bound by ancient traditions. Some are ultra-capitalist, some are communist and centrally planned, while most are mixed economies in varying degrees.

The fact is that the world is not sharply divided into two classes of countries, one rich and one poor. There is more of a continuum, and in many ways it might be more useful to distinguish four or five classes of countries representing different 'stages' of development. Five such classes would be:

- the really mature developed countries (e.g. the United States, Canada, France and Germany);
- the poorer among the more developed countries, many of which are rapidly catching up (e.g. Italy, Spain, Greece and Japan, and presumably also the USSR, Czechoslovakia, Poland and Yugoslavia);
- the more developed among the poorer countries, many of which have an intermediate status and many of which also are rapidly catching up (e.g. Taiwan, Singapore, Israel, South Korea and Turkey);
- the OPEC countries are in a class all of their own, rich in wealth but often possessing primitive and weak socio-economic infrastructures incapable of absorbing the enormous income they earn;
- finally, there are the really poor countries (e.g. India, Indonesia, Bangladesh, Haiti, Ethiopia and Chad), which illustrate a great variety of circumstances.

The developing countries are not all poor countries, though the overwhelming majority of them certainly are. We must carefully avoid, therefore, using the increase in per capita income as an *identification* of development. This would be an extremely narrow view. An increase in per capita income, reflecting an increase in production, in many ways is merely the end product of factors or forces that cause economic development, rather than its cause or essence. Even the ultimate objective of development is a great deal more than a mere increase in per capita income; questions relating to the use and distribution of this income are as important dimensions of development policies as its increase. The good society is not identical with the affluent society, nor a better society with a more affluent one. Indeed, an important question raised by a study of development concerns ultimate aims and objectives. An increase in production at the expense of the total destruction of the ecological balance nationally or internationally is clearly undesirable. Similarly, the destruction of the cultures and traditions of the peoples of the Third World is not necessarily a universally acceptable cost of development. The formulator and executor of development policies must recognize that development implies political and social change. The justification of specific policies may be sought, not in the application of narrow economic criteria, but rather on the basis of a socio-political consensus that defines the objectives of national development policy. These objectives would usually be related to the desire for material well-being, social and economic security, freedom from grave want, preservation of national institutions, etc.

The fact that the per capita GNP and aggregate GNP are inadequate as measures of the progress of the LDCs can be further substantiated in the case of India, as the result of an interesting study made by two Indian economists. These two authors analysed India's progress during the decade 1954–64 on the basis of twenty-one factors that can be taken as indicators of increase in the development potential. These include: number of factory establishments; power capacity; transport capacity (various indicators); net area irrigated; postal and other communications; output and imports of intermediate and capital goods; number of bank branches; enrolments in primary schools, secondary schools, universities and polytechnics; number of wage and salary earners in factories; patents registered; and fertilizers consumed. On the basis of these indicators, the authors concluded that the rate of progress of India during that decade was 7.3 per cent per annum – over double the rate of growth in national income at constant prices, which was only 3.5 per cent per annum. The authors concluded that 'this appears to suggest that, provided the momentum of the development process is maintained, the growth rate in national income could accelerate after the adaptation lags are completed'.[2] A similar discrepancy would seem to apply to the LDCs in general, though the relationship between

41

real growth and GNP growth might be reversed in some cases. Thus there is evidence, for India as well as many other countries, that the situation, as measured by the number and proportion of people living below a very low poverty line, has actually worsened rather than improved.[3] The overall evidence is thus confusing and difficult to interpret.

Although the physical environment and the resource endowments of the developing countries differ widely, it is nevertheless possible to identify a more or less common set of economic processes and relationships that prevent a full utilization of their resources. Economists often indicate these processes by stressing that development is hindered by the operation and domination of a series of interlocking vicious circles. Different characteristics of the economy are related to each other in such a way that a general breakthrough is difficult, if not impossible. We can identify, in an aggregative and general sense, a number of characteristics that determine the structural relationships peculiar to poor countries.

One important characteristic has been the relatively fast rate of population growth. It would, of course, be hazardous and perhaps unrealistic to argue that a specific country had reached, or exceeded, its optimum population level. This level is a limit that recedes continuously with increases in the efficiency of factor utilization and with technological progress. However, in the poor countries today, unlike in the developing countries of the last century, population growth pre-empts some of the growth in productive capacities.

The higher birthrate of the poor countries means that the proportion of children and young people at any point of time is very much higher there than in the richer countries. Typically, in the poor countries nearly half the population is under 15 and almost two-thirds is under 25. This means that the poor countries have to devote much more of their resources to the task of raising a new generation of producers, besides providing services of a given standard to an enlarged and rapidly urbanizing population.

The low per capita incomes of the poor countries prevent the generation of a sizeable investible surplus. New sectors of modern economic growth thus remain very small, especially in terms of employment, and are often foreign-controlled. The national economy at large remains deprived of new capital infusion. In the poor countries, agricultural production accounts for about 40–50 per cent

42

of GNP, while in the rich countries the ratio is about 5 per cent. Moreover, about three-quarters of the total population of a poor country is engaged in the agricultural sector.

It has been contested ever since Ragnar Nurkse proposed turning the rural 'surplus labour' into capital, and since Arthur Lewis in his famous Manchester School paper talked of 'unlimited labour supply' in developing countries,[4] whether the people in the agricultural sector could be said to be unemployed or underemployed. The problem of lack of productive employment in the poor countries is, however, by no means confined to agriculture. It also exists in the urban and non-agricultural sectors to a significant degree. Indeed, the underutilization of all factors of production (capital, labour, etc.) is a central feature of the economy of a poor country. The underutilization of labour is both the cause and effect of a distortion of the consumption and investment patterns and of high and rising inequalities of income distribution. The poor country cannot afford to allocate resources to any but the most essential uses, and yet such a concentration may clash with the demand structure reflecting a highly unequal income distribution. The result is that investment in the socio-economic infrastructure is well below its optimum level. The low level of expenditure on education, health, transportation facilities, credit and marketing arrangements, etc. leads to the prevalence of high mortality rates, the inadequate provision of health, education and nutrition needs, inadequate access to public services and support, and a widening of the gap between the different income classes within the poor country. Governments often, and usually wrongly, believe that such conditions must be tolerated and unequal income distribution fostered in order to create an investible surplus, and that this leads to growth of the economy, which will later benefit the masses.

These structural bottlenecks of a 'typical' poor economy reflect its basic inability to evolve and use a technology that caters to its own resource endowment and resource potential and deals with rapid population growth. The great scientific and technological upsurge that the world has been experiencing since the turn of the century has almost completely bypassed the poor countries. These countries are, with few exceptions, dependent on the richer countries to meet their technological needs.

Capital-surplus oil exporters are not confronted with low investment rates. They have financial resources in plenty, but the underdeveloped socio-economic infrastructure of these countries impedes structural change. Thus despite abundant foreign exchange and investment funds, investment opportunities are severely limited and technological backwardness thwarts their development effort. The desire to participate in the management of the international economy and to influence the diffusion of technology internationally is thus shared by all nations of the Third World.

Almost all world expenditures on science and technology take place inside the richer countries, and research and development are therefore quite naturally directed towards solving *their* problems by methods suited to *their* circumstances and resource endowments. The problems of the poorer countries, however, are not the same; for instance, they need research to design simple products, to develop production for smaller markets, to improve the quality of and to develop new uses for tropical products, and above all to develop production processes that utilize their abundant labour. Instead, emphasis is placed on sophisticated weaponry, space research, atomic research, sophisticated products, production for large high-income markets, and specifically a constant search for processes that save labour by substituting capital or high-order skills.

The accumulation of knowledge in directions broadly irrelevant and sometimes harmful to the poorer countries hurts them in so far as the new knowledge inevitably tends to destroy or submerge the old knowledge, which often was more relevant and useful to them. Thus, where the long line of economists looking hopefully to science and technology for easing the task of development went wrong, was in placing great emphasis on the *volume* of knowledge without paying equal regard to the *composition* of that volume. Some economists and other scientists have the rather naive idea that the accumulation of scientific and technological knowledge provides a growing stock or inventory of possibilities, and so constantly widens the spectrum of technological possibilities open to LDCs. What this view neglects is that in practice only the 'latest', most 'advanced' or most 'modern' of the known technologies is actually available; the others have been displaced or destroyed. Thus the spectrum of technologies available to developing countries is not widened; on the contrary, the range of *suitable* technologies – suitable that is for the LDCs – is constantly diminished. Partly this is no doubt the fault of the LDCs themselves, since they often accept the identification of 'suitable' with 'modern' or 'advanced'. As 'modern' and 'advanced' nearly always mean more capital-intensive and less labour-intensive, i.e. less employment-intensive, the use of such technologies exacerbates the rising unemployment and underemployment that have often assumed frightening proportions in the poorer countries, particularly among the younger job seekers pouring from the rapidly expanding ranks of primary and secondary school leavers.

Paradoxically, simply to increase scientific and technological expenditures within the underdeveloped countries within the present system may be no remedy at all. Their present expenditures are much too small and scattered to be effective and they also suffer from the shortage of trained research people (particularly just below the top level). To be more effective, these expenditures would have to be multiplied to a degree clearly beyond the resources of many of these countries without extensive financial or technical assistance. More important and feasible is a reversal of policies that presently often discourage and harass such elements of national and labour-intensive technologies as are found particularly in the informal sectors of these countries. In the case of private foreign investment, all the forces are working in the direction of the investors, especially the multi-national corporations, using their own home-made technology. The widespread use of labour is often further discouraged by the relatively high wages – high relative to rural incomes – paid to regularly employed workers, wages strongly pressed for and often readily conceded. Aid and technical assistance work in the same direction: aid is available for imported capital goods, but much less so for local employment-creating expenditures, while technical assistance fails to be adapted to different local conditions, especially considering the short duration of the assignments of most experts from the more developed countries. Training fellowships for nationals of the poorer countries all too often are synonymous with training in methods that are more suitable for rich countries and sometimes positively harmful for the trainees' countries.

Technological dependence intensifies what, for want of a better word, is called 'dualism'. Most LDCs have a large, stagnant, agricultural sector that is linked to a small, modern, large-scale, industrial sector mainly through the supply of resources, both labour and capital, from the former to the latter. The growth of the industrial sector neither initiates a corresponding growth process in the rural sector nor generates sufficient employment to prevent a growing population in the stagnant sectors. The industrial sector of the poor countries is really a periphery of the metropolitan industrial economies, critically dependent on them for the technology it uses. Hence its pattern of production fails to make an impact on the economy as a whole. The central task of development planners is to integrate the industrial and agricultural sectors in such a manner that growth and structural change in one sector initiate and support corresponding developments in the other, while the human and natural resource potentials of the country are more fully utilized. The flood of migration from the depressed rural sector, combined with the small employment potential of the modern industrial sector, results in an increasingly large, overflow shanty-town district in urban areas.

This section has looked at a few of the salient characteristics of a 'typical' less developed economy. Such an economy, we have seen, is characterized by low income levels, high rates of population growth and technological dependence. These characteristics lead to low saving rates, small foreign exchange earnings and lack of integration between the rural and the urban sectors of the economy. The process of economic development must break the vicious circles of poverty and stagnation that prevent economic growth and structural change. The few rich Third World countries do not experience this vicious circle, but even here dualism is no less pronounced and real development is limited by the absence of an adequate technology. The next section is addressed to an analysis of the major aspects of this development process.

The Development Process

The theoretical literature on economic development has been growing at a very rapid rate since the end of the Second World War. There exists no central body of doctrine that is generally accepted as *the* theory of economic development, as different authors have emphasised different aspects of the development process. Indeed

some authors – such as Deepak Lal – question the legitimacy of the
sub-discipline of development economics and by implication deny
the possibility of the construction of a general theory in this field. A
strikingly important aspect of the development process is its
complexity; economic, political, social, demographic and cultural
factors all interact to produce growth and change. A comprehensive
analysis of the relationship and the behaviour of all these factors is
not possible given the existing state of knowledge in the social
sciences. Social, and particularly economic, theory deliberately
seeks to abstract from the complexity of the process, in order to
focus attention on those relationships considered to be crucial. All
unifactor theories of development attempt to identify the dominant
vicious circle, in the sense that they hypothesize about the particular
set of relationships between a few variables that are considered the
prime cause of underdevelopment.

It is impossible, and unnecessary, in a book of this nature to
undertake a comprehensive survey of the major theories and schools
concerning development. Excellent surveys are available.[5] We are
here interested mainly in understanding the role of the external
sector as a stimulant for development – more specifically, the role of
foreign trade, foreign capital, foreign technology and foreign skills
in the process of development. We wish to know not only how the
level of production is affected by different levels of foreign
resources, but also what would be the effects of substituting foreign
for domestic resources, and vice versa.

One analytical tool developed by economists that could help in
this is the production function. This is a technical relationship
expressing the quantity of output in a production process as a
function of the quantity of imputs consumed. *For a given technology* a
production function indicates how the level of output varies with
different levels of imputs. It enables the marginal productivities of
the different inputs of production to be calculated, and also their
degree of substitutability. For our purposes, therefore, we could use
a production function to assess the contribution of foreign resources
to production and the consequences (in terms of output) of
substituting domestic for foreign resources.

If domestic saving or production can easily be substituted for
foreign exchange earnings or imports respectively, the external
sector is not critically important for development policy and a

vigorous fiscal policy or other promotional policies may suffice. On the other hand, if such substitution is difficult, the domestic economic policies of the government will not be adequate to meet a foreign resource shortage. The value of the substitution parameter in a constant elasticity of substitution (CES) production function can measure the structural characteristics of an economy.[6] Theoretically there is no reason why we cannot first define a CES production function that specifies as its inputs domestic capital and foreign exchange, and then estimate the elasticity of substitution between those factors.

The formulation of the CES production function has enabled economists to focus attention on the problem of factor substitutability. Many theories of economic development, especially the 'two-gap' models[7] first put forward in the early 1960s, explicitly recognized the importance of factor substitutability. All the main approaches to the problem of economic development have made assumptions about factor substitutability. The classical theory assumes that the only limit on development is the savings of the society; given this saving, which is thought of in the form of a surplus over 'subsistence' consumption, factor substitutability is infinite. The 'stage' theories in the tradition of Walt Rostow assume, like the classical theory, that savings is the main constraint on development. The 'balanced growth' theories stress external economies, market conditions and demand in general. Hirschman, in his theory of 'unbalanced growth', stresses the low substitutability between capital and the 'ability to invest', i.e. entrepreneurial and managerial skill; he recommends concentration of effort on 'induced' rather than 'autonomous' investment because then an increase in capital is matched by entrepreneurial ability. Finally, the 'capital' theories in the Harrod–Domar tradition and the 'labour surplus' theories (Lewis, Ranis and Fei, etc.) assume that factor substitutability is infinite and that savings is the only constraint on growth.[8].

The problem of factor substitutability has been dealt with extensively in the two-gap models. Growth may be constrained because the resources that are available cannot be substituted for resources that are not, i.e. a minimum amount of each factor of production is necessary if the structural bottlenecks that limit development are to be overcome. The 'three-gap' models identify a 'savings constraint', a 'balance-of-payments constraint' and a 'skill constraint' which may limit development. These constraints represent gaps between the demand and supply of capital, foreign exchange and skills respectively. It is argued (and considerable empirical support has been provided to back this assumption) that capital, labour and foreign exchange cannot be substituted for each other freely, i.e. that the elasticity of substitution between these factors is low. Investment and growth in most developing countries may be regarded as being highly influenced by the foreign exchange available to import capital goods. Chenery has shown that the development of a large number of poor countries is limited mainly by their lack of foreign exchange and that these countries cannot substitute domestic resources for foreign exchange in order to achieve their planned growth targets. Similarly, Weisskopf and Marris and a large number of other researchers have shown that poor countries have extensive foreign exchange requirements. Half the countries in Marris's sample had their growth limited by the scarcity of foreign exchange; the other half had the required foreign exchange and skilled manpower but were short of domestic savings. This shows that the external sector can play a crucially important role in determining the pace and direction of a poor country's development.[9]

The growth rate that can be attained by a poor country under given supply and demand conditions of the factors of production is determined at the lowest level where the *tightest* constraint becomes operative. If the economy functions at this level, the other factors of production are, of course, not fully utilized, because they cannot be substituted for the factor that is limiting growth. The gap may therefore be defined as the difference between (1) the quantities of the factors of production that are required if the country is to grow at a maximum possible rate (where the least limiting constraint is operative), and (2) the existing supplies of the factors. For example, if the attainable growth rate on account of domestic savings availability is higher than that on account of the availability of foreign exchange, the foreign exchange constraint may be said to be dominant and an import gap exists.

The view of the development process thus unfolded is a complex one. It emphasizes the importance of the availability of the requisite factors of production in the *right proportions* to the developing societies. The three-gap models have shown that the strategy of development must concentrate on the alleviation of the dominant constraint. An increase in foreign exchange earnings will not be useful when the savings gap is dominant, and an increase in domestic savings will be of little value when skilled labour is the main constraint, except to the extent that substitution exists or can be promoted.

Development Strategy: National and International

During the 1950s and 1960s many developing countries tried to eliminate the structural bottlenecks that limit growth and change through the extensive use of national economic plans. In most developing countries in Asia, Africa and Latin America, economic planning took place within the context of a 'mixed economy'. The planners thus have usually thought in terms of financial balances. The core of a 'typical' development plan of a 'typical' poor country in the 1950s was the sections that described how savings (private and public) were to be mobilized and allocated between alternative (private and public) investment uses. Implicit in the plans was a preoccupation with growth models of the Harrod–Domar type, which see a saving deficiency as the main hurdle for a developing economy. Admittedly, some plans adopted a more disaggregated approach and identified a number of different sectors of the economy. Professor Mahalanobis's plan for the Indian economy deserves special mention in this connection. However, neither the aggregate nor the disaggregated approach dealt explicitly with the problem of factor (or resource) substitutability.

In the 1960s some poor countries adopted the two-gap models as the framework within which their plans were constructed. Pakistan's Third Five-Year Plan (1965–70) and Perspective Model (1965–85) were based on the two-gap theories. The planners sought to use the foreign resources available along with other factors in such a way that dependence on foreign assistance would be eliminated by 1985.[10] This, the planners foresaw, would involve both an increase in the capacity of the economy to earn foreign exchange and a substitution of domestic produce for imports. In other words, a change in the coefficients of the inputs of the aggregate and sectoral production functions was envisaged, by substituting (1) foreign assistance for domestic savings and export earnings in the initial stages, and (2) domestic savings and export earnings for foreign assistance in the later years.

Development planning went out of favour in the 1970s and 1980s owing both to problems experienced in policy implementation within the domestic economy and to the near impossibility of adapting national economic strategies smoothly to unforeseen and unpredictable external trade and exchange rate shocks. Five-year plans have given way to 'rolling' plans, annual development plans, etc. and international agencies have generally encouraged the move away from medium-term and perspective planning. Nevertheless, the concern with providing estimates of medium-term foreign exchange requirements and availabilities has endured. Thus, the World Bank now provides increasingly detailed time series data on the debt profiles of a very large number of developing countries and these estimates are supposed to provide an important input for the development of IMF stabilization programmes. As we shall see in Chapter 9, these so-called stabilization programmes encompass a wide range of macroeconomic policies. Changes in these policies are required, the IMF argues, to increase efficient utilization of a country's scarce foreign exchange resources – particularly the component of foreign exchange that is made available in the form of concessional foreign assistance.

There are very real constraints on the useful utilization of foreign assistance. In the 1940s and 1950s, when underdevelopment was thought of merely as a state of capital scarcity, it was assumed that all money obtained as foreign assistance by a poor country would be spent entirely on investment and capital imports. There was nothing in conventional theory on which such an assumption could be based, for clearly some of the foreign assistance would be allocated to consumption purposes.[11] Recently it has been claimed that foreign aid and investment contribute very little in the way of additional saving. A number of time series and cross-section studies have found a negative association between foreign inflows (including foreign assistance and investments) and domestic saving rates. The greater the foreign inflows, the lower are the domestic savings. This may be because increased foreign aid may permit governments to lower public savings (realized through taxation) or because foreign capital may reduce investment opportunities for domestic savers and thus induce them to increase their consumption levels.[12] The precise estimates provided by these studies have limited validity, however, because of the rather imprecise concepts and methodologies on which they are based. To find a negative correlation between two variables is not synonymous with discovering a causal pattern. That domestic savings are negatively associated with foreign inflows need not mean that foreign aid availability causes a reduction in domestic savings. Both saving rates and foreign inflows may be associated with another factor that causes the former to fall when the latter rises. According to Papanek, low savings and high foreign inflows are both caused by exogenous factors, and the negative statistical association between the two variables says nothing about the contribution that foreign aid and assistance can make in the development process. The utility of foreign assistance differs from country to country. Countries well endowed with natural resources, e.g. the oil-rich, Middle Eastern states, have no serious savings or balance-of-payments problems, although trade receipts are a vitally important source of development finance for these countries. Foreign aid can thus make very little contribution towards their development. On the other hand, countries that have limited natural resources and low levels of export earnings depend critically on foreign assistance. Semi-industrialized countries, experiencing difficulties in selling their manufactured exports, find foreign aid and capital inflows very useful in the alleviation of savings and balance-of-payments problems.

An important fact pinpointed by many researchers is that, whatever the relationship between saving and foreign aid, the association between savings and growth on the one hand, and between savings and export earnings on the other, is significantly positive. A country with low export earnings has less chance of developing. The external sector is thus of crucial importance – it can stimulate growth and facilitate structural change by providing resources that cannot be obtained domestically.

However, the economic policy-makers of a poor country are usually confronted with a large number of factors beyond their control when they attempt to accelerate the inflow of foreign resources. This reflects the generally weak position of the poor countries in the international goods and factor markets. Because the production methods and powers of technological innovation of the richer countries are much more efficient than those of the poor countries, the former can substitute for the produce of the latter much more easily or can totally dispense with the need for it. In the short run, however, this may be difficult, and the OPEC countries have in the recent past demonstrated their ability to influence the volume of their export earnings and to determine the terms at which their exports will be traded in international commodity markets. However, they now face the problem of safeguarding their gains in the face of falling oil prices. As things stand, the development of the vast majority of the poor countries is critically constrained by the availability of certain imports. The advantage that the rich country has within the international economy is articulated in the trade patterns and tariff arrangements that exist in the world today.

There is therefore a need for the formulation of an international development strategy, supported and indeed pioneered by the rich countries, that will provide assistance in an increasing flow of resources through trade, aid capital and the transfer of skills and technology to the poor countries. Both multilateral organizations and individual rich countries have a vital role to play in this. Such a strategy must provide for some discrimination in favour of the poor countries in international trade and payment arrangements. The trade and aid policies of the rich countries and of the multilateral organizations (which they largely finance and control) must be designed to supplement the ability of the poor countries to obtain those products and services from the outside world that are required to overcome the bottlenecks now limiting development. This implies that the poor countries must have at their disposal not merely a larger volume of goods but also more appropriate goods. They must be able, in the main, to import a technology that allows them to increase employment, raise productivity levels, improve income distribution patterns and develop their socio-economic infrastructure. Such international strategies were developed by the United Nations, though these strategies may be criticized in detail and in any case have not been effectively implemented.

As we have shown above, foreign exchange shortages became particularly acute constraints on the development of a large number of poor countries during the 1980s. Most seriously affected have been the sub-Saharan African countries – such as Tanzania, Uganda, Sudan and Ethiopia – which have developed highly import-dependent economic structures. Foreign exchange scarcity has led to large-scale economic dislocation, a rapid increase in the rate of capacity underutilization and in some years there has also been massive starvation and malnutrition in these countries. The crisis has also seriously affected those economies that had during the 1970s pinned hopes upon expanding export markets and easy access to international finance. Such countries – Brazil, Mexico and South Korea – have seen a rapid growth in debt-servicing obligations leading to a choking off of domestic economic growth. This has been combined with an increase in the level of protection, which limits the exports of these countries to western markets. The rise in repayment obligations and the slackening of export growth have meant that the debt-service ratio – defined as the ratio of annual debt-service payments to export earnings – went up for virtually every newly industrializing country over the period 1977–84.[13]

Both the poorest and the most rapidly growing economies of the Third World are thus vulnerable to external economic shocks. The external sector plays an important role in determining the pace of their development. The virtual collapse of the North–South negotiations has grave implications for these countries as it does for the West, which can in the not so long run incur substantial losses by the growth of economic and political instability in the Third World. The revitalization of the North–South dialogue – entailing a rapid increase in both trade and concessional development finance flows between the West and the Third World – must therefore be accorded high priority on the international agenda.

Notes

1   W. Brandt, *Common Crisis* (London: Fontana, 1983).
2   V. V. Divatia and V. V. Bhatt, 'On measuring the pace of development', *Banca Nazionale del Lavoro Quarterly Review*, June 1969, p. 73.
3   R. Dandekar and N. Nath, *Poverty in India* (New Delhi: Ford Foundation, 1971).
4   W. R. Lewis, 'Economic development with unlimited supplies of labour, *Manchester School*, 1954, pp. 17–39.
5   For detailed bibliographies see M. Todaro, *Economic Development of the Third World* (London: Longman, 1985).
6   The CES production function was first presented by K. Arrow and H. Chenery, B. Minhas and R. Solow in 'Capital labour substitution and economic efficiency', *Review of Economics and Statistics*, August 1961.

7   The two 'gaps' are the foreign exchange gap and the domestic savings
    gap.
8   A detailed discussion of these theories may be found in H. W. Singer
    and R. Schiavo-Campo, *Perspectives of Economic Development* (Boston:
    Houghton Mifflin, 1970) and A. Thirlwall, *Growth and Development*
    (London: Macmillan, 1983).
9   These studies are discussed in G. Papanek, 'The effect of aid and other
    resource transfers on savings and growth in less developed countries',
    Economic Journal, September 1972, pp. 934–50.
10 Pakistan's economic performance has not been in accordance with these
    expectations and the need for foreign assistance has in fact increased.
    This is recognized by the Sixth Plan, which covers the period 1983–88.
11 This is by no means totally undesirable. If foreign assistance leads to an
    increase in the consumption level of the children, the rural workers or
    the urban poor, it may in effect contribute more towards development
    than the proportion of foreign assistance that finances a highly capital-
    intensive project which, while inflating the GNP, does not contribute
    towards an increase in employment or an improvement in the pattern of
    income distribution.
12 For a discussion of these studies see Papanek (n. 8), pp. 939–50. More
    recent evidence is provided by G. Abbott, 'Two concepts of foreign
    aid', *World Development*, 1 (9), 1973.
13 UNCTAD, *Trade and Development Report 1985* (New York: UN,
    1985), Ch. 3, p. 1.

PART II

Trade

4   *Trade and Development*

Trade and Growth

Chapter 3 has shown that the importance of the foreign trade and
investment sector in the economy of a developing country is
determined by the cost at which domestic resources can be
substituted for foreign inputs during the process of development.
However, development is not synonymous with an increase in GNP
per capita. The cost involved in substituting domestic resources for
foreign exchange may entail changes in the level of employment, the
pattern of income distribution or the structure of public revenue and
expenditure, which may be detrimental to the long-run development prospects of the poor country. The concern with overall
growth rates tends to obscure the fundamental objective of reducing
poverty. Consequently, attempts to isolate the determinants of
GNP growth are by their very nature incapable of going to the real
causal links in the development chain. Little is to be gained therefore
by concentrating attention on the relationship between growth of
GNP per capita and changes in the size of the foreign sector of the
poor country. Foreign trade orientation is not merely reflected in an
association between levels of GNP per capita and ratios of trade to
income. In any case, attempts to relate foreign trade fluctuations to
aggregate variables such as investment, government expenditure
and prices have failed to identify any simple consistent form of
association.[1] The only quantitative relationship that seems firmly
established associates the ratio of exports to investment (both public
and private) with the size of the country. The smaller the country,
the greater is the importance of exports relative to investment.
Otherwise, it has also been estimated that the impact of changes in
export earnings on income generation will be rather limited in the
short run in most poor countries.[2] This finding, however, has been

questioned on the basis of more recent analysis,[3] and clearly much depends on the nature of the exported commodity, its mode of production and the policies of the exporting country.

Yet trade has traditionally been regarded as the main engine of growth. Adam Smith's 'vent for surplus' theory demonstrated that colonial trade could lead to welfare gains – since such trade permitted the colonies to utilize 'surplus' labour and natural resources that would have remained idle in the absence of international trade because of low levels of domestic effective demand. The 'opening up' of Latin America in the fifteenth and sixteenth centuries, and Africa three hundred years later, enabled these economies to move from a point well within their production possibility frontier to a point on this frontier. Such a movement would generally be associated with an increase in the aggregate consumption level – but how much of this was consumption by the expatriates who owned the new plantations and how much consumption by the local people remains an open question. Moreover, gains in trade may create a reservoir of funds for export from the colonies to the capital markets of the mother countries. The surplus on the current account may eventually be converted into a growing deficit on the capital account. Bagchi has shown that the 'opening up' of the Indian economy by colonialism led to a substantial drain of resources and a curtailment of investment, particularly within the Indian industrial sector.[4]

The classical economists did not, however, address themselves to such questions. Their main contribution in the field of trade theory was the theory of comparative advantage, which provided a rationale for holding the view that trade would equalize world prices of commodities and eliminate international differences in the incomes of factors of production. Developing trade between rich and poor countries may be expected to induce international specialization in accordance with the comparative advantage and factor endowments of the trading partners, and to raise labour incomes and reduce the cost of capital in the poorer countries. It should be noted that this factor price equalization is achieved as a consequence of international differences in the true costs of production. If trade patterns do not reflect such specialization, there is no reason to believe that trade will lead to development.

International trade in the modern world does not reflect the

assumptions that underlie the simple (Ricardian) theory of comparative advantage. The theory assumes: (1) that technological knowledge is a free good, or at least is equally available in both countries;
(2) that the trading countries are not too different in their relative
availabilities of capital and labour; (3) that trade is free, i.e.
unencumbered by the existence of tariffs, quotas, etc.; and (4) that
the prices of factors and products represent their true scarcities,
values, etc. However, technological knowledge is not a free good. It
is concentrated in rich countries, and much of it is exclusive to the
international firms. Trade patterns are determined by domestic
policies that require barriers to be placed by governments to regulate
the quantity and the direction of imports and exports. The international differences in resource endowments are enormous, and all the
existing evidence suggests that the gap is widening. Moreover, the
differences are complex and by no means reducible to simple
capital/labour ratios. International trade patterns between rich and
poor countries reflect the bargaining power of the trading partners.
Because the world markets in which trade takes place are characterized by oligopolistic competition, there is no indication that the
economic bargaining position of the poor countries is being
improved. Factor and commodity prices are distorted in all countries
by multiple government and institutional intervention.

If trade is not a simple engine of growth and even less so of
development, it is because the pattern of world trade thwarts
international specialization in accordance with the principle of
comparative advantage. Hence trade does not equalize commodity
prices or factor income. Presbisch and Singer[5] separately have
argued that there are systematic forces at work in world markets that
tend to reduce the gains of the poor countries in international trade;
consequently, trade may actually widen the gap between the rich and
poor countries. Furthermore, the adverse movement in the terms of
trade of the poor countries transfers the benefits of technological
innovations from the poor to the rich and, what is more important,
acts as an impediment to the development of the poor countries. The
theoretical possibility of this has been formally recognized within
the neo-classical tradition since Jagdish Bhagwati developed the
concept of 'immiserising' growth – i.e. growth that remained
concentrated in a sector producing exportables that faced a (price and
income) inelastic demand curve. Bhagwati showed that product-

ivity growth within such an economy would lead to a deterioration in its terms of trade.[6] During the 1950s and 1960s, however, a number of economists challenged the view that the terms of trade of primary producing developing countries had shown a secular declining tendency. But recent empirical evidence conclusively establishes the existence of such a trend. In an authoritative study, John Spraos has shown that the double factorial terms of trade corrected for employment changes and defined as

$$ECDFIT = \frac{V}{p_m ll_m^x}$$

(where V = the index of output of exportables valued at current prices, p_m = the price index of the North's manufactures, ll_m^x = output per person employed in the manufacturing sector of the North) declined for most agricultural goods exports of the South by 2.0–3.5 per cent per annum over the period 1960–78.[7] The net barter terms of trade deteriorated between 1950 and 1970 by about 25 per cent and by a further 9 per cent over 1970–7 for the non-oil-exporting LDCs. Various indices of the terms of trade for primary producing developing countries showed a declining trend over the periods 1900–70[8] and 1973–82.[9] This shows that the structure of international markets is an important determinant of the impact that trade can have on development. It has recently been argued that an export-oriented development strategy is effective only when the international economy is itself expanding and protectionist levels are generally low.[10] This question will be further examined in Chapter 6.

Trade cannot be an agent of development if it does not facilitate structural change within the economy, for development is growth *plus* change. In the case of the oil-producing countries, for example, trade had phenomenal growth long before OPEC but in the past the impact of trade on their economic structure – on poverty, on employment and on income distribution patterns – was less than optimal. The argument that foreign trade and foreign investment may tend to sustain dualistic tendencies within the developing economy reflects the view that the benefits of international specialization in the existing framework of world markets are not shared either efficiently or equitably between different regions and different social groups within the developing country. This brings us to a consideration of the relationship between trade, employment and income distribution.

Trade, Employment and Income Distribution

If development is conceived of as a human (rather than a technical or mechanical) process, it becomes immediately obvious that we cannot speak of development without reference to employment and income distribution. If the GNP of a poor country is growing at a rapid rate but more and more people are finding themselves to be socially and economically useless, and if the wealth and income of the country are being increasingly concentrated in the hands of a microscopic elite of businessmen, landlords and government officials, it is surely wrong to think that such a country is developing. Policies aimed at growth maximization to the exclusion of employment and income distribution considerations have often proved disastrous. Pakistan, Iran and some Central American countries have in the recent past paid a heavy price for pursuing such development strategies.

The most important lesson that must be learnt from such cases is that a great deal of harm can be done by those theorists and practitioners who (explicitly or implicitly) assume a necessary contradiction between growth and equity. There exists no convincing empirical evidence in support of this presumed contradiction, but much to the contrary. Indeed, real development can occur only if there is a sustained increase in the skill and productivity of the mass of the producers of the country concerned. This implies that output growth must go together with improved incomes in the poorer groups, as a result of the more productive employment of labour.

The impact of trade on development can only be properly assessed if we look at the relation between trade and changes in employment and in the pattern of income distribution. A country that uses its export proceeds to import sophisticated capital goods for capital-intensive projects benefiting a small elite cannot expect to derive real benefit from an expansion in trade. The same is true of a country that has no proper policy of maximizing the linkage or indirect employment and income effects of export production, or of concentrating export production among smaller farmers and indigenous firms so as to place the export and related activities within the context of a proper development policy. The rich oil economies earn immense foreign exchange revenues each year, but unless the use made of these funds ensures an increase in both the living standard of all – including the poorest sections of the population of these countries – and the productivity of their labour force, they will simply squander their money.

Existing patterns of trade do not automatically contribute towards desired changes in income and wealth distribution in the poor countries. The emphasis upon the small 'modern' urban sector and the neglect of agriculture, rural development and small-scale industry have invariably resulted in increased levels of income concentration in the poor countries. This change in the pattern of income distribution has in no small measure been assisted by the trade policies of both the poor and the rich countries. The developing countries have often sought to emphasize the necessity for becoming 'self-sufficient', in terms of presently imported goods, and 'industrially modernized'. In the past it was thought this could be achieved if emphasis were placed on import substitution, i.e. on producing goods that were previously being imported for home consumption. Such import substitution was conceived of as a fairly simple process, involving a transfer, usually with the help of aid and foreign investment, of capital and technology. Ambitious programmes of industrialization were drawn up, and attempts were made to divert resources towards the financing of these programmes. This involved a shift to relatively capital-intensive production technologies. Poor countries ran up enormous foreign debts and paradoxically the dependency of these countries on the industrial countries increased rather than diminished. This dependence was mainly technological, for the developing countries essentially failed to devise an indigenous technology based upon domestic resource endowments and capable of increasing the skill and efficiency of the labour force. (Nor did the technologically powerful countries do so on their behalf.) Moreover, the domestic financing of the industrialization programmes invariably involved the impoverishment of both the rural sector and the unskilled urban workers. The gap between the rich and the poor within the developing countries continued to widen, with the result that the goods produced by the newly established import-substituting industries faced a limited market. This tended to reduce the incentive for further saving and investment, and it became difficult either to operate these industries at full capacity or to invest in more sophisticated import-substituting industries.

Trade patterns that can lead to employment expansion and desired changes in the pattern of income distribution in the poor countries are easily conceivable. A country specializing in the export of processed mineral and agricultural goods, or of labour-intensive manufactures, should be able to link trade expansion with employment levels and income distribution patterns. A nation importing relatively simple technology and inputs geared to the small producer in country and town (e.g. small tractors, fertilizers, light software and licensed know-how) should also be able to relate growth through trade to desired structural changes in employment and income distribution. The strategy of development suggested above (provided the trade policies of the rich countries make it possible – a big proviso!) emphasizes the relevance of increasing the productivity of the whole mass of the working population of the poor country and of reorienting its production structure so that it finds it possible to specialize in accordance with its long-run dynamic comparative advantage. It can be a means for combining the best elements in both the import-substituting (IS) and export-oriented (EO) strategies that have often been thought of as mutually exclusive in the past. The trade strategy, in both export and import structure, of a country must reflect its overall development policy. Most developing countries have a comparative advantage in the production of labour-intensive manufactured goods and processed agricultural commodities. Economic policy must aim at developing a production structure in which specialization in the production of these goods, and the use of the resulting foreign exchanged proceeds, increases the skill and efficiency of the labour force, so that expansion in the efficient production of more sophisticated manufactures and in agricultural mechanisation becomes possible in the future – the comparative advantage of the country changing as its production structure becomes more complex.

During the late 1960s the exponents of the EO strategy advocated just such a shift in the trade strategy of the LDCs. Attempts were made to identify exportables with strong employment multiplier effects.[11] It was shown, however, that there were very few exportables and very few countries that were likely to combine an employment-inducing organizational production and trade structure, a favourable technology of production and desirable saving and expenditure patterns. Thus low-income countries may possess a technology that is labour-intensive and employment-inducing but the organization of production within these countries – the dominance of the multinational corporations, the bias of their governments towards technology-intensive production methods, the high propensity of their saver groups to import luxuries – may offset these advantages. Agricultural commodities may be particularly suitable candidates for export expansion because their production processes are labour intensive. However, owing to the generally low international income elasticities of demand with which they are confronted, the rapid growth of synthetic substitutes, the vulnerabilities of their output level to seasonal variations and the weak bargaining position of the labour force employed, the employment gains generated by expansion of agricultural exports are not likely to be particularly significant over a long time-period. Manufactures on the other hand are becoming increasingly competitive at world market prices; their linkage effects on Third World economies are, however, not as great as those of agricultural exports and they generally employ a labour-saving technology of production.

It is thus important that in studying the employment impact of trade expansion we do not stop at an identification of the structural characteristics of production processes – their organization, their technology, their impact on demand, etc. It is necessary to go a step further and treat these structures as variable and open to modification through appropriate policies. We must ask: to what extent is it possible to combine methods of organization of production that enhance the bargaining power of developing countries in world markets with a technology of production that is conducive to employment expansion within them? We must seek in other words to combine organizational forms, technological structures and inter-sectoral relationships that exist at present in different markets and in different countries. In order to do this we must focus attention clearly on the processes of policy-making by the major actors in the developing countries, in international markets that absorb the major exports from the Third World, and in the developed countries. We must study the objectives, strategies and organizational structures of the major buyers and sellers, producers and consumers of products that are of export interest to the LDCs. Our task must be to seek to understand the extent to which modifications within these policies can be brought about to enhance the employment potential of export expansion in different markets and different countries. These modifications should aim at reconciling the economic strategies of different actors in such a way that the conflict between output growth and employment expansion within the LDCs is gradually eliminated. Export expansion should, in other words, contribute not just to an increase in the number of jobs available. It should contribute to an enhancement of the skills of those employed within these jobs and to their ability to participate within the processes of decision-making in these organizations.

Trade can be a means of development only if the international environment is favourable to the poor countries. It is obvious that only if world markets do respond to the developing countries' efforts to specialize in the production of processed commodities and simple manufactures will international trade be able to play a major role in the development process. The international environment, reflecting as it does the economic relations of the rich and poor countries, is an important determinant of development and of world trade patterns. Let us now look at the actual patterns of the international trade of the developing countries.

Developing Countries: Trade Patterns

Table 4.1 summarizes the structure of world trade. Over the period 1961–72 the share of the LDCs in world exports declined while that of the developed countries increased by about 3 per cent. Since then, however, the developing countries have recorded significant gains – their share of world exports going up from 18.8 per cent over the period 1967–73 to almost 26 per cent during 1981–3. The chief beneficiaries have been the oil-exporting countries, which have gained owing to the massive increases in the price of crude during 1973–4 and again in 1979–80, and several newly industrializing countries, particularly the East Asian 'Gang of Four' – Hong Kong, Singapore, South Korea and Taiwan – which have also enjoyed high

Table 4.1 *World exports by destination, 1961–83 (%)*

	Developed OECD	Exports to LDCs	Centrally planned economies[a]
Exports from OECD:			
1961–66[c]	73.8	22.0	3.8
1967–72[c]	76.7	19.1	3.8
1972–74	75.5	19.3	3.7
1975–77	70.1	23.5	4.5
1978–80	71.5	23.0	3.8
1981–83	69.6	24.6	3.9
LDCs:			
1961–66[c]	71.9	21.3	5.7
1967–72[c]	73.6	19.8	5.4
1972–74	73.7	21.1	3.6
1975–77	70.7	23.3	3.9
1978–80	70.7	24.4	3.1
1981–83	64.6	29.7	3.7
Centrally planned economies:			
1961–66[c]	20.9	14.4	64.6[b]
1967–72[c]	24.1	15.0	60.7[b]
1972–74	27.1	13.1	56.2
1975–77	27.2	13.8	56.0
1978–80	29.1	14.9	52.7
1981–83	29.3	17.2	50.7
World:			
1961–66[c]	67.1	21.0	11.4[b]
1967–73[c]	70.5	18.8	10.2[b]
1972–74	70.7	19.4	8.3
1975–77	66.6	22.8	8.9
1978–80	67.5	22.9	7.7
1981–83	64.4	25.6	7.8

Notes:
[a] includes only East European centrally planned economies
[b] includes both East European and Asian centrally planned economies
[c] estimates for 1961–6 and 1967–73 not strictly comparable to those below because of difference in sources.

Sources: IBRD/IDA *Annual Report 1973* (Washington, 1974); UNCTAD, *Handbook of International Trade and Development Statistics 1985, Supplement* (New York: UN, 1985), pp. 66–7.

rates of export growth. Taken as a group, the export growth rate of the non–OPEC developing countries during 1981–3 substantially exceeded that of the OECD countries. During this period the highest growth rate was recorded by trade between developing countries. The annual average rate of growth of exports of non–oil–exporting LDCs to developing countries was 13.5 per cent during 1981–3. Exports to the OECD grew by only 7 per cent per annum. The annual average rate of growth of exports of the OECD countries was only 3.6 per cent during this period.

Despite the relatively rapid rate of growth of intra Third World exports, almost two-thirds of Southern exports are still absorbed in western markets (Table 4.1). Table S.3 shows that the share of the OECD in total Third World imports also stands at over 60 per cent. The share of intra Third World imports increased from 19.0 per cent in 1970 to 30.3 per cent in 1982. Although some of this increase was undoubtedly due to higher prices paid for oil imports, Table S.3 shows that the share of non–OPEC intra-LDC imports also increased from 12.9 per cent to 16.7 per cent over this period.

There has been some change in the commodity composition of Third World trade. The share of manufactures in total Third World exports increased from 16.3 per cent in 1970 to 21.9 per cent in 1982.[12] For a very large number of LDCs, however, agricultural products and minerals still account for the lion's share of export earnings. Depressed commodity prices in recent years have meant that the terms of trade have turned sharply against the LDCs since 1981 (Table S.7). Moreover, the export performance of the LDCs substantially lagged behind that of the rich countries in both 1984 and 1985 – in 1985 developing country exports were virtually stagnant. UNCTAD expected little change in this situation during 1986.[13] This brings home the point that the recovery that began in 1984 has largely by-passed the poor countries. The international trade system has not been an effective conduit for the transmission of growth from the rich to the poor countries. Given the continuing importance of the OECD countries as the predominant trade partners of the LDCs, it is appropriate to turn to an examination of their trade policies to see what changes in these policies are needed to reduce existing imbalances within the world economy.

Notes

1 See, for example, A. MacBean, *Export Instability and Economic Development* (London: Allen & Unwin, 1966), pp. 58–108.
2 ibid., p. 94.
3 UNCTAD, *Trade and Development Report 1985* (New York: UN, 1985), p. 3.
4 A. K. Bagchi, *The Political Economy of Underdevelopment* (London: Cambridge University Press, 1982), pp. 78–90.
5 R. Prebisch, *Towards a New Trade Policy for Development*, UNCTAD Document E/Conf/46/3 (New York 1964); and H. W. Singer, 'The gains from trade', *American Economic Review, Papers and Proceedings*, 1950. The theme of 'unequal exchange' has more recently been further developed by A. Emmanual, *Unequal Exchange* (London: New Left Books, 1972).
6 See J. Bhagwati, 'Immiserising growth. A geometric note', *Review of Economic Studies*, 25, 1957–8, pp. 201–5.
7 J. Spraos, *Inequalising Trade* (Oxford: Clarendon Press, 1983), pp. 70–9, 104–14.
8 ibid., pp. 63–8.
9 H. W. Singer, 'The terms of trade controversy and the evolution of soft financing', in G. Meier and D. Seers (eds), *Pioneers in Development* (London: Oxford University Press, 1984).
10 R. M. Kavoussi, 'International trade and economic development. The recent experience of developing countries', *The Journal of Developing Areas*, 19 (3), April 1985, pp. 379–92.
11 The following paragraphs are based on H. W. Singer and J. A. Ansari, 'Trade access and employment in developing countries', *Canadian Journal of Development Studies*, 1 (2), 1980, pp. 288–302.
12 This is an underestimate since UNCTAD defines manufactures as products in SITC categories 5–8 (less 68 and 69). Many manufactures are included in SITC categories 2, 3 and 4. For a broader definition of manufacturing, see UN Industrial Development Organization, *Industry in the 1960s* (New York: UNIDO, 1985), pp. 37–60.
13 UNCTAD, *Trade and Development Report 1985* (New York: UN, 1985), p. 187.

5   *Trade Policies of the Rich Countries*

The International Trade System

One of the most significant features of the Bretton Woods era (1946–73) was the very rapid growth of international trade: it exceeded the rate of growth of output throughout the 1950s and 1960s. The collapse of the Bretton Woods regime (discussed in Chapter 11) has had a devastating impact on both the volume and pattern of international trade.

Table 5.1 presents estimates of the rate of growth of world trade over the period 1982–6. Negative growth rates in the volume of world trade were recorded in both 1982 and 1983 and there was a sharp fall in the growth rate in 1985. Table 5.1 shows that the developing countries have been particularly severely affected. Export volumes fell in both 1982 and 1983 and were virtually stagnant during 1985. Moreover, the terms of trade of the LDCs continued to decline throughout this period. UNCTAD estimates that the

Table 5.1   *World trade: annual rates of change in volume, 1982–6 (%)*

	1982	1983	1984	1985[a]	1986[b]
OECD countries	−1.0	1.0	9.7	3.0	4.8
Developing countries	−6.3	0.9	8.5	0.5	4.6
World	−3.0	−3.0	8.7	—	4.8

Notes:
[a]   Estimate from UNCTAD TDB/1081, 1980, p. 4.
[b]   Forecast of UNCTAD Secretariat.

Source: UNCTAD, *Trade and Development Report 1985* (New York: UN, 1985), pp. 187, 188.

purchasing power of the exports from the developing countries fell by an annual average of 6.5 per cent over 1982–6, leading to an annual average fall in import volumes of 3.8 per cent.[1]

The slowdown in world trade volumes has been accompanied by an erosion of the rules, norms and procedures governing international trade that had been agreed to in the late 1940s and embodied in the General Agreement on Tariffs and Trade (GATT[2]). GATT committed its contracting parties to seek trade liberalization through a process of successive negotiations aimed at achieving significant cuts in levels of protection. These negotiations were to be based on the principles of non-discrimination and reciprocity. Negotiated concessions were to be extended to all GATT members on the basis of the 'most favoured nation' (MFN) clause, and 'concessions' (i.e. reductions in import barriers) made by one trading partner were to be roughly balanced by 'concessions' from other negotiators. The original agreement also committed the members to a gradual phasing out of all non-tariff protectionist measures in order to ensure the 'transparency' of protectionist measures.

Seven rounds of multilateral trade negotiations (MTNs) have been held under GATT auspices and an eighth is currently under way.[3] During the 1950s and 1960s the system was strengthened in two important respects. First, the process of bilateral, item-by-item negotiation was superseded by multilateral, across-the-board procedures in 1962 at the Kennedy Round. This enhanced the scope of trade negotiations significantly and also reduced the scope for 'free riding' – i.e. for enjoying the benefits of liberalization negotiated by major traders without liberalizing one's own trade – within the system. Secondly, GATT showed increasing awareness of the need to facilitate the integration of the developing countries within the international trade system. In 1955, Article XVIII of the Agreement was amended to take account of the special needs of the developing countries. A decade later, largely in response to the challenge presented to GATT as a result of the creation of a new organization – the United Nations Conference on Trade and Development (UNCTAD) – in which the LDCs enjoyed a voting majority, a new Part IV was added to the General Agreement. This promises to 'accord high priority' to reducing trade barriers to products of export interest to LDCs. Developed countries committed themselves to paying special attention to the trade interests of the developing countries when devising their own trade policies, and in Article XXXVI(8) it is stated that 'the developed contracting parties do not expect reciprocity for commitments made by them in trade negotiations . . . to the trade of less developed contracting countries'. All developed countries agreed to operate a system of generalized preferences with regard to LDC trade in 1970.

Since the early 1970s there has been a gradual and persistent departure from the trade patterns and procedures established during the Bretton Woods period. Although substantial tariff cuts on trade among developed countries were negotiated during the Tokyo Round of GATT negotiations, nation after nation has opted to ignore GATT regulations and procedures in the conduct of an increasing proportion of its international trade. Every country violates the principle of 'non-discrimination' and openly uses trade policy as a means to discriminate against partners regarded as 'disruptive'. The GATT provision permitting emergency import controls to deal with structural balance-of-payments disequilibria (Article XIX(1)(a)) is increasingly misued. The tariff is now an insignificant instrument of trade policy. It has been replaced by the voluntary export restraint agreement (VER), other non-tariff barriers (NTBs), exchange rate manipulation and government subsidization of 'national champion' export industries. 'The actual trading "system" is simply a series of improvisations. While trade may still grow in such a world the functioning of international prices which is a fundamental aspect of international competition has been steadily impaired.'[4]

Developing countries have been particularly seriously affected by the disintegration of the liberal trading regime of the Bretton Woods era. The regime had never covered trade in agricultural products or in textiles, areas of paramount interest to most LDCs, but the rules did apply to most manufactured exports from the Third World. Although tariff reduction in these product groups was significantly less than in the product groups that were of primary interest to the West during both the Kennedy and the Tokyo rounds,[5] the South nevertheless benefited from the existence of a relatively liberal regime and experienced high rates of growth of manufactured exports throughout the 1960s and 1970s. Today the norms of non-discrimination, continuity and transparency have ceased to apply to the bulk of North–South trade. There has been a proliferation of VERs and orderly marketing arrangements (OMAs) involving developed and developing countries. Tariff concessions granted earlier are now altered through OMAs and without reference to Articles XIX and XXVIII of the GATT. A large and growing proportion of trade between the South and the West is administered by a wide range of non-tariff barriers. Anti-dumping and counter-vailing measures and other forms of quantitative restriction are increasingly imposed on products and areas where developing countries have demonstrated comparative advantage. These measures clearly contradict the commitments to a 'standstill' and a 'rollback' of protectionism made at a series of GATT meetings by western representatives since 1982. Two seasoned observers of the world trading system wrote in 1986: 'The breakdown of [the GATT system] is nowhere more evident than in trade relations between developed and developing countries. Here an undeclared trade war is in progress.'[6]

The inability or unwillingness of the OECD countries to fulfil the pledges contained in Part IV has created a great deal of acrimony and bitterness. Many developing countries opposed the holding of the Eighth MTN during 1982–5, arguing that the West had an obligation to meet its earlier commitments on the imposition of a 'standstill' and gradual phasing out of restrictions on LDC imports and a reform of the hitherto indiscriminate use of 'safeguard' and 'emergency' measures by western countries. Some progress on these issues must be achieved during the current MTN if the international trade regime is to be saved from total disintegration. The need for the creation of an efficient and equitable trade regime is particularly urgent in the world's commodity markets.

Trade in Primary Commodities

The predominant role of primary commodities in the trade of the LDCs cannot be ignored. If the broad category of primary products is defined to include raw materials, fuels and unprocessed edibles, exports of primary products have constituted over 75 per cent of the export earnings of the LDCs in the recent past. If oil is excluded, exports of primary products account for about a quarter of the total.

The share of primary products in world trade, however, has been declining since 1950–1 – the short-lived Korean War boom. Long-run prospects for expanding (or even maintaining) the level of external demand for both food and industrial raw materials are rather limited. According to Engel's well-known 'Law', as income rises, expenditure on food tends to constitute a smaller proportion of consumer spending. Hence the overall income elasticity of food exports is low (though there are exceptions) and this is often also the case with exported industrial raw materials. As modern industrial production expands, there is a relative economy in the use of raw materials. Moreover, industrial raw materials produced in the poor countries are confronted in world markets today with competition from synthetic substitutes. The relatively high price and output instability of the raw materials of the LDCs in comparison to these synthetics may also tend to work against an expansion in export demand in the long run.

Yet the sluggishness in the world demand for the primary goods exported by the LDCs cannot be attributed entirely to the change that has occurred in the structure of production in the developed countries. Nor can it be explained merely by reference to the very real increase in the productivity of the agricultural sector of the rich nations. An important element in the reduction of the import demand for primary goods exports from the poorer countries is the protectionist policies being pursued by the industrial countries with respect to their agricultural sector.

By almost any standards, the protection rates of the rich countries against the exports of the LDCs are excessive. Levels of agricultural protection are substantial. The Common Agricultural Policy (CAP) of the European Economic Community (EEC), maintains high domestic prices for agricultural commodities by a system of 'variable levies', which ensure that prices do not fall below those specified by the CAP.[7] The United States also has a highly protectionist policy concerning agricultural trade; support to domestic farm policies is given by a whole range of import quotas. The traditional UK method was less directly protectionist, relying on income deficiency payments to farmers instead of import levies or controls.

The national agricultural policies of the rich countries constitute the most important impediment to the liberalization of trade in agricultural commodities. Such policies have entailed substantial

75

cost to the rich countries themselves. The rich EEC countries, the United States and Japan have devised farm policies in order to increase the income of their rural population and to reduce dependence on food imports. This is usually done by raising the price of agricultural goods and limiting the import of agricultural commodities into the economy. This is by no means the most efficient method of giving assistance to the farming sector, if such support is considered necessary. Support could and should be given in the form of direct income subsidies and the extension of auxiliary agricultural services. This would at least allow for a reduction in the domestic prices of agricultural goods in the rich countries and enable the LDCs to compete through their agricultural exports. Some progress towards the reduction of agricultural protection by the EEC has been made through the Lomé Convention[8] signed in 1975 and ratified in 1979 and in 1984, but much remains to be done.

At present, agricultural trade patterns are disadvantageous from the point of view of the poor countries. The (effective) protection of agricultural production is increasing over time in most countries. The rich countries dominate international agricultural trade, both as sources of exports and as destinations of imports. During the period 1960–84 the share of the poor countries in agricultural trade declined and their reliance on food imports increased. If present protectionist policies are not relaxed the situation is likely to be even more grim in the future. The trade policy of the rich countries is a major contributor to the increasing lack of productive employment in the rural hinterland of the Third World. Improved agricultural technology has made it possible for agricultural production to increase considerably, but, if the fruits of this increased productivity are denied to the small farmers and agricultural workers of the poor countries, the 'Green Revolution' will not facilitate these countries' development.

Developed countries have in recent years significantly increased trade discrimination against primary commodity imports from the LDCs. Tariffs on meat, vegetables, sugar, cereals, tobacco, dairy products and molasses have been traditionally high in the EEC, Japan and the United States. Variable levies and NTBs apply to the import of cereals and dairy products in the EEC. Variable levies are used by the US to restrict imports of sugar. Internal taxes levied in many developed countries on agricultural imports from LDCs are frequently higher than those on domestically produced agricultural products. This has been a major cause of the restriction of the growth of coffee, tobacco, sugar, tea and cocoa exports from the LDCs.[9]

A major feature of the structure of tariffs and non-tariff measures affecting agricultural products in all markets is the general tendency for tariffs to escalate with the stage of processing, and for non-tariff measures to weigh more heavily on the more processed forms of commodities. Very often no tariff or non-tariff measure is applied against imports of a commodity in raw form, but once some processing is undertaken these barriers rise rapidly. Even for such tropical products as coffee, tea and cocoa, not generally grown in the developed countries, there is a considerable degree of trade barrier escalation as soon as some processing is undertaken. Other products of export interest to developing countries that are hard hit by trade barrier escalation (tariffs and/or non-tariff measures) are meat, fish, vegetables, fruits, cereals, oilseeds, hides and skins, rubber and wood.

The main cause of the high level of agricultural protection in the West is the commitment of most governments to a high level of agricultural subsidization. As Table 5.2 shows, agricultural subsidization is at very high levels in the major western countries. Moreover, there has been a substantial increase in the level of subsidization in ten out of the fourteen cases recorded in Table 5.2.

Table 5.2   *Producer subsidy equivalents[a] under price support and related programmes in the USA, EEC and Japan, 1979/80 and 1984/5*

	1979/80			1984/5		
	USA	EEC	Japan	USA	EEC	Japan
Milk	20.8	89.0	23.9	21.2	62.0	23.1
Sugar	14.7	64.7	46.2	139.6	142.1	84.1
Wheat	1.2	50.4	77.9	17.2	37.6	79.9
Rice	0.1	24.9	78.1	55.7	27.0	79.4
Maize	1.7	54.7	—	7.6	22.1	—

Note:
[a] Producer subsidy equivalents comprise all transfers to farmers effected through trade measures and domestic support programmes as a proportion of receipts from sales of the respective commodity.

Source: Food and Agriculture Organization, 'International agricultural adjustment, Fifth progress report', C.85/21 (Rome; FAO, August 1985), table 1.7.

Developed countries that were in the fairly recent past net importers of agricultural commodities are today not merely self-sufficient but large-scale exporters of these products. The traditional export markets for LDCs have been reduced owing to the rapid growth of subsidized exports from the developed countries.

The existence of tariffs, administrative barriers, quota restrictions, etc., on the imports of agricultural commodities, required as a consequence of subsidies and high prices granted to local farmers, is often economically irrational and very harmful to the poor countries, especially to the poorer sections within this group. Their removal, however, is rendered difficult by the simple fact that they have existed for so long. It is commonly recognized, for example, that little or no political or economic disadvantage would accrue to the developed countries if trade restrictions on coffee, cocoa and spices were to be considerably lowered. This is because these products do not compete with commodities produced in the industrial countries, nor have synthetic substitutes for coffee, cocoa or spices as yet been found.[10]

For the majority of primary product exports from the LDCs, however, competition from synthetic substitutes is a very important problem. Synthetic substitutes for both textiles and rubber have now established world markets for themselves. Moreover, once a market has been created for a synthetic commodity, occasioned perhaps by a rise in price and a relative scarcity of the competing primary good, a subsequent fall in the price of the primary good has little effect. The advantage that the synthetic industry enjoys in terms of economies of scale and low variable costs is usually overwhelming.

Some synthetic fabrics, synthetic rubber and synthetic leather are all part of 'petrochemical' production, and their production processes have the technical and financial characteristics of the petrochemical industry, which are as follows:

- it employs a highly sophisticated technology,
- it exhibits marked economies of scale,
- it has a long gestation period,
- it requires heavy financial investment,
- it is highly capital-intensive (in the factor proportions sense of a high capital/labour ratio),

- it is dominated by large international concerns and the financial barriers to entry are formidable.

It is not surprising therefore that the product of such an industry has important technological competitive advantages over the 'natural' product of perhaps the most backward sector of the poorer countries. Some of these advantages are:

- synthetic products can be standardized to a degree that is not possible with corresponding primary goods;
- it is usually much more possible to cater for quality changes in demand in the production of the synthetic products;
- synthetic goods are usually more durable than primary products; and
- coordination of decisions and forecasting of market trends is considerably easier in the case of the synthetic products because they are produced by a few large and highly sophisticated industrial enterprises, whereas primary goods are produced by a large number of small units in many different countries.

Thus, whatever the scarcity-induced advantages that occur to primary products from time to time, in the long run the synthetic products have the most important advantages – unless of course the production of the synthetic product is based on a scarce or very costly raw material that cannot easily be substituted.

The poorer countries cannot in the foreseeable future hope for major domestic development of any of the big synthetic substitute industries because, as pointed out earlier, the financial and technological barriers to entry into such industries are formidable. However, a number of LDCs can, especially within the context of a comprehensive regional integration programme, aim at the establishment of an economically viable synthetic fibre or synthetic rubber industrial complex. Even so, it would be quite some time before such an industry became truly competitive in world markets.

This is perhaps too bleak a picture of the prospects of agricultural export products as, in a short-run sense, primary commodities undoubtedly stand a much better chance than synthetics. When a synthetic substitute is introduced for the first time the public is (in general) quite slow in its response. It takes some considerable time before synthetic goods create their own markets. The growth in the demand for such commodities is gradual, and the primary good that is under threat from a synthetic substitute can expect to hold its own for quite some time. For example, despite the availability of different types of synthetic fibre since about the turn of the century, natural fibres still have the greater share of the market, though the proportion is continuously declining. Moreover, the successful large-scale introduction and public acceptance of most synthetic substitutes often depends upon a critical impulse provided by the existence of abnormal circumstances. In the case of both rubber and fabric synthetics, the two world wars, the Great Depression of the 1930s and the Korean War provided the critical impulses necessary for their worldwide popularization. Hence most of the poorer countries have a chance of planning for the change in their production structure that takes into account the growth of synthetic products. Export diversification is an unavoidable necessity for those of the LDCs that have to depend critically on their external trade sector to initiate and/or sustain the development process.

Two important conclusions emerge from the foregoing analysis. First, if export diversification is to become possible for a large majority of the poor countries, it is clear that international cooperation and coordination are inevitably required. Moreover, it is futile to talk of international action to thwart the development of synthetic substitutes; such action would be strongly resisted not merely by multinational corporations but also by the governments concerned. (Additional technical research on natural products and tropical materials and associated production problems may, however, be more easily conceded.) It is much more realistic and sensible to urge the developed countries to assist the LDCs in their programmes of export diversification by easing the social cost of resource reallocation in both the rich and poor countries. Above all, it is time to begin to distribute research and development expenditures and technological progress more evenly over the rich and poor countries.

Second, it is also important to tackle the problem of price and revenue instability that confronts the primary exporters. The introduction of synthetic substitutes for primary goods will in fact tend to increase the price stability for primary products. There exists at this moment little doubt that export instability is a far greater problem for the poor than for the rich countries, though it is not possible to make blank statements about the relative importance of this problem for all LDCs taken together. Clearly, not all developing countries suffer from significant and frequent fluctuations in their export earnings, but a large proportion – including perhaps all the least developed countries – of them do.[11]

Moreover, commodity price movements during the recession of the early 1980s and the subsequent recovery have been highly disappointing. In the course of previous cycles, price fluctuations of commodity exports have been an important mechanism for the transmission of growth from the rich to the poor countries. Increased demand in the developed world has usually led to an increase in the international price of most traded primary commodities. But in the recent recovery (which began, roughly speaking, in 1983), while the volume of primary commodity exports by LDCs has increased, the gain in price has been modest and has remained confined to the earlier part of the upswing. The peak had been reached in the case of all categories of primary products[12] in the first quarter of 1984. Commodity price indices continued to decline for the next two years despite the sustained economic growth in the West. Moreover, they have throughout this period remained substantially below the levels achieved during the previous peak of 1980. If commodity prices are deflated by the export unit value of manufactures, the resulting 'real price' also shows a declining tendency since the first quarter of 1984.[13] Prospects for significant price improvements in the medium run are not particularly encouraging for a whole range of primary products – including sugar, cereals, coffee, cocoa, cotton, rubber and most minerals and metals – of export interest to the LDCs.

Many explanations have been offered for the persistence of weak commodity prices despite economic recovery in the West. It is argued that the appreciation of the dollar during 1982–5 led to an increase in commodity prices (usually denominated in dollars) in terms of other currencies. This led to a slackening of demand, increased substitution by synthetics and a subsequent decline in dollar commodity prices. Another factor has been the large-scale devaluation undertaken by several LDCs. This has stimulated production (because of the favourable domestic prices for exportables) and led to a fall in international commodity prices. Moreover, as inflation has fallen and real interest rates have stabilized at high levels, speculators have tended to move out of 'real' assets such as primary commodities into financial ones. Manufacturers have also tended to hold lower stocks in an era of high and rising interest rates. Most importantly, primary commodities' prices have remained low because growth in the West – particularly in the EEC – has been modest and, significantly, a large proportion of this growth has occurred in the service sector. Manufacturing, which has been the main user of both agricultural and mineral raw materials, has stagnated in recent years. Its share in GDP has continued to decline in the United States and most Western European countries.

This would suggest that there are important structural changes taking place within the developed countries that are likely to lead to a gradual decline in the world demand for primary commodities. The poor countries require international assistance to enable them to adjust to this structural change. Such assistance can take the form of export stabilization measures, such as the STABEX scheme of the EEC and the IMF's Compensatory Financing Facility.[14] It can also be a means for facilitating the industrial development of the LDCs, enabling them to process a larger proportion of their commodity output and to expand manufactured exports.

Trade in Manufactures

Developing countries have sought to expand manufactured exports, as this promises to offset the uncertainties and fluctuations in their primary export receipts. As early as 1964 a major theme at the first UNCTAD conference was the need for both the rich and poor countries to take measures that would enable the latter to expand their exports of manufactured goods to the former. Chapter III of *Towards a New Trade Policy for Development*, the report prepared by UNCTAD's first Secretary-General, Raul Prebisch, for the 1964 conference, discussed the problem of accelerating industrialization in poorer developing countries, laying particular stress on (1) the difficulties created by policies of import substitution based on excessive protectionism, and (2) the consequent uncompetitiveness of so many products on world markets. The report also drew attention to the substantial tariff and non-tariff barriers in the industrialized countries against manufactured goods produced in the poor countries.

The manufactured exports of the Third World none the less grew rapidly during the period 1970–83. At the beginning of this period the developing countries' share of world manufactured exports was only 5 per cent. By 1983 this share had risen to about 11 per cent. UNIDO estimates that the share of manufactures in the total non-oil exports of the developing countries increased from 25.9 per cent in 1970 to 53.3 per cent in 1982.[15] Nine LDCs accounted for over 50 per cent of total manufactured exports from the Third World.[16] The bulk of manufacturing exports from a typical LDC consisted of a relatively small range of products and, as Table 5.3 shows, a large proportion was destined for OECD markets. The share of the OECD countries in the total manufactured exports from the Third World increased by 4 percentage points over the period 1963–82, while intra-LDC trade declined by a roughly similar proportion.[17] In 1982, 42.4 per cent of all clothing imports and 20 per cent of all textile imports by the West originated in the Third World. The growth of clothing, textiles and many other light manufacturing imports into the West is, however, severely restricted by a wide range of protectionist measures. If market restrictions remain in force, there is every likelihood that the relationship between LDC export expansion and developed country growth – which was highly unstable throughout the 1960s and 1970s – may finally break down.[18]

As observed above (p. 73), tariffs are now the least important protectionist measure employed by the developed countries. Nevertheless, tariff discrimination against LDC imports continues. Both the Kennedy (1962–7) and Tokyo (1973–9) rounds of GATT negotiation resulted in an increase in the level of discrimination

Table 5.3 *Destination of developing countries' manufactured exports, 1963–82 (current prices)*

| | 1963 | | 1975 | | 1982 | |
	Value ($m.)	Share	Value ($m.)	Share	Value ($m.)	Share
To OECD countries	1,902	55.8	18,352	58.3	65,046	59.0
To East European countries	102	3.0	1,172	3.7	3,760	3.4
To LDCs	1,404	41.2	11,935	37.9	41,520	37.6

Source: UNIDO, *Industry in the 1980s* (New York: UN, 1985), p. 39

against the developing world. Table 5.4 summarizes the impact of the Tokyo Round tariff cuts on Third World exports. It is clear that, except in the case of industrial raw materials, the reduction in tariffs on LDC exports were lower than the average reduction on products in the same tariff range as the LDC exports prior to the Tokyo negotiations. Thus we see, for example, that products within the tariff range 5 had an average reduction of 32 per cent as a consequence of the MTN, but the reduction on agricultural exports of the LDCs (which were originally in this tariff range) was only of the order of 12 per cent. Similarly, tariffs on finished manufactures exported by LDCs went down by 24 per cent, but the average reduction in tariff on products in the tariff range that includes most Third World manufactures (i.e. 10–15 per cent) was as high as 40 per cent. Thus the MTNs are unlikely to have significantly reduced the bias against Third World exports in the markets of rich Western countries.

Whereas textile imports into the rich countries are both restricted by high tariffs and also subject to discriminatory quotas and quantitative limits, the labour-intensive 'other manufactures' may encounter highly effective tariff barriers but are only rarely subject to quantitative restrictions. Engineering product exports from the poor countries have also been growing very rapidly. These products

Table 5.4   *Impact of the Tokyo Round on Third World trade with the rich countries*

LDC exports	Average level of tariffs on LDC exports prior to Tokyo Round	Average level of reduction in Tokyo Round on LDC export (%)	Average level of reduction in Tokyo Round on all products in same tariff range (%)
Agricultural products	7.9	12	32
Industrial	7.5	26	32
Raw materials	1.1	60	28.5
Semi-manufactures	4.6	27	28.5
Manufactures	13.6	24	39.6

Source: M. Allen, 'The multinational trade negotiations', *Finance and Industry*, September 1979, Tables 1 and 2, p. 23.

are often manufactured and exported by the multinational corporations operating in the LDCs, and consist mainly of components and re-exports of products brought in for contract processing. Lower protection rates on these products are thus of mutual benefit to both the rich and poor countries.

Many proposals for increasing the trade access of the LDCs have been presented. However, before we go on to consider any detailed policy questions, it is important to try and sort out the real nature of the problem with which they are intended to deal. The most superficial study of the arguments and policy proposals concerned with the expansion of the poorer countries' trade in manufactures suggests that there is a good deal of confusion as to whether the purpose of such proposals is merely to permit the realization of existing comparative advantage in favour of the poor countries. In other words, would the desired growth of trade take place if barriers were removed, or is it necessary to go beyond merely removing barriers to introduce positive measures to help developing countries improve their competitive position?

The answer depends on the country and the product. Some of the poorer countries are competitive in strongly resource-based products (e.g. metals, timber and timber products, and processed foods) or have deliberately set out to build up the export potential of parts of their industry. Other countries would find it difficult to compete on the open market in almost any product, either because their own industries are very high-cost – often as a consequence of excessive protection – or because, as in the case of many smaller African countries, the economic base is so small that industries of the necessary size and sophistication do not exist. Finally, there are a few countries that are competitive in a wide range of manufactured products, possessing a broad industrial base and the management skills needed to make effective use of the potential cost advantage imparted by their low wage rates – an advantage that in most poor countries is largely dissipated by low productivity, management deficiencies and government policies that discourage its exploitation. Hong Kong, South Korea and Taiwan are current examples of economies in this last position, and thirty years ago Japan might also have been so regarded. The difficulties that are still being experienced in integrating the Japanese economy with the other free market economies of the industrial world are perhaps a pointer to

85

problems that lie ahead as other developing countries achieve Japanese levels of industrial efficiency.

Only in cotton-type textiles does it appear that almost all the poorer countries with significant domestic textile industries are competitive with almost all industrial countries. However, it does not follow that the removal of barriers is the only action necessary, at least not if considerations of the relative needs of individual developing countries are allowed to influence policy. Of the poorer countries that have a significant share of international trade in cotton-type textiles, India is one of the least competitive. But India and its problems loom so large in the Third World that it may be desirable for importing countries to take special measures to protect India's share of the market – or at least to prevent the lowest-cost exporters from snapping up all the business going. This sort of reasoning, which is applicable to many different exporters in different product groups, underlies the provision in the EEC's general preference scheme that restricts any one exporting country to 50 per cent of the total tariff-free imports of any given product.

Lastly, it should be observed that a similar degree of confusion exists over the attitudes adopted towards affected domestic industries in the importing rich countries. Put in its sharpest form, the question is: should adjustment assistance measures be designed to slow down the rate of change – and even perhaps, through re-equipment subsidies and training programmes, to encourage these industries to develop a 'positive' competitive response – or should they be directed towards accelerating structural change in the rich countries and enabling labour to move out of the declining industries? Most of the measures so far considered or adopted have reflected an uneasy compromise between these two opposing objectives, with, on the whole, a balance in favour of slowing down rather than speeding up change. It will be argued that the emphasis should be the other way round, because more rapid structural change is in the best long-term interests of rich as well as of poor countries.

Measures to remove barriers to trade

UNCTAD's General System of Preferences (GSP) is still the single most important tariff-reducing measure as far as the LDCs are concerned. The scheme was 'in principle' adopted within

UNCTAD at the first UNCTAD conference in 1964, but six years were to elapse before the resolution resulted in formal proposals. The main difficulties encountered in devising a workable scheme were product coverage, the depth and extent of the tariff cuts that importing countries were prepared to make, the special problems arising from the fact that some of the countries classed as 'developing' are more competitive than others, and the need to take account of different existing preference systems.

In effect, what has happened in the development of the UNCTAD scheme is that the 'donor' countries (the term is significant) have agreed to differ in the scope of their offers. The language used to describe the scheme – 'donors', 'recipients', 'offers' – is indicative of some muddled thinking about its purpose. Many leading exponents of international trade theory (e.g. H. G. Johnson) have argued with undeniable logic that a scheme that enables consumers in industrial countries to increase their real income by buying imported goods more cheaply than goods from their own domestic producers, and that thus also helps to reduce inflation, benefits importing as well as exporting countries.[19] But in practice it is clear that the rich countries see the scheme as a concessionary one in which they are being asked to give away something (i.e. tariff protections) without any return, and this explains why so much stress seems to have been laid on equitable burden-sharing in the discussions that have taken place – mainly in the Development Assistance Committee (DAC) of the OECD. The major reason why the rich countries have taken this view is their apprehension about the adverse effects of increased imports on competing domestic industries – their fears that unemployment might rise and both money and real incomes fall despite the increased purchasing power of given domestic incomes. The question as to how far these apprehensions are justified, on the basis of experience to date and such estimates as can be made of what might happen in the future, will be examined below (pp. 90–4). The GSP was renewed in 1981, although it is generally acknowledged that its impact on LDC exports has been modest.[20]

Non-tariff barriers

Non-tariff barriers are more significant in relation to trade between rich and poor countries than in relation to trade among the rich

87

countries, if only because the poor countries are less well informed about the nature of the barriers they face and much less well placed to find out how these can be overcome in practice.

GATT lists over 1,000 barriers, ranging from quotas to rules determining government procurement procedures, health and safety standards, and many minor administrative and customs regulations that restrict the free flow of goods across national frontiers. Additionally, there is growing concern about the extent to which multinational corporations can control the trade of their subsidiaries in different countries, as regards both the products marketed and countries of marketing. In certain circumstances, for example, a chemical or fibre company might seek to prevent its subsidiary in a developing country from exporting or to restrict its exports to a limited range of markets where they would not come into competition with the exports of a subsidiary in another country. The government of the developing country involved might well be prepared to cooperate in this policy if it needed the subsidiary badly enough, with the capital and know-how it represented.

NTBs have become extremely important means for trade discrimination against LDCs. Table 5.5 presents estimates of the proportion of total imports in developed countries that are affected by non-tariff measures (NTMs) in terms of different product groups and different import sources. It will be seen that the proportion of Third World exports (excepting fuel) to the developed countries affected by NTBs is significantly higher than the corresponding proportion for intra developed world imports. The aggregate level of imports affected by NTBs declined for all groups of countries over 1981–4 – but this is explained almost entirely by the termination of the automatic licensing requirement for fuel imports into the United States in 1983. When fuel imports are excluded from the calculations, the ratio of imports affected by NTBs is seen to go up for all groups of countries – the increase being roughly equal in the case of intra-western imports and imports from the Third World. Currently the proportion of LDC imports to the West affected by NTBs is higher than in intra-LDC imports in the case of oil seeds, vegetable oils, agricultural raw materials, iron and steel, non-ferrous metals, textiles, clothing, footwear and all other manufactured products. This ratio tended to increase over 1981–4 in most LDC categories.

Table 5.5 Import coverage ratios of selected non-tariff measures and tariffs applied by selected developed market economy countries[a] against different groups of countries (%)

SITC	Product coverage	World			Developed market			Developing countries			Socialist countries		
		NTMs 1981	1984	Post-MTN tariffs	NTMs 1981	1984	Post-MTN tariffs	NTMs 1981	1984	Post-MTN tariffs	NTMs 1981	1984	Post-MTN tariffs
0+1+22+4	ALL FOOD ITEMS	34.3	38.2	6.0	43.1	45.4	5.6	21.6	28.1	6.0	41.7	42.8	7.3
0	Food and live animals	36.4	40.5	6.2	48.2	50.0	6.3	22.4	29.6	6.1	42.8	44.1	7.6
22	Oil seeds/nuts	23.6	23.6	0.1	23.0	23.0	0.1	26.8	26.8	0.4	32.7	32.7	1.1
4	Animal/vegetable oils	47.8	47.7	4.1	36.3	36.3	2.4	52.3	52.3	5.0	77.1	77.1	6.1
2 (less 22+27+28)	AGRICULTURAL RAW MATERIALS	3.4	5.5	0.5	2.0	4.1	0.5	4.1	5.6	0.5	9.9	14.2	0.7
27+28+67+68	ORES AND METALS	7.0	14.8	2.2	7.1	17.2	2.8	6.4	9.9	1.0	11.0	13.3	2.5
67	Iron and steel	21.4	42.1	5.2	19.9	40.7	5.9	15.0	42.3	3.1	54.4	59.2	5.4
68	Non-ferrous metals	5.9	8.9	2.1	3.8	8.4	3.0	9.3	9.7	1.1	10.4	10.4	1.9
3	FUELS	42.1	15.2	0.6	59.7	23.0	0.9	39.4	11.7	0.7	46.4	43.3	0.8
5	CHEMICALS	16.4	17.2	5.5	17.6	18.1	6.0	11.7	12.7	3.7	10.5	14.2	4.0
6–8 (less 67+68)	MANUFACTURES OTHER THAN CHEMICALS	15.7	16.9	6.1	13.0	14.4	5.7	29.8	28.9	7.7	33.1	34.2	9.3
61	Leather	6.0	12.3	4.0	5.2	11.6	5.1	7.0	7.7	3.1	14.4	15.1	5.1
65	Textile yarn/fabrics	35.4	37.4	10.5	17.8	17.8	11.9	57.5	60.0	8.2	71.6	74.1	9.4
84	Clothing	58.5	65.0	16.9	35.7	38.0	14.8	75.9	77.0	17.2	57.7	58.1	15.6
85	Footwear	49.0	11.2	11.4	44.1	9.4	9.8	52.3	11.2	11.7	42.6	33.3	11.3
0–9 less 3	ALL ITEMS, excl. fuels	16.9	19.2	—	15.0	17.2	—	20.8	22.9	—	23.6	34.7	—
0–9	ALL ITEMS	25.4	17.9	3.7	18.9	17.7	4.5	32.9	15.5	3.0	34.0	33.5	3.3

Partner group

Notes:
[a] Australia, Canada, EEC(10), Finland, Japan, Norway, Switzerland and the United States.
The accuracy of the NTM information has been verified by certain developed market economy countries. The basic data are currently being verified by other countries. Accordingly the figures in the table are to be regarded as preliminary and subject to revision.

Source: UNCTAD Data Base on Trade Measures (unpublished).

In 1982, the developed countries committed themselves to a 'standstill' and 'rollback' of protectionism. Table 5.5 provides evidence that this commitment has not been met and developing country manufacturing imports are being increasingly restrained by price and quantity surveillance measures and by quantitative restrictions. Moreover, the future does not look particularly bright. The passage of the Textile and Apparel Enforcement Act (the Jenkins Bill) in both the houses of the US Congress in 1985 bodes ill for the clothing industry of South Korea, Taiwan and Hong Kong. The bill seeks to limit the import of textiles, footwear and clothing very substantially. It was vetoed by President Reagan in December 1985 but it is by no means dead. The pressure for protection in the advanced countries continues to grow from the declining industries. In recent years attention has focused increasingly on the problem of structural adjustment in the West and its likely impact on the trade and development problems of the Third World.

Structural adjustment policies

Declining industries in the West include textiles, apparel, leather, wood products, iron and steel, shipbuilding and rubber products. The developed countries have lost their comparative advantage in these areas. But, as a recent UNCTAD study has shown, shifts in comparative advantages are not a major determinant of structural change in the developed countries: 'A 10 per cent change in the comparative advantage indicator is likely to induce at most a 4 per cent change of the corresponding output share [of the industry concerned]; with the rates of output change lying around 1 per cent in the majority of cases'.[21] Structural change in the developed countries – i.e. changes in the relative share of different industrial branches in aggregate manufacturing output or employment – has mainly been in response to the policies pursued by the governments.

Since the late 1970s many western governments have adopted a strongly anti-interventionist stance. In this view industrial change should be determined by market forces and governments should as far as possible stand aside. This view was forcefully expressed in the OECD Ministerial Council 'Statement on Positive Adjustment Policies' adopted in 1982.[22] This statement asserts that defensive policies should be subject to strict criteria, government intervention should be temporary, concerned mainly with improving competitiveness, and the objective of self-sufficiency should be significantly downgraded. The macroeconomic policies pursued by monetarist governments have emphasized price and wage flexibility, deregulation and privatization, and the avoidance of inflation. These measures are seen as a substitute for direct microeconomic intervention.

The shift away from domestic microeconomic intervention has meant in practice that protectionist measures have gained in importance – intervention has shifted from the domestic to the foreign sector. There has been increased reliance on VERs, bypassing the MFN clause and other GATT rules, and the mere threat of new protective measures has increasingly undermined the multilateral trading system, with unfavourable consequences for countries having little bargaining power.

More emphasis has been given to policies directed towards increasing the flexibility of markets, notably capital and labour markets. For example, in capital markets in some countries increased competition among providers of finance has been encouraged by such means as less reliance on quantitative control over credit flows, freeing interest rates, easing exchange controls, permitting increased competition from foreign financial enterprises, and the use of new specifically tailored financial instruments. In labour markets in some countries there has been a movement away from heavily centralized wage bargaining towards pay deals on the basis of individual plants, greater use of bonus payments, profit-sharing and worker participation in ownership. In these respects, deregulation has played a crucial role in a few countries, but other changes in fiscal policies, collective bargaining and administrative structures have also been important.

Perhaps the most sweeping changes in the capital markets were brought about by tax reforms that reduced the cost of capital. In essence, the measures adopted in the United States in 1981 combined tax credits for investment with a shortening of the period of fiscal depreciation and the general substitution of degressive for linear depreciation. In its application, the tax reform provided a particularly strong stimulus to investment in vehicles, R&D and, more generally, machinery and equipment.

These reforms had an important macroeconomic impact, notably in accelerating the inflow of foreign capital into the United States.

They also had appreciable – and partly unforeseen – microeconomic effects. There was a fast increase in R&D expenditures, thereby accelerating technological progress. Since the tax reform benefited only profit-making enterprises, or ventures with ensured profits in the short run, it helped to channel new investment to capital deepening and to service industries.

Thus tax reform has been a potent factor in accelerating structural change in the direction of an expanding service economy geared to high technology and capital deepening. This was not sufficient to restore the competitiveness of manufacturing (and agriculture) affected by the overvalued dollar and was one of the factors that contributed to the increase in exports of manufactured goods by some developing countries.

Several European countries have also taken measures to raise the return on productive investment, but their margin of manoeuvre was limited by restrictive fiscal policies. Capital deepening took place within stagnating (or even declining) total investment. Improvements in productivity in manufacturing may thus have been due more to the increasing service content and falling employment than to rising labour-saving investment.

Job creation has, however, remained an important motivation. The gradual reduction of sectoral and regional programmes of assistance to industry tended to be accompanied by a variety of employment programmes, principally directed towards young people. In many schemes dedicated to vocational training (or retraining), the beneficiaries were simply removed from the unemployment register but without increasing opportunities for non-subsidized employment. Furthermore, the greater use of early retirement schemes and compulsory reductions in working hours were meant to make room for the unemployed, as did measures to repatriate migrant labour and/or reduce immigration.

There is evidence of accelerated structural change since 1979, in terms of employment, trade and output, within the western economies. However, it is difficult to assess precisely the impact of the policy measures described above on economic structures. In principle, measures reducing the cost of labour to employers and increasing the flexibility in its use should have helped to improve the competitive position of labour-intensive industries and to slow down the substitution of capital for labour. However, despite the evidence of overall real wage moderation in recent years, there is concern that labour markets remain too rigid. With regard to investment, various incentives have tended to reduce the cost of capital, leading to a fairly general decline in the cost of capital relative to labour, despite the high interest rate structure.

It is difficult to detect any explicit concern about developing countries in the OECD policy statements on structural adjustment. The major agreed international policy statement on structural adjustment adopted in 1976 and reiterated in 1979 is not even mentioned in the 1982 OECD Ministerial Council 'Statement on Positive Adjustment Policies'. These policies have been concerned very ·largely with the problem of adjusting the structure of developed countries to changes underlying the structure of trade among themselves or with changes in the structure of the domestic economy.

Moreover, the positive effects of structural adjustment policy within the West on developing countries have been vitiated by contradictions in these policies and by inter-country discrepancies in policies. For example, policies influencing the cost of labour and the cost of capital have not always been consistent or in the interest of redeployment of labour-intensive industries to developing countries. In some countries, too, the shift away from direct government intervention at the industry level has encouraged resort to protectionist trade measures, including so-called voluntary export restraints and threats of new trade barriers, in the interest of preserving jobs. In other countries, vigorous action has not been pursued to phase out support that defeats the principle of industrial redeployment based on dynamic comparative advantage. Outstanding examples of industries in which such support continues are agriculture and agro-industries, textiles and clothing, leather, light engineering products, steel, and shipbuilding. In the case of agriculture and steel, these anti-redeployment measures have actually tended to increase.

Within individual countries, macroeconomic policies have been pursued for anti-inflation purposes but they have also nullified or severely weakened the capacity for adjustment through their negative effect on investment, technological progress, growth and employment. Discrepancies in the use of macroeconomic policies have constrained the capacity for inter-country structural adjustment and limited the opportunities for industrial redeployment to developing countries that could have materialized in an environment of more comprehensive world economic growth.

Finally, and perhaps most importantly, there are the doubts to which the experience of the last few years gives rise about the potential effectiveness, so far as the developing countries are concerned, of structural adjustment policy in the West. The concepts of 'conscious efforts' and 'active cooperation' do not seem so far to embrace on a sufficiently wide scale the expenditure, taxation and regulatory measures needed for identifying new technologies, encouraging research, providing education and other infrastructure, assisting with financing and start-up cost, promoting export markets and assisting, financially and educationally, displaced workers in the planned decline of older and uncompetitive industries. There are, of course, exceptions, but, if structural adjustment policies in the West are to have a more effective impact on the industrialization of the developing countries, these issues will have to be addressed more fully in the future.

The principle of structural adjustment assistance – i.e. that the rich countries should bear the cost of adapting to changes in the structure of world industrial production and trade – commands general assent, but more consideration and more experimental programmes are required if it is to be applied successfully. Adjustment assistance programmes should generally make it easier for the governments of rich countries to take the initiative in liberalizing trade and enabling the poor countries to expand their processed and manufactured exports.

Future Trade Prospects

Fruitful cooperation between developed and developing countries is an essential prerequisite for the orderly growth of world trade as well as for a dismantling of protectionist barriers. GATT has addressed itself to these questions and the ongoing eighth MTN provides an appropriate forum for the development of a framework of North–South cooperation. The fact that the talks got under way in September 1986 owes much to the mediation of South Korea – the leading newly industrializing country from the South – which succeeded in bringing together developed and developing countries with widely divergent views on the timing and the content of these negotiations. The success of these negotiations depends crucially upon cooperation and reconciliation between the rich and poor countries.

The eighth MTN and the future of GATT

Developing countries have approached the eighth MTN in a spirit of cynicism and disillusionment. This is mainly because of their general dissatisfaction with the results of the Tokyo Round and the inability of the developed countries to implement the decisions announced in 1982 to roll back protection.

The seventh MTN agreements did not go a long way towards improving the position of the developing countries in world trade. We have seen in Table 5.4 that the average reduction of tariffs on products of export interest to LDCs is considerably lower than the average reduction of tariffs on all products covered by the seventh MTN. The World Bank estimates that the most important cuts in the manufacturing sector were concentrated in non-electrical machinery, chemicals, transport equipment and wood products. As against this, industries like textiles and leather processing, in which LDCs enjoy a comparative cost advantage, received less than average tariff reductions. In agriculture, the most significant reductions were concerned with tariffs on beef and dairy products.[23] LDCs expressed deep disappointment with concessions on the import of tropical products announced by the EEC and other developed countries in 1979.[24] They were unhappy about product coverage, depth of tariff cuts, and insignificant reduction of non-tariff barriers.

The Tokyo seventh MTN tariff reductions eroded the advantages enjoyed by LDCs due to the operation of the GSP. An UNCTAD investigation has found that:

> the [MTN] tariff cutting exercise fell short of fulfilling the objectives in regard to developing countries of the Tokyo Declaration . . . [The implication of the implementation of the concessions contained in the General Protocols] is an across the board erosion of preference margins offset only slightly by

exceptions to tariff cutting among products covered by the GSP. Some GSP margins are not just eroded, they are eliminated. The hoped for deep tariff cuts on non-GSP products are insufficiently numerous to compensate for the erosion of preference margins; too many important non-GSP products are not affected by the MTN.[25]

The limited and generally unsatisfactory results of the seventh MTN are, to a considerable extent, explained by the limited and ineffectual participation within these negotiations by the developing countries. Of the ninety-nine participants, no less than sixty-nine came from the Third World. But active LDC participants totalled no more than a handful. Moreover, their intervention was sporadic and disjointed. They simply did not have concrete offers to make in the negotiating process. Only the more industrialized developing countries could make realistic offers on a wide range of issues and only they had the necessary technical and negotiating experience. The least developed countries hardly participated at all – only four or five had permanent delegations in Geneva.

The developing countries were hampered at the MTN by the form the negotiations took and the institutional context within which they were organized. From their earliest days the talks quickly developed into bilateral discussions between major traders. Formal meetings of the Trade Negotiating Committee and of its constituent groups were indefinitely prorogued. Negotiation processes became heavily tilted in favour of some form of reciprocity. LDCs increasingly found themselves in bilateral or very small multilateral negotiating forums dealing with world traders such as the United States, the EEC countries and Japan, and the temptation to strike separate deals and work out bilateral compromises became strong. Joint action on specific issues between LDCs became difficult, and on a wide range of issues they found themselves seriously divided. The GATT institutional machinery has not been designed to serve the developing countries as an instrument for significant modification of international trade policy.

The disintegration of the GATT system has continued unchecked in the years since the conclusion of the Tokyo Round. The situation that exists today has been well described by Martin Wolf: 'If one regards the GATT as being an agreement on a number of basic principles and norms of behaviour it would appear to be moribund. The GATT has become little more than a forum for commercial diplomacy or a historical record of particular decisions. It no longer embodies living norms.'[26] The eighth MTN is thus perhaps a final attempt to rescue GATT from impending oblivion and to prevent the rebirth of the international trade system of the 1930s in which 'beggar my neighbour' policies were the norm.

The developed countries regard the eighth MTN as an opportunity to expand the scope of international economic negotiations. They are therefore pressing for new agreement in the area of trade in services and in high-technology products. They would also like to see progress made towards the establishment of 'performance criteria' reflecting the treatment by governments of foreign investment located in their countries. They would like attention to be focused on the safeguarding of international property rights and on the reform and strengthening of GATT's dispute settlement procedures. They would also like to link international trading and financial arrangements to minimize the effects on trade of erratic foreign exchange fluctuation.

Some of these issues are likely to be of significant concern to the LDCs: for example, the orderly regulation of trade in services and technology transfer is likely to yield significant benefit to them. Developing countries have, however, opposed the expansion of the eighth MTN agenda to incorporate trade in services and other developed country concerns, arguing that progress must first be made in the traditional areas where agreement had already been reached in the seventh MTN and in the GATT ministerial meetings of 1982 and 1983. Above all, the 1982 commitment to 'standstill and rollback' protection must be implemented – the 1983 decision to advance the Tokyo Round cuts by a year has been described 'as a gesture of impotence if ever there was one'[27] – before new questions need be addressed. They therefore emphasize issues such as:

- establishment of a code regulating emergency protection,
- trade in agricultural and tropical products, expansion of North–South trade,
- structural adjustments and trade policy,
- quantitative trade restrictions and other NTBs,
- trade in textiles and clothing,

- trade in natural resource based products,
- the implementation of the Tokyo Round agreements, and
- rollback or phasing out of restrictions on LDC imports to the West inconsistent with GATT rules or based on waivers from them.

The divergence of opinion on what should be the main concerns of the eighth MTN between the developed and developing countries may mean that the present round lasts longer than the previous one – which took no less than six years to produce a final agreement. Trade policy cannot be allowed to remain in a state of permanent drift, with unilateral protectionist measures gradually but inexorably destroying the international trade system. There is a need therefore to rethink the basic approach to the problem of successfully integrating the developing countries within the international trade system. We need to establish procedures for international negotiation that can produce genuinely development-inducing trade policies. In order to do this we will almost certainly have to go well beyond the mechanisms of the present GATT system.[28] We need a new international organization – something along the lines of the international trade organization suggested by Keynes in the Bretton Woods Conference of 1946. Such an organization would be concerned not merely with the liberalization of trade but also with its management. It would attempt to use international trade policy as an instrument for the stimulation and sustenance of growth and for the reduction of income disparities within the world economy. Failing such a development, it is almost inevitable that, in the not too long run, the international system will be decomposed into several regional units – each incorporating both developed and developing countries.

The EEC and its developing associates

One such regional system is represented by the EEC and its associated partners in Africa, the Caribbean islands and the Pacific region (known as the ACP countries). UK entry into the EEC in 1973 involved the dismemberment of another such system, in which the United Kingdom discriminated in favour of the commodities it imported from Commonwealth countries under a system of imperial (later retitled Commonwealth) preferences. The price of Indian textiles in the United Kingdom was not inflated by import levies, whereas French textiles were subject to custom duties, etc. before UK membership. The United Kingdom not merely had to end the preferences that were previously accorded to Commonwealth products, but also had to discriminate against these imports; thus, the United Kingdom has had to impose the common EEC tariff on Indian textile imports as well as subject India to the quota restrictions stipulated by the Community.

For the poor Commonwealth countries the institution of such a system of discrimination could have created enormous problems. The EEC had over the years developed a trade policy that was then generally regarded to be highly unfavourable for the poor countries. The major exceptions were of course the African countries that had been 'associated' with the EEC, i.e. the countries that were French colonies and had been associated with the EEC for nearly a decade. The Commonwealth countries in Africa, the Caribbean and the Pacific – but not those in Asia – became 'associable' as a consequence of the agreement that marked UK entry into the EEC. Later, special arrangements were arrived at between the EEC countries and some Mediterranean developing countries also, including both Arab countries and Israel. The countries that were not made 'associable' were the Asian Commonwealth countries, including populous and poor countries like India, Bangladesh and Sri Lanka.

The main benefit that the ACP states have obtained from the EEC has been through the policies established within the framework of the Lomé Convention. In early 1975 the EEC and forty-six developing countries from Africa, the Pacific and the Caribbean signed the first Lomé Convention, which considerably extended the concessions that had been granted by the EEC under the First and Second Yaoundé Conventions. The sixty-six developing countries that have signed the present Lomé Convention have a population of about 300 million and include the whole of independent black Africa (with the exception of Angola). The first Lomé Convention provided for continuous consultation between the EEC and developing countries and for the elimination of all tariff and non-tariff barriers on most exports from developing countries that were a party to the Convention. These concessions, however, were not granted to products covered by the CAP of the EEC. The

99

Convention reorganized the principle of non-reciprocity of trade concessions granted to the developing countries and established an Export Stabilization Scheme.[29] The Convention aimed to strengthen the socio-economic structure of the developing countries, to promote rural development, to support schemes for regional and inter-regional cooperation, and to provide aid to small-sized industrial firms.

The Convention was renewed and extended in 1979. In spirit, the second Convention lacked much of the atmosphere of the partnership that characterized the negotiations leading up to Lomé I. The EEC insisted on retaining safeguard provisions that could be applied to offset import growth unilaterally.[30] Rules of origin – which stipulated that even products with 60 per cent of value-added originating in an ACP state had to be excluded from preferential treatment – were also not liberalized. ACP participants in both the Lomé II and Lomé III negotiations have pointed out that the percentage of ACP exports going to the EEC has actually declined over the period 1975–85. Nor have the ACP countries achieved export diversification. The ACP's access advantages have steadily been eroded by the tariff reductions negotiated at the MTNs and by the development of the Community's Generalized Preference Scheme. ACP states have also expressed concern about the volume of EEC aid channelled through the European Development Fund (EDF) and the inordinate slowness with which it is distributed. Finally, although several joint EEC–ACP institutions have been established and there is a continuing emphasis on the 'contractual' nature of Lomé, which gives formal equality to all signatories, the ACP states have not been equal partners in the major decision-making processes.[31] It has also been argued that the overall impact of the Lomé system, with its discrimination against labour-intensive manufactured imports from the ACPs and the ever-present threat of the imposition of 'safeguard' measures, has contributed to a slowing-down of the growth of investment within the ACP.

The negotiations leading up to the signing of Lomé III at the end of 1984 saw new initiatives by the EEC Commission. According to the EEC proposals, development assistance was to be targeted towards agriculture, particularly the food-producing sector. This was to be achieved by linking the provision of assistance to the effective use of resources by recipients. The Commission argued that a 'policy dialogue' should be developed to ensure that there was consistency in activities financed by its aid and the related policies pursued by the government.

The concept of policy dialogue was viewed with suspicion by the ACP delegates and no new mechanisms have been established within Lomé III to increase the conditionality of EEC aid. The new agreement does include an insistence on the need to improve efficiency but does not provide a basis for the joint EEC–ACP determination of the economic priorities of individual countries. Total aid envisaged under Lomé III stands at 8.5 billion ECUs (European Currency Units) – higher than the 5.5 billion ECUs allocated under Lomé II, but lower than the 10 billion ECUs considered necessary by the ACP. The agreement incorporates small improvements in the conditions of access of both agricultural and service imports from the ACP. However, rules of origin applicable to ACP exports have not been revised. Provisions have been made for fighting desertification in Africa and for improving the access of the ACP states to EEC agricultural surpluses. Measures have also been included for the strengthening of the STABEX scheme and for assisting ACP states in developing coherent trade strategies.

ACP countries have expressed cautious optimism about the likely impact of Lomé III. However, the EEC has refused significantly to reduce protectionist barriers and the ACPs have refused to accept international coordination of development assistance policies even when this is to be geared to the objective of achievement of agricultural self-reliance. Nevertheless, these negotiations do represent a small step forward in the development of international economic cooperation between rich and poor countries.

Notes

1 UNCTAD, *Trade and Development Report 1985* (New York: UN, 1985), p. 189.
2 GATT is the name of the agreement signed between the contracting parties in 1948 and also the name of the permanent secretariat with headquarters in Geneva that has been established for facilitating the conduct of this agreement.
3 The Eighth Multilateral Trade Negotiations commenced in September 1986 and are discussed above (pp. 95–8).

4   M. Wolf, 'Fiddling while the GATT burns', *The World Economy*, 6 (1), March 1986, p. 6.

5   See above pp. 95–8.

6   G. Curzon and V. Curzon, 'Diffusing conflict between traders and non traders', *The World Economy*, 6 (1), March 1986, p. 20.

7   Suppose the domestic price of commodity X is fixed at £100 per ton and the import price is £50 per ton; then the levy will be £50 per ton. If the import price falls to £10 per ton, the levy will rise to £90 per ton in order to maintain the CAP-determined domestic price. CAP prices have at times been below world market prices, so that the need for variable levies has disappeared.

8   See above pp. 100–01.

9   For evidence on agricultural protectionism in the 1980s see UNCTAD, *Agricultural Trade Expansion and Protectionism*, TD/B/C.1/259.

10   However, synthetic substitutes may not be long in coming in even these instances.

11   We have assumed that export instability is a 'bad thing', but it can be argued that this is not always the case. The large majority of economists would certainly agree with our view, as would UN opinion. However, see also A. MacBean, *Export Instability and Economic Development* (London: Allen & Unwin, 1966).

12   Broadly, food and tropical beverages, vegetable oil seeds and oils, agricultural raw materials, and minerals.

13   See UNCTAD, *Monthly Commodity Price Bulletin*, 17 (2), April 1986, and UNCTAD, *Trade and Development Report 1985* (New York: UN, 1985), pp. 23–32.

14   Discussed in Chapter 6, pp. 129–30 and 127–9, respectively.

15   UNIDO, *Industry in the 1980s* (New York: UN, 1985), pp. 38–9.

16   South Korea (15.2 per cent of LDC manufactured exports in 1981), Hong Kong (11.9 per cent), Singapore (8.0 per cent), Brazil (7.3 per cent), Kuwait (2.0 per cent), Malaysia (1.8 per cent), Argentina (1.4 per cent), Thailand (1.4 per cent), Mexico (1.3 per cent); UNIDO (n. 15), p. 42. The level of concentration would increase significantly if figures for China and Taiwan were also included in these calculations.

17   According to W. Arthur Lewis this has been the major cause of the declaration of export growth in the LDCs. See W. A. Lewis, 'The slowing down of the engine of growth', *American Economic Review*, 70 (4), 1980, pp. 555–64.

18   For a discussion of this relationship see B. Scott, *Has the Cavalry Arrived?* (London: Trade Policy Research Centre, 1984), pp. 89–90.

19   H. G. Johnson, *Economic Policies towards Less Developed Countries* (London: Allen & Unwin, 1966).

20   See above p. 96.

21   UNCTAD, 'Problems of protection and structural adjustment', TD/B/1081 (Part II) (New York: UN, 1985), p. 17. The comparative advantage index is derived from B. Balana, 'Trade liberalisation and

revealed comparative advantage', *The Manchester School of Economic and Social Studies*, 33 (2), 1965, pp. 99–123.

22 Organization for Economic Cooperation and Development, *Positive Adjustment Policies: Managing Structural Change* (Paris: OECD, 1983).

23 M. Allen, 'Multilateral trade negotiations. A background note', *Finance and Development*, September 1979, p. 22.

24 R. Krishnamurti, 'The MTN and developing countries', *Third World Quarterly*, April 1980, p. 260.

25 UNCTAD TD/B/178 Add. (Geneva: UN, 1980), p. 8.

26 M. Wolf, 'Fiddling while the GATT burns', *World Economy*, 4 (1), March 1980, p. 5.

27 ibid., p. 6.

28 Some limitations of GATT are discussed in J. A. Ansari, *The Political Economy of International Economic Organisations* (Brighton: Wheatsheaf, 1986), Ch. 2.

29 For a discussion of this scheme see Chapter 6.

30 Although safeguard measures have never been applied, the threat of their application has been a means for forcing ACP countries to accept VERs in a number of instances (e.g. Mauritian textiles).

31 The question is discussed in detail in I. V. Gruhn, 'Lomé convention renegotiations', in R. Boardman *et al.* (eds), *Europe, Africa and Lomé III* (London: Centre for African Studies, Dalhousie University, 1985), pp. 26–32.

6   *Trade Strategy*

Has Import Substitution Failed?

During the 1940s and 1950s many less developed countries (LDCs) pursued what is known as an 'import-substituting' (IS) trade and development strategy.[1] The essence of such a strategy was the provision of macroeconomic incentives for the growth of industries whose output could increasingly substitute for goods that had hitherto been imported. The most important set of incentives involved the creation of prohibitive protectionist barriers to keep out simple manufactured imports and the development of a system of import licensing and foreign exchange controls that turned the domestic terms of trade against the sector producing exportables (usually agriculture) and in favour of import-substituting industries.

Development economists in the 1940s and 1950s put great emphasis on the necessity of a deliberate, intensive and guided effort to promote and encourage industrialization in LDCs. A number of authors, including Rosenstein–Rodan, Nurkse, Singer, Prebisch, Hirschman and Dobb, while concerned with a variety of issues, argued that a radical transformation of backward economies with limited or no industrial base requires a deliberate and conscious industrial strategy because the market mechanism, notably in the context of LDCs, is an inadequate means of ensuring rapid industrial development.

The theoretical rationale for a deliberate industrial strategy, as discussed by those authors, rested on a number of grounds, including infant industry, external economies and, broadly speaking, the dynamic benefits associated with industrialization. Another closely related argument favouring a deliberate industrialization strategy rested upon the existing structural rigidity in the composition of LDCs' exports and its implications for growth and terms of trade. The Prebisch–Singer thesis of a secular decline in terms of trade for primary exporters implied that market forces can work to the secular disadvantage of the poorer countries (identified as exporters of primary commodities) and to the advantage of the more advanced industrial countries (identified as exporters of manufactures) in international trade and investment.[2]

Industrialization in the context of this early literature implied import substitution. It was difficult in 1950 to visualize large exports of manufactured goods from LDCs when they lacked an industrial base and the age of the MNCs had only just dawned. Moreover, import substitution with the help of protective tariffs was the traditional and proved policy for infants (late-comers) in industrialization. The 'infant industry' argument lent itself readily to generalization into an 'infant economy' argument. The critics of import-substituting industrialization (ISI) often accuse development economists of this school and UNCTAD of a bias in favour of ISI and against export-oriented strategy. They also maintain that too much state intervention, including high levels of protective duties relied upon to encourage ISI, induces inefficiency and is thus an obstacle rather than an instrument for viable industrial development in LDCs. On the other hand, it can be argued that the critics do not take into sufficient consideration the impact of external pressures and obstacles on the development efforts of LDCs, and that they presume that the export-oriented strategy is a real possibility for all LDCs, disregarding international trade barriers as well as internal technological and capital constraints in many LDCs.

Moreover the critics of ISI, such as Ian Little for the OECD,[3] Bela Balassa for the World Bank[4] and Krueger and Bhagwati for the National Bureau of Economic Research,[5] all tended to disregard or underestimate the importance of a previous phase of IS as a necessary base for subsequent or even simultaneous export-led growth. This is confirmed by the actual experience of the two often-mentioned examples of successful exporters, South Korea and Taiwan. Both countries pursued an IS strategy in the 1950s; and even in the 1960s and 1970s, when substantial emphasis was laid on development of manufactured exports, still a considerable degree of IS took place in a number of industries in both countries.[6] In the case of Korea, it can be shown that IS and export promotion were carefully and consciously interlinked as alternating phases in shifting industrialization between the different sectors. In the case of Brazil also, exports of manufactured goods were in those industries where large-scale IS had been successfully accomplished. This is not to underrate the importance of export-promotion policies that were introduced in these countries in the 1960s. Nevertheless it is true that such export-promotion policies simply appeared as a way of exploiting the export potential that had been built up during the IS phase. The critics tend to argue that the shift from IS to export orientation (EO) was the result of enlightenment and of bad experience with IS. Yet the shift can equally be presented as a rational and natural sequential development in the progress of industrialization. (It can also be presented as due to a shift in the external environment in a more expansionist/optimistic direction at around 1960.) Prior learning about the technology and product via production for the home market is usually considered a prerequisite for effective competition in world markets for manufactured goods; hence the emphasis by List on the 'transitional' or temporary nature of infant protection. Also IS was often needed to provide the necessary basis for competitive export production. Seen in this light, IS and EO are complementary rather than alternative strategies.

Turning to the second criticism of ISI – too much intervention and interference with the play of market forces and consequent departure from comparative cost principles – neo-classical critics of ISI have maintained not only that too much intervention has led to bureaucratic inefficiencies, corruption and delays but also that the imposition of a high level of protective duties for import-substituting industries has induced the establishment of high-cost inefficient industries, allowed overvaluation of the domestic currency, and led to the neglect of agriculture and other sectors, etc. The policy implications drawn from this analysis are that protective duties should be substantially reduced, the exchange rate should be devalued and the play of market forces should be encouraged. These policies are supposed to be a prerequisite for successful export-oriented industrialization (EOI). Of course, EOI is not a crude laissez-faire strategy, but also requires appropriate government measures, incentives and subsidies to encourage exports, and to provide equal economic incentives to production for domestic and foreign markets. While the extent as well as the duration of government intervention, from this perspective, should possibly be reduced, the main requirement is a change in its direction, and 'degrees' of intervention are not easily measured or compared. But criticism of intervention and statism is not identical, although it may overlap, with criticism of ISI.

The fact that IS policies in certain instances have led to 'inefficiencies' and other undesirable side-effects should not be interpreted to imply that extensive state intervention is not of crucial importance for rapid and viable industrial development. Excluding special cases of city states like Hong Kong, the industrial development of other newly industrializing countries (NICs) has been accompanied by a substantial degree of state intervention, far beyond what is often realized by the critics of ISI. But it must certainly be acknowledged that there are many other kinds of government intervention that may be more important and more constructive than 'distortion' (or correction) of market prices.

The high degree of intervention and 'statism' that has prevailed in Latin American NICs, including Brazil and Mexico, is well known. Moreover, the detailed study of economic policy in most NICs shows that industrial development has been accompanied by a high degree of centralized planning and government regulation, with strict import, banking, credit and foreign exchange controls. South Korea 'is a country where a strong state overrides market forces without hesitation, with an effective tightly-planned economy, with strict controls, an essentially nationalised banking system, and a private sector organised in government-sponsored trade associations for easier control. It is as far removed from free market policies as it is possible to be'.[7] The government's overwhelming control over the banking sector has provided the most important tool in influencing the direction and distribution of investible funds by varying the interest rate charged according to the field of investment, depending on the priorities attached to the different lines of economic activities.

Likewise in Taiwan, rapid growth of the industrial sector in general and of manufactured exports in particular during the 1960s and 1970s was not accompanied by the adoption of a free trade regime, or anything approaching it. By the late 1970s, more than a quarter of imported items were subject to quantitative restrictions and import control.[8]

The purpose here is not to provide a blanket argument for any sort

107

of state intervention, or to dismiss the fact that extensive state intervention in a number of instances has not been particularly successful in the development of a viable industrial base. Nevertheless, it is becoming increasingly clear that it is not the extent and the duration of state intervention that determine the success or failure of ISI or EOI but rather the economic–political situation the state faces both internally and externally, its political commitments, and its administrative capacity. The state is not a *deus ex machina*, but neither is the international market. Which is the better guide, or rather which combination is best, depends on country-specific, or even sector-specific, conditions.

Effective and efficient implementation of any trade policy, whether IS or EO or a combination of both, depends on the organizational ability of the state as well as the economic and political peculiarities of any given economy. This point has been well demonstrated by Datta Chaudhuri in his comparative study of South Korea and Philippines.[9] Both countries are similar in terms of population size and in the early 1960s the two countries also had comparable levels of GDP per capita. Moreover, both countries, Datta Chaudhuri argues, adopted more or less similar trade policies in the 1950s and 1960s, in the sense that in the early 1960s both countries shifted their trade policies to encourage manufactured exports. Nevertheless, the performance of the Korean economy in terms of overall growth, employment generation, rise in real wages and particularly expansion of manufactured exports was far more spectacular than that of the Philippines in the 1960s and 1970s. In explaining the differences between the two growth processes, Datta Chaudhuri outlines certain factors that might have stronger explanatory power than trade policies, including the relation between the state and the industrialist class, the administrative capability and political commitment of the state to formulate carefully and implement effectively an appropriate industrial strategy, etc. In the case of South Korea, the state since the early 1960s devised a discretionary and selective regulatory system to guide the allocation of resources in the desired direction. Also, export promotion policies were accompanied by close collaboration between the state and a relatively well-developed industrialist class, so that the development priorities were defined in consonance with entrepreneurial interests. In the case of the Philippines, on the other hand, the dominant class with which the state collaborated was the agrarian hierarchy, and the efficiency and planning capacity of government and administration were far inferior to that of South Korea.

It is clear therefore that ISI has worked in some cases – in Germany and Japan in the nineteenth century and in Korea and Taiwan in the twentieth[10] – and has failed in others, notably in Latin America. During the 1970s it was fashionable to suggest that the cost of protection had been too high and countries throughout the Third World should switch to EOI. The next section examines the possibility of such a change in policy.

Is Export Orientation Possible?

The cost of protection to the LDCs has been high, owing to the artificial reduction of the relative price of agricultural commodities on the one hand and to the restriction of imports on the other. It is no easy matter to assess what the cost of protection is to a particular country. The dynamic (i.e. long-run) effects cannot be adequately assessed by means of the methodology that is currently employed to measure the cost of protection.

The static costs of protection reflect the allocative effects of protection. These result from the distortions that are introduced by protectionist policies into the domestic price structure. The country is forced to forgo the advantages of specialization in accordance with existing comparative cost advantages, both on an inter-sectoral level (i.e. between primary production and manufacturing) and on an intra-sectoral level (i.e. within the manufacturing sector itself). These price distortions entail both a consumption cost, which arises from the fact that by distorting prices protectionist policies interfere with consumer choice, and a production cost, which exists because protectionist policies induce a shift of resources from low-cost to high-cost activities. However, if all protection were abandoned, most LDCs would find that an expansion in their exports would be offset by a reduction in export prices and an inevitable exchange devaluation. Therefore, the static costs of protection should not be measured at existing exchange rates. They should be measured by the net effective rate of protection (ERP) of the import-competing goods (see Appendix, pp. 151–2), against which should be set the higher foreign prices that the smaller volume of exports obtains under protection.

A number of countries producing consumer durables have found the c.i.f. value of material inputs to exceed the value of output, if valued at world prices. Pakistan is a good example.[11] In cases like these it is obvious that, even allowing for gains from exchange overvaluation, the static costs of protection are formidable.

Protection is usually justified on the grounds that, as time goes on, the static costs will be reduced and eventually the protected industries will become efficient and competitive. This is the gist of the 'infant industry' argument, according to which protection is justified if a reallocation of resources increases national economic productivity sufficiently to offset the initial static costs of protection. But there are important reasons why the protected industries never seem to outgrow the 'infancy' stage: they are sheltered from foreign competition and are induced to produce for relatively small domestic markets. The production patterns thus established entail a very important dynamic cost of protection. Moreover, it has commonly been observed that industries producing for sellers' markets and deliberately ignoring economies of scale, owing to low levels of demand, usually lag behind in terms of productivity and efficiency.

Protectionist policies induce producers in LDCs to set up plants that are well below the optimum size to realize scale economies, and underutilization of capacity becomes a common phenomenon. Protectionist policies that aim at the development of import-substituting industries encourage production for the home market rather than for export and thus opt for a development strategy that sacrifices the short-run gains of international integration along lines determined by existing national comparative advantages. This is one dynamic cost of protection.

Another dynamic cost is the impact of protectionist policies on technological change within the industries of the poor countries. The structure of protection of the LDCs has discriminated strongly against technological innovation, a bias resulting from two factors. First, there has been a concentration on the development of the light consumer goods industries and a discrimination against the production of investment goods. The result has been an inappropriate pattern of industrialization as far as the technological development of

110

the poor countries is concerned. The protected consumer goods industries could easily import the capital and technological know-how from the West and have, therefore, paid no attention to developing indigenous technologies and production methods that are more labour-intensive and that exploit indigenous resource endowments more appropriately. Indeed, the oligopolistic position of firms in protected LDC markets has been a second obstacle to technological development. Both domestic and foreign firms have found that import-substituting policies have invariably resulted in assured high profitability levels. The restriction on imports has led to an elimination of competition, with the consequence that firms operating in such insulated markets have increasingly adopted monopolistic practices and, in the absence of incentives, have imported technology from abroad despite its obvious unsuitability. They have tried to compensate for inefficiency by insisting that the level of protection should be raised even more, so that they can offset the high cost of maintaining and replacing their capital equipment by corresponding increases in product prices and in their profits.

The unwillingness of developing countries to protect production processes that promise to lead to the development of appropriate technologies has had serious consequences. The protectionist policies that the LDCs have followed – and it must be remembered that the concept of ERP shows that protection of a production process is determined not only by tariffs and trade restrictions but also by domestic fiscal policies – have neither encouraged local producers to develop an indigenous technology nor induced foreign investors to import more suitable technical and scientific materials. In fact, the net effect of the protectionist policies has been to discourage technological innovation. Most LDCs have allowed the so-called import-substituting consumer goods industries to import capital goods at subsidized prices, and no one in the LDCs – business, government or public opinion – has stopped to question the suitability of the technology being imported. The cost involved in deliberately permitting the introduction and consolidation of alien and unsuitable technologies into developing countries is colossal. It cripples the chance of balanced development for the economy and of full employment and leads to a chronic dependency of developing on developed countries. There is no indication that even the oil-rich developing countries are paying adequate attention to the question

111

of the impact of their trade policies on the technology transfer process (though for some of them with very small populations a capital-intensive technology may well be 'appropriate', at least as long as the oil lasts).

The effects of the protectionist policies of the LDCs have not been what one would have wished. Protection has involved both short- and long-run costs. Protectionist policies have aimed at promoting the rapid industrialization of the LDCs, but the types of indus- trialization that they have in fact promoted have entailed a heavy cost in terms of economic efficiency. Such industrialization has usually had a negative impact on the pattern of income distribution within the developing countries. More often than not the industries that have been encouraged are capital-intensive, employ a relatively small labour force and tend to accentuate income disparities. Moreover, the import-substituting industries that have been de- veloped often show no sign of becoming competitive in the foreseeable future. It seems that protectionist policies have resulted in more poor countries having the worst of both worlds: on the one hand, by promoting import substitution they have discriminated against exports and thus reduced their own ability to earn foreign exchange, while on the other they have increased their technological dependence on the West. It is the widespread recognition of the very high cost of the protectionist policies adopted by most Third World nations that has induced many analysts to conclude that the associated strategy of import substitution based industrialization has failed.

The alternative industrial strategy proposed by the critics of ISI is an outward-looking strategy of EOI. There is no doubt that development and expansion of manufactured exports are of crucial importance for LDCs. Apart from the well-known 'vent for surplus' principle (i.e. that the surplus part of the domestic production, for which there is no domestic demand, can be exchanged through exports for those goods and services required by the domestic economy),[12] a country can, by export promotion, overcome obstacles of a limited domestic market in those lines of industries that are highly susceptible to economies of scale. Also, by competing in the world manufactured markets, industries would be forced to attain a high standard of efficiency and product quality.

Nevertheless the viability of the EOI strategy for LDCs as a whole must remain subject to controversy, notably in the restrictive international environment of the 1990s. The question is not whether EOI is *desirable* but whether it is *possible*.

To begin with, it is wrong to assume that what is possible for one or some of the LDCs or NICs can work for all, or the great majority, if all or most LDCs seek to pursue export-led growth at the same time. A recent analysis has indicated, on the basis of a simulation exercise, that if all LDCs in the mid-1970s had had the same export-intensity as South Korea, Taiwan, Hong Kong and Singapore, adjusting for differences in size and level of industrialization, this would have involved a more than 700 per cent increase in Third World manufactured exports.[13] This would have resulted in untenable market penetration into industrialized countries and a protectionist backlash would have been inevitable. Hence, it is seriously misleading to hold up the East Asian Gang [i.e. Hong Kong, Taiwan, South Korea, Singapore] as a model for development because that model almost certainly cannot be generalized without provoking protectionist response ruling out its implementation.[14] Even present market shares provoke a protectionist response – is it conceivable to increase total trade in manufactures seven times over and still maintain present market shares?[15] Although there is scope for the expansion and promotion of South–South trade,[16], access to the markets of the OECD countries, which are the major markets for LDCs' manufactured exports, is of considerable importance for the successful implementation of an EOI strategy, and will remain so for some time. It is the continued likelihood of this market access by LDCs that requires careful assessment, notably in the 1990s.

In contrast with the unprecedented expansion of global trade between 1950 to the mid-1970s, as the 1970s wore on the rate of global economic growth declined drastically, as did the rate of growth of world trade (trade seems highly sensitive to the rate of growth, with a multiplier effect[17]). The prospects for pursuing an EOI strategy in the 1990s clearly look less promising for LDCs that were not in 'the first wave' – even if we consider that the first wave is safely 'home'.

The post-war expansion of global trade was greatly facilitated by a significant reduction in trade barriers administered by GATT. This situation has changed considerably since the late 1970s and the prospects for the outcome of the 8th MTN are anything but

113

promising. Although there has been a general commitment to reduce tariff barriers, nevertheless non-tariff barriers (NTBs) have served as the main form of protective measures in major OECD countries in recent years. GATT has recorded over 600 different types of NTBs; UNCTAD, which recently began to compile an inventory of NTBs, within two years recorded over 21,000 product-specific measures and a similar number of general measures.[18] Furthermore, as in the case of tariff measures, NTBs appear to be disproportionately directed at LDCs' exports, and increase as the degree of processing increases. Moreover, protectionism appears to be particularly high in the labour-intensive sectors that constitute most of LDCs' manufactured exports and are particularly important to them for employment and more equal income distribution, as emphasized by the critics of ISI. If the economic problems now confronting the major industrial countries continue for some years, which seems a distinct possibility, the protective trade barriers are more likely to grow than decline. In view of this the EOI strategy seems highly problematic and difficult to execute for most LDCs.

The debate about ISI versus EOI is, in one sense, misplaced and hence partially senseless. Probably the best position in the light of available evidence is that neither ISI nor EOI is the superior strategy in any overall and absolute sense; rather, each depends for its relative advantages and disadvantages on assumptions about the external situation facing LDCs. The early advocates of ISI, consciously or unconsciously, made pessimistic assumptions about global growth and trade policies of industrial countries; such pessimistic assumptions were natural around 1950 when the more recent experience of the Great Depression of the 1930s was put together with the disruption and heavy setbacks caused by the war. Similarly, twenty years later, it was equally natural for critics of ISI to project the favourable external environment of the 1950s and 1960s into the future. Given the recent much less favourable international outlook, it is as natural that ISI should have regained a great deal more respectability. Apart from explaining some of the fluctuating fortunes and fashions in ISI versus EOI, such a position would also indicate that the optimal industrial strategy in LDCs would be something that is flexible between ISI and EOI – switching emphasis towards ISI in times of global recession and towards EOI in times of

Measures to Stimulate North–South Trade

The LDCs have sought cooperation with the developed world through international export stabilization schemes, the most important of which are commodity agreements and schemes for supplementing shortfalls in export earnings.

Commodity agreements are set up for a number of reasons, but traditionally they have been justified as a means of stabilizing the export earnings and/or prices of a particular commodity. Compensatory financing schemes deal with the problem of stabilizing the aggregate export earnings of poor countries, and supplementary financing schemes are devised to offset the effects of unexpected deficits in a poor country's budget as a result of shortfalls in export earnings. In the following paragraphs some of the more important export stabilization schemes will be discussed.

Commodity agreements

Commodity agreements may take several forms, but basically they involve agreements between producers and consumers. The countries concerned agree to regulate the price and/or production of the commodity in question so as to prevent fluctuations in export prices beyond a predetermined range. In practice, it has been found extremely difficult not only to fix this range but also to adhere to it over a number of years. Commodity agreements have had a high failure rate. Largely as a result of the divergence of interests between sellers and buyers there is disagreement about what constitutes a 'reasonable' price range. One popular economic objective is that agreements should aim to smooth short-term fluctuations in prices that do not reflect long-term changes in supply and demand. An opposing view is that agreements should aim to maintain prices at current levels either in money terms or in terms of the manufactured products for which the export earnings can be exchanged. A further suggestion is that agreements should incorporate an element of aid; i.e. they should affect the market so as to allow an additional flow of resources from the rich to the poor countries.

One of the biggest drawbacks to the idea of widespread international commodity agreements is that the poor countries do not always benefit from maintaining (or raising) price levels. Most exports of temperate foodstuffs that compete with domestic demand in the rich countries have high elasticities. Similarly, many raw materials exported by the poor countries face stiff competition (actual or potential) from synthetics. Petrol and tin have low elasticities of demand, but copper (from Zambia, Chile and other poor countries) has to compete with aluminium. However, among the category of tropical foods and beverages, several commodities would benefit from price increases. The Food and Agriculture Organization (FAO) cites coffee, tea, bananas and citrus as having particularly low elasticities of demand.

The significance of low demand elasticities becomes apparent on consideration of those commodities in which agreements have been made. The principal agreements operating for varying periods since 1945 have been for coffee, sugar, tin, wheat, olive oil, jute and cocoa. These are all formal agreements involving some degree of international supervision. There have also been intergovernmental informal agreements for tea, sisal and abaca. Not all these agreements have worked to the benefit of the poor countries. For example, one study suggests that Tanzania has suffered financially as a result of the informal agreement to raise and stabilize the price of sisal.[20] As the world's major exporter of sisal, Tanzania has found herself undercut by non-participants in the agreement and seriously hit by the relatively elastic demand for sisal. This elasticity seems to result from the availability of synthetic substitutes.

Undoubtedly the most successful attempt of the Third World countries in managing an international commodity market has been achieved in the case of oil. The oil-producing countries came together in the early 1960s and established a producers' association, OPEC, initially in order to resist moves by international oil companies aimed at reducing their tax commitments to the host countries. It was expected that OPEC would not last very long, for it contained member states with widely different economic and political interests. However, OPEC has not merely survived; it enormously increased its influence in the oil market during the period 1973–81. Since 1982 the price of oil has dropped dramatically and differences between those (like the Saudis) who would prefer to conserve stocks and those (like Nigeria and Iran) who would like to sell all they can at the going market price have seriously reduced OPEC's effectiveness. Moreover, OPEC's share of the international oil market has also dropped sharply. Nevertheless, despite the routine violations of OPEC-determined production quotas and heightened political tension among its members,[21] formal unity has been maintained and an improvement in market conditions may well lead to a rapid increase in OPEC's organizational influence in the future.

Primary-producing countries that do not produce oil have found it difficult to organize producers' associations. They have lent support to international commodity agreements between producing and consuming countries. The actual mechanisms used to stabilize world prices have varied with different countries, the principal devices used being buffer stocks, production quotas and multilateral contracts. A look will now be taken at the devices that have been utilized in four major agreements.

The large-scale usage of buffer stocks has proved possible only in the case of the non-perishable commodity tin. The **Sixth International Tin Agreement**, which entered into force in June 1982,[22] provided for a buffer stock of 500,000 tons. Since some major tin producers (Bolivia and Brazil) and consumers (the USA and the USSR) chose not to join the agreement, the capacity of the buffer stock was reduced to about 40,000 tons. Financial contributions for maintaining the buffer stock remained very limited and during 1982–5 buffer stock operations to maintain the agreed price were financed largely by commercial borrowings.

The increase in the value of the US dollar during 1983–5 resulted in an increase in sterling tin prices and made it possible for the International Tin Council (ITC) to service these borrowings and to maintain the value of its collateral on an ever-increasing debt. At the same time, however, the rise in the value of the dollar meant that the prices defended under the agreement rose markedly in non-dollar currencies at a time when there was already a situation of over-supply in the market resulting from a continued decline in consumption (in part encouraged by the high price of tin) and the entry into the market of new producers. While the agreement made provision for adjustment of the prices defended, no action was taken to revise the price levels, largely because the ITC needed to maintain the value of the tin held as collateral.

To support the buffer stock operations at the beginning of the Sixth Agreement the export quotas put into effect towards the end of

119

the Fifth Agreement were continued and set at about 65 per cent of annual output in the year 1981/2 – subsequently reduced to 60 per cent. This failed, however, to prevent a market disequilibrium. Demand continued to decline, partly as a result of the continuation of the general downturn in the world economy and partly as a result of substitution and productivity improvements in end-uses. Moreover, the effectiveness of export controls was significantly reduced, on the one hand because of the smuggling of tin from some member countries, and on the other hand because of increases in production in countries not subject to these controls.

In the course of 1985 the situation deteriorated rapidly. There was a sizeable increase in the stock overhanging the market and at the same time the dollar began to decline, thus reducing the value of the tin held as collateral and making it increasingly difficult to match fixed-price forward purchases off against unpriced forward sales. The ITC's creditors sought to reduce their exposure by reducing their credit lines or placing limits on the amount of business they were willing to do with the Council. This meant that, faced with a sharp drop in the price of tin, the Buffer Stock Manager was no longer in a position to support the agreed prices under the agreement and had to suspend operations in October 1985.

The failure of the International Tin Agreement has led some experts to assert that the buffer stock mechanism was an inappropriate means for market intervention in this case. The buffer stock system has the advantage (in the eyes of many economists) that it does not distort the long-term supply and demand forces of the market. It is seen as a device for ironing out erratic short-term fluctuations in price, and there is some evidence to suggest that it has been successful in this objective. However, by itself a buffer stock does little, if anything, to increase the export earnings of the poor countries that are the major tin exporters. In the Tin Agreement it was especially stated that such an increase in export earnings was a desired objective. To achieve this end it was necessary to introduce a production quota system, under which quotas were allotted to each producing country and were subject to revision by the ITC. This introduced a divisive influence among the exporter countries, which tended to compete among themselves for higher quotas.

Such a conflict of interests played a major part in the evolution of the **International Coffee Agreement**. This agreement rests almost exclusively on the control of production through export quotas. It was initiated in 1962 with almost total support from all consumer and producer nations after a steady decline in the price of coffee from a peak in 1954. Since then the price decline has been halted. Export earnings by many producers, all of which are poor countries, have risen. Thus, despite disagreements among themselves about the allocation of export quotas, the exporting countries were content to sign four agreements over a twenty-one-year period. The present agreement gives marginal quota increases to many of the new producer countries in Africa and Latin America at the expense of the big traditional producers (Brazil and Colombia). The latter nevertheless retain their dominant role in the world market, and there is no doubt that they consider their interests better preserved with an agreement than without one. The agreement has set up a diversification fund to assist the structural changes necessary to prevent the recurrence of over-supply. Minor alterations have also been made to the enforcement procedure that proved a major weakness during the first agreement. In general it is the big producer countries that press for strict enforcement of quotas, while the smaller ones consider they have most to gain from exceeding them.

On the consumer side, one of the principal objectives of the Coffee Agreement is to 'assure adequate supplies of coffee to consumers . . . at reasonable prices'. A stable coffee market is regarded by many consumer countries as desirable for both economic and non-economic reasons. Since the late 1950s, US governments have seen stable coffee prices as a prerequisite to political stability in Latin America. France, with the objective of retaining its political influence in Africa, actively canvassed for an increase in the price of coffee during the 1962 negotiations. There is therefore a degree of self-interest uniting all signatories to the agreement. Recently, however, a growing parallel market in coffee traded outside the agreement has emerged and efforts are being made to revise national quotas and improve monitoring procedures in order to curb this market.

International sugar agreements, though structured similarly to the Coffee Agreement, proved less resilient to internal destructive forces. They never covered more than the residual portion of the market not covered by preferential schemes such as the (now-expired) Commonwealth Sugar Agreement. With this basic structural weakness, the 1959 Sugar Agreement never recovered from the

US unilateral boycott of the Cuban quota in 1960. By 1962 the agreements had ceased to function. During the mid-1960s the price fell below 2 cents per pound weight, about half the planned price of the 1959 agreement. A new agreement was signed in 1968, and during the 1970s the situation improved dramatically. Prices rose steadily and passed through the upper price limits of the agreement despite the selling of national reserve stocks. This improvement in the position of the producers can certainly be partly attributed to the agreement, but it can also be seen as a consequence of the response of producers to the very low prices of the mid-1960s. The gestation period for sugar (cane) is such that it takes a number of years to build up production again after a fall-back during a price slump.

In July 1984 the International Sugar Agreement collapsed. This was due to the unwillingness of major producers to agree to new export quotas or to the establishment of some new mechanism for the stabilization of sugar prices. Meanwhile, major importing countries continued to heavily protect their domestic sugar industries, thus reducing the world demand for sugar. The collapse of the agreement led to a major weakening of sugar prices, which, according to the Director of the International Sugar Organization, in 'real terms reached an all time low in early 1985'.[23] Prospects for the renegotiation of an agreement have appeared somewhat remote ever since.

The third mechanism used in commodity agreements is the multilateral contract. Such contracts have operated in the past for wheat and have been allowed for under the terms of the 1971 **International Wheat Agreement**. In practice, however, the supervisory body, the International Wheat Council (IWC), has in recent years preferred to act simply as a clearing house for trade in wheat rather than to encourage price negotiations. The significance of this agreement to the poor countries is different from that of the other commodity agreements, in that for most of them wheat is not a major export crop but a source of food imports. One part of the agreement – the Food Aid Convention (which is the humanitarian arm of the IWC) – allows for the use of wheat as 'food aid'. Certainly there are advantages to the poor countries in encouraging the smooth flow of wheat when they need it; on the other hand, the incentive to expand wheat production for export by the poor countries themselves is severely reduced.

122

During the 1980s there was considerable debate within the IWC for a revision of the 1971 convention, but continued opposition from the United States prevented the adoption of substantive provisions for the maintenance of a mutually acceptable price structure. Provisions were made for increasing the IWC's information-gathering and disseminating activities and for raising the resources of the Food Aid Convention. Total aid provided under the convention exceeded the minimum obligations of donors for most of the 1980s.

In an assessment of the role of commodity agreements, the issues of economic inefficiency and waste should certainly not be ignored, for they are often criticized on these grounds. However, our concern is primarily with the question: do the poor countries benefit from commodity agreements? This question can best be answered by pointing to the fact that the poor countries have considered it in their interests to sign a number of agreements already and that at the fourth UNCTAD conference in 1976 they advocated the adoption of a wide-ranging International Commodity Programme (IPC). Perhaps a more relevant question is therefore: what form of commodity agreements will most benefit the poor countries? To recapitulate some of the points made earlier, the poor countries should benefit from agreements affecting their exports that include the following:

- measures to reduce the sharp fluctuations in their export earnings;
- measures to increase the price of those of their exports that have a low elasticity of demand;
- measures to encourage diversification of production where the prospects for expanding a particular commodity export are slight;
- measures to increase consumption of a commodity in the rich countries;
- measures to encourage the smooth flow of exports.

The IPC incorporated many such measures:

1 the establishment of international stocks of commodities on a scale sufficient to provide assurance of the disposal of production

123

undertaken on the basis of a realistic assessment of demand, as well as assurance of adequate supplies at all times for importing countries;

2 the creation of a Common Fund for financing international stocks on terms capable of attracting international capital to the fund;

3 the building-up of systems of multilateral commitments on individual commodities, which were linked to the operation of international stocking mechanisms and compensatory schemes;

4 compensatory arrangements for commodities for which international stocking, etc. could not secure suitable price-production incentives.

The original UNCTAD estimate for the establishment and commencement of operation of the Common Fund was of the order of $6 billion. However, in 1979 (at the fifth session of UNCTAD held at Manila), agreement was reached to establish the fund with a capital of $750 million for financing international stocks and offset export earning shortfalls. The fund had not commenced operation in 1987 owing to continued opposition from the USA and the USSR, both of which have refused to ratify the Common Fund Agreement. Presently both these countries hold an effective veto against the fund.[24] Even when the fund starts operations it will find it difficult to offset major destabilizing movements in world commodity markets because of the very meagre resources with which it has been endowed.

During the period 1974–9, when the establishment of a Common Fund with adequate resources seemed possible, a large literature was produced that questioned the need for buffer stocks, financing facilities and other forms of governmental intervention for the regulation of commodity markets.[25] However, as Thirlwall points out, these studies were concerned exclusively with the microeconomic and static efficiency effects of price stabilization.[26] A number of economists – most prominent among them being Keynes[27] and Kaldor[28] – have asserted that there is a strong *macroeconomic* basis for advocating commodity price stabilization at the international level because commodity price instability creates balance-of-payments crises for the LDCs.

[It] imparts inflationary bias combined with tendencies to depression in the world economy at large. When primary prices fall the demand for industrial goods falls but their prices are sticky downwards; when primary product prices rise industrial goods prices are quick to follow and governments depress demand to control inflation. The result is stagflation.[29]

Keynes was very much concerned with such issues throughout the course of the Second World War. He proposed the establishment of an international commodity organization – known as Commod Control – representing both major producer and consumer nations with adequate funds for financing large buffer stocks and linked to the world's central monetary agency, the International Clearing Union.[30] These proposals were abandoned owing to opposition by the Bank of England and the British Ministry of Agriculture, but echoes of the original Keynes proposals are to be heard in UNCTAD's integrated commodity plan, in the EEC's STABEX and STYMIN (Mineral Export Stabilization Programme), and in the compensatory finance scheme developed over the years by the IMF.

Compensatory financing schemes

The major difference between the effects of a commodity agreement on the one hand and a compensatory financing scheme (CFS) on the other may become clearer with the help of a little geometry. In Figure 6.1 the initial equilibrium in the market for a certain commodity is established at the intersection of S and D. Total revenue at this point is measured by p_2q_3. If demand falls to D_1, total revenue will fall to p_1q_2. If a commodity agreement is in operation in order to maintain revenue at the level of p_2q_3, changes in price and output of the commodity will be manipulated; the new price will be p_3 and the new output q_1 (since $p_2q_3=p_3q_1$). On the other hand, if a CFS exists, the new equilibrium price in the market will be p_1 and the new equilibrium output will be q_2. The CFS will ensure that the difference in revenue between p_2q_3 and p_1q_2 is made up in the form of compensation; alternatively, the compensation may be only partial.

The main point is that under the CFS (unlike the commodity agreement) the market will be allowed to find its own equilibrium and the necessary compensating adjustments will not directly interfere with the market-determined pattern of resource determination. In the real world, it is found that if a CFS is operative the exporting country is tempted to restrict output so as to extract the maximum benefit from the CFS in question. In such a situation, of course, the neutrality of the CFS on the resource allocation process is no longer maintained.

A large number of CFSs have been proposed since the early 1950s. Some can hardly be called a CFS at all. They are specific commodity compensatory schemes, which compensate exporters for deviations of the price and/or output of specified commodities from agreed 'normal' levels. The most far-reaching CFS aims at evening out total export proceeds from the specified commodities.

On the other hand, general compensation schemes focus attention on the fluctuations of the total export earnings or the terms of trade of a particular country. A number of sophistications have been suggested within the compensation mechanism. UN proposals, for instance, have argued that compensation should be automatic on

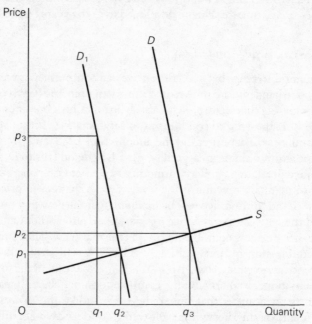

Figure 6.1   *Effect of a compensatory financing scheme on revenue*

126

specified shortfalls in export proceeds. It should not be left to the discretion of the compensator to determine the action to be taken in each specific case, because political and strategic considerations will invariably influence decisions if this procedure is adopted. It has been suggested that compensation should come out of a permanent insurance fund rather than in the form of *ad hoc* payments, or alternatively that compensation should be in the form of interest-bearing loans rather than outright grants. Both of these proposals aim at increasing the automaticity of the compensating mechanism. The rich countries have, however, argued that some exporting countries may deliberately limit sales so as to maximize their gain from the CFS; hence some discretionary element in the compensation procedure is called for. If a durable and successful CFS is to be launched, it is essential that some form of compromise between these two opposing standpoints should be worked out.

Two important CFS proposals will now be briefly considered. The Compensatory Financing Facility (CFF) of the International Monetary Fund (IMF) was inaugurated in 1963. The basic criteria for the use of the CFF have remained largely unchanged since its inception.[31] Apart from the general requirement of a need for the drawing, a member must demonstrate that it has experienced a shortfall in its export earnings, that the shortfall is temporary and attributable to circumstances largely beyond its control, and that it is willing to cooperate with the Fund in efforts to find, where required, appropriate solutions for its payments difficulties. The amount of a drawing is constrained by the size of the calculated shortfall, subject to a limit on outstanding drawings. Following approval of a request by the Fund's Executive Board, a drawing is made in one instalment and normally repaid in eight equal quarterly instalments spread over the fourth and fifth years after the drawing. The 'rate of charge' on outstanding CFF drawings is the same as that applied to other drawings from the general (quota) resources of the Fund.

While the underlying rationale for the use of the CFF has not changed since 1963, there have been major changes in the scope and method of its operations. In particular, these changes have affected (1) the coverage of the facility, namely the items of the balance of payments included in the calculation of the shortfall, (2) the method of calculating the shortfall, and (3) the maximum level of drawings in terms of quota limits.

Originally coverage was limited to shortfalls in merchandise exports. In 1979, earnings from tourism and workers' remittances were also included in calculations to estimate export shortfalls. In 1981, compensatory payments were also accepted to cover increases in the costs of cereal imports.[32] The CFF – unlike STABEX – is thus not a commodity-specific scheme and the calculation of a shortfall is related to total merchandise and service export earnings and increases in payments for cereal imports.

The shortfall to be compensated is calculated in any twelve-month period in relation to a medium-term trend defined as an average of values for a five-year period centred on the shortfall year. Estimates thus involve forecasting export levels for two years after the period for which compensation is sought. Various methods have been used for estimating the trend and for forecasting,[33] but calculations have always been made on the basis of nominal rather than real values.

Drawings under the CFF are since 1984 limited to cover 83 per cent of the export shortfall and excess in cereal import payments. It is also stipulated that such drawings must not exceed 105 per cent of a country's IMF quota. Drawings on the CFF were initially subject to low conditionality, but since 1975 relatively stringent conditions are applied to drawings above 50 per cent of a country's quota. Since 1983 a 'special arrangement' for correcting the balance-of-payments situation has to be negotiated with the Fund before CFF drawings above 50 per cent of a country's quota are permitted. Developing countries have argued that CFF drawings are increasingly being associated with the typical IMF stabilization programmes (discussed in Chapter 11), which require an LDC to institute a deflationary set of macroeconomic measures and thus inhibit development prospects. However, as Table 6.1 shows, drawings remained very small until 1975 when the scheme was substantially liberalized. Drawings were particularly high during the two recessionary periods 1976–8 and 1981–3. During 1976–85, annual average CFF drawings represented about a quarter of total Fund credit. Since 1983, CFF drawings have declined and repayment obligations have increased sharply. In 1985 for the first time in its history *net* use of the facility was negative – repayments exceeded new credit obtained. During 1986 and 1987 net negative outflows increased substantially. Reflecting these trends, total outstanding drawings have continued to fall – from a peak of SDR 7 billion in 1984. Moreover, the terms of CFF financing have stiffened in recent years. Most drawings – for example ten out of a total of thirteen in 1985 – are now in excess of 50 per cent of a country's quota and thus subject to strict 'upper tranche conditionality'. An expansion of the CFF is required particularly because of the failure of primary commodity prices to recover during 1984–7, but such an extension can be effective only if (1) the link between the CFF and the monetarist stabilization programmes of the IMF is severed and (2) repayment conditions are significantly modified to ensure a sizeable net outflow of funds to the poor primary exporters in the years ahead.

Another important CFS is the STABEX scheme operated by the EEC since the signing of the first Lomé Convention in 1975 (see Chapter 5). STABEX aims at stabilizing earnings from primary (mainly non-mineral) commodities exports by the ACP countries. The list of commodities included in STABEX has continued to expand, although no major manufactured or semi-manufactured product is covered by the scheme. In recent years – particularly during the recession of 1981–3 – claims from ACP countries seeking compensation have significantly exceeded the resources of the STABEX (sanctioned by the different Lomé Conventions and provided by the EEC members). The processing of claims has usually been slow and ACP states have frequently found themselves facing long delays. Moreover there are no mechanisms to ensure that

Table 6.1   *Gross annual CFF drawings, 1963–85*

Year	Number of drawings	Amount (SDR million)
1963	2	76
1966	2	24
1970	3	3
1975	5	113
1976	48	2,308
1980	15	980
1981	29	1,243
1982	28	2,628
1983	24	2,839
1984	8	816
1985	13	929

Source: R. Kaibrui, 'Evolution of the CFF', *Finance and Development*, 23(2), June 1986, p. 26.

the compensation payments actually find their way to the farmers. 'Often they are simply pocketed by recipient governments for their own good or bad purposes'.[34] In general, funds provided under STABEX are untied and made available unconditionally.

It has been argued that the primary purpose of the STABEX scheme is to ensure a stable supply of primary commodities to the EEC.[35] The operation of STABEX provides 'a form of disguised protection to European processing industries . . . [and] tends to preserve the existing division of labour between Europe and the ACP'[36] by discouraging export and production diversification in the latter countries. Moreover, compensation for individual claims remains entirely in the hands of the EEC members, whose evaluation of individual claims sometimes reflects a bias against both commodity and market diversification of an ACP country's external trade. STABEX therefore does not provide 'the comprehensive security against the uncertainties of the market place to which the ACP states had aspired [in 1975]'.[37] Since STABEX coverage is limited to only forty-eight commodities, it is inevitable that a high proportion of available resources is directed to a very small number of countries. Lomé III (1986–90) has increased the EEC's control over the use of STABEX resources. It has been agreed that switching of compensatory financing should now be justified by the ACP countries and, if not satisfied, the Community has the right to suspend future STABEX payments to the country concerned. Resources allocated to STABEX under Lomé III stand at 925 million ECU, which represents a 72 per cent increase over Lomé II.[38]

Supplementary financing and structural adjustment schemes

A supplementary financing scheme (SFS) aims at providing additional resources to LDCs so that they may deal with the problem of export instability.

The first major SFS proposal was formulated by the World Bank in 1964. It was designed with the intention of allowing for adjustment to take into account the varied effect of export earnings instability on different economies. The amount of finance to be provided and the conditions under which it would be made available would be determined by the conditions existing in the recipient country. The primary concern of the World Bank's SFS was to offset the disrupting effects of export earnings shortfalls on the national plans of the poorer countries. The scheme aimed at supplementing the efforts of these countries in adjusting to unexpected export shortfalls. Only the part of the shortfall that would pose a serious problem for the implementation of the LDC's development plan would be offset under this scheme, export shortfalls being estimated on the basis of the development plan's own projections of export earnings. Each country would be offered a 'policy package' in accordance with its requirements and circumstances, and the supplementary finance offered as part of the package would of course be additional to the aid funds already committed to the LDC.

During the 1970s both the World Bank and the IMF enlarged the scope of their SFS operations. Emphasis was shifted from stabilizing export earnings to provide support for macroeconomic programmes that sought to address the problem of the impact of structural disequilibrium on the country's balance of payments. Early steps in this direction were the opening of the so-called 'third windows' at the Bank and the establishment of the 'oil facility' at the Fund in the mid-1970s. In 1974, the Fund created the Special Fund Facility to provide medium-term support to overcome serious balance-of-payments maladjustment. This was renewed in 1985. It provides finance for essential import purchases. Operations are very limited, however. Thus in 1985 only $2 billion were allocated and were used by only three countries.[39] In 1981, the Fund established the Enlarged Access Facility (EAF), which incorporated the SFS operational since 1977. LDCs that have large balance-of-payments deficits in relation to their quotas are under the EAF permitted to obtain loans up to 115 per cent of their quotas for structural adjustment purposes.[40] Borrowings under the EAF are related to the stabilization agreements worked out by the Fund and subject to the standard conditionality provision.

In 1986, the Bank and the Fund took the first steps towards combining the structural adjustment programmes sponsored by the two organizations.[41] In that year the IMF approved a Structural Adjustment Facility (SAF) designed to assist low-income member countries with protracted balance-of-payments problems adopt medium-term macroeconomic and structural adjustment programmes. The World Bank's Executive Board agreed to the broad outlines of the facility's most innovative feature: closer Bank–IMF

131

collaboration in assisting member countries with the design of these programmes. For the drawings under the SAF, a policy framework paper, to be developed by the member country in close collaboration with the IMF and the World Bank staffs, will provide the broad outline for a three-year macroeconomic and structural adjustment effort. Annual programmes will complement this framework, detailing the specific goals to be pursued and the policies to be implemented. The policy framework papers are to be updated and reviewed in connection with the presentation of each subsequent annual programme.

The new facility is financed by reflows to the IMF for loans made over the four and a half years of its Trust Fund operations. The Trust Fund, which was established in 1976 to meet the requirements of low-income developing countries for additional concessional financing for balance-of-payments needs, was itself financed by the sale of a portion of the IMF's gold holdings. Between 1977 and 1981 the Trust Fund lent nearly $3 billion to fifty-five countries. The SAF, which may become a catalyst for additional financing, is expected to make available an estimated $2.7 billion in low-interest loans by 1991.

The SAF provides ten-year loans at an interest rate of 0.5 per cent. Each of the annual programme loans has a five and a half year grace period. Disbursements will be limited to 47 per cent of a member's quota, and will be stretched over a three-year period. They will be determined on the basis of a detailed review of the borrowers' needs, objectives, investment priorities and macroeconomic policies, conducted on an annual basis. The operation of the SAF is expected to coordinate – and eventually fuse – the lending strategies of the Fund and the Bank.[42] These provisions are likely to ensure (1) that resources placed at the disposal of the SFS will remain relatively limited, (2) that the disbursement of these resources will remain conditional on strict IMF/World Bank surveillance. As long as these institutions retain their commitment to monetarist doctrine it is unlikely that the operations of the SFS will lead to a significant acceleration of growth within the Third World.

The inability of the international community to evolve a satisfactory mechanism for dealing with the problem of export instability reflects the fact that there are no universally accepted criteria of what would constitute a satisfactory compensatory or supplementary financing scheme. The developed countries generally feel that such a scheme should not involve a long-term net transfer of resources and that, if it does so, an element of discretionary control should be incorporated into the financing mechanism. On the other hand, the LDCs feel that a CFS/SFS of this nature would offer no more than marginal help in their endeavours to cope with the problems of fluctuations in export receipts. If a financing scheme is to have real rather than symbolic significance, it must involve a transfer of funds much larger than the transfers envisaged under the current schemes. Moreover, the poor countries resent the fact that the rich want to use the compensatory or supplementary financing mechanism as a means for ensuring that the LDCs accept some limitation of their national economic sovereignty. The fact that the poor countries are obliged to listen to the IMF and World Bank and not to the United States or EEC countries is of little relevance here, for in the 1980s the World Bank and IMF are not bodies that are regarded by the poorer countries of the world as highly representative of their interests. A compromise between the radically different positions taken by the rich and poor countries on this issue is necessary before the problem of export instability can be effectively tackled through a comprehensive international financing scheme.

Another approach to the problem of export instability is that adopted by the General System of Preferences operated by UNCTAD since 1979. This calls for preferential access for Third World exports to the developed countries. However, as the next section shows, the operation of the scheme leaves a great deal to be desired.

The General System of Preferences (GSP)

The main idea behind the GSP is that manufacturing exports from developing countries should be given preferential access to the markets of the rich countries. In a sense, however, it is erroneous to talk of the GSP as an entity, because the rich countries have not been able to agree on one single scheme. The United States, Australia, the Nordic countries, the EEC countries and Japan all operate separate preference schemes, which differ with regard to product coverage and the method of preferential treatment. The rich countries argue that processed agricultural goods and other semi-manufactures should be excluded from the scheme, and different rich countries give different product classifications. Generally speaking, the schemes evolved by the Nordic countries are the most liberal, those of the EEC countries and Japan are the most restricted. The rich countries have agreed that specified manufactured exports would have duty-free access to their markets, but Japan and the EEC members have set quantitative ceilings beyond which imports of manufactured goods from the LDCs would no longer have preferential treatment. Other rich countries have specified that they would withdraw the preferences if domestic problems necessitated such action. On top of all these limitations on the utility of the scheme, there is the further problem that there is no legal guarantee that the rich countries will in fact continue to implement the schemes that they have formulated. Hence the poor countries justifiably have not been very enthusiastic about the GSP's impact on trading patterns. As a Yugoslav economist has commented:

> The System . . . contains no built-in guarantee and donors can shut off the carefully built export drives of an LDC. Exceptions [by the rich countries] have been taken in precisely those products where LDCs enjoy comparative advantages and can compete effectively . . . Product coverage is not broad enough . . . Ceilings and quotas to be applied by certain donors [can] be utilised in a dangerous manner.[43]

Results achieved as a consequence of the operation of the scheme can be described as marginal.[44] Efforts continue to be made to improve beneficiary lists, product coverage and tariff cuts, but such improvements have at best been modest. There has also been a tendency to restrict further the preferential limits on certain categories of products under the major schemes. A number of LDCs have thus been denied the opportunity to realize their full export potential under these schemes. Total imports by preference-giving countries from LDCs amounted to over $225 billion in 1984. More than half ($124 billion) of these imports were MFN dutiable and could therefore fall within the scope of the GSP. However, only half ($64 billion) of these dutiable imports consisted of products eligible for preferential treatment. Of these covered imports only $32.3 billion actually received preferential treatment. Although the share of LDC exports granted preferential treatment in total dutiable imports of the OECD countries has been rising gradually over the years, it still accounts for only about a quarter of total dutiable imports from LDCs into the OECD.

The trade effects of the GSP continue to be constrained, first of all by the large exclusions of key products from the schemes, second by the various limitations on preferential imports, and third, to a lesser extent, by the difficulties encountered in complying with origin rules. Since the GSP covers mostly industrial products, LDCs with a broader industrial base and diversified industrial exports have benefited more than those relying heavily on exports of agricultural and industrial raw materials. It should be stressed, however, that a number of LDCs seldom avail themselves of preferences on products subject to very low rates or having a low margin of preference, while others have unwittingly disqualified themselves from preferential treatment by failing to comply with the notification requirements under the rules of origin.[45] It is none the less clear that major changes will have to be made in the schemes operated by individual OECD countries – product coverage will have to be significantly expanded to include non-manufactured products and provision will also have to be made to reduce arbitrary changes in rules of operation – if the GSP's effectiveness is to be enhanced. Every round of tariff cuts negotiated under GATT auspices reduces the value of the GSP,[46] and it may well be the case that when the present scheme expires in 1991 it will be allowed to fade away altogether. This will be a great pity, for integrating the Third World into the world trade system must remain an important priority of international economic policy. The national GSPs – whatever their limitations – provide an important means for doing this and for slowing down the 'trade war' (described in Chapter 5) that exists between the rich and poor countries. A strengthened GSP can significantly stimulate the orderly growth of North–South trade.

South–South Trade

Discussion of the trade policy of the LDCs countries centres on North–South issues. This is natural because, as Table 6.2 shows, South–South trade still accounts for less than a third of total Third

World exports and imports in most major product categories. The two main exceptions to this rule are agricultural raw material imports and manufactured exports,[47] but in both these cases the share of intra Third World trade declined during 1975–82. The share of intra Third World trade in global exports and imports is currently about 8 per cent.[48] Intra Third World financial flows are also very small: in 1975 aid from OPEC accounted for 14.6 per cent of total financial flows to the LDCs; by 1983 this share had fallen to 7.2 per cent (see Table S.5 in Statistical Appendix). Commercial borrowing by LDC governments is almost entirely located in the Eurocurrency markets and in the United States. Finally, as Chapter 10 shows, although Third World transnationals are increasing investment in the LDCs, their share of total direct foreign investment remains very low. This low level of intra Third World trade and finance has induced an UNCTAD group to describe 'South–South economic relations as the weakest link in the network of international economic relations'.[49]

Table 6.2   *South–South trade*

	Year	Share of LDCs in exports of LDCs	Share of LDCs in imports of LDCs
Total	1970	19.8	19.0
	1975	23.3	24.5
	1982	29.8	30.3
Food items	1970	15.0	27.8
(SITC 0+1+4+22)	1975	22.4	28.9
	1982	26.7	30.5
Agricultural raw materials	1970	21.4	48.6
(SITC 2−22−27−28)	1975	26.5	41.5
	1982	31.0	38.0
Ores and metals	1970	9.3	14.8
(SITC 27+28+67+68)	1975	13.6	10.2
	1982	25.0	19.4
Fuels	1970	20.5	82.4
(SITC 3)	1975	20.9	89.7
	1982	28.2	84.7
Manufactured goods	1970	33.3	8.4
(SITC 5 to 8−67+68)	1975	37.1	9.6
	1982	36.3	14.0

Source: UNCTAD, *Handbook of International Trade and Development Statistics 1985* (New York: UN, 1985), pp. 74, 94.

Many authors – including Arthur Lewis[50] – have argued that strengthening this link is of vital importance in an era of sluggish growth and production in the industrialized countries. Lewis believes that rapid growth of South–South trade can 'compensate' for stagnation of western demand for Third World exports, but it is widely recognized that intra-LDC trade cannot automatically fill the gap created by the slow growth of demand in the rich countries. Specific policies are needed to increase intra Third World economic transactions. The strengthening of economic relations within the Third World requires the development of long-run initiatives involving the creation of relatively expensive socio-economic infrastructure. LDCs are unwilling to commit funds to such schemes, particularly during a period of severe foreign exchange shortages and rising debt burdens. The impact of the debt crisis on inter-regional trade can be seen in the case of Latin America (the region most seriously affected by the debt crisis). Intra Latin American exports fell by 17 per cent over 1981–2 and their share in total exports was lower in 1984 than in any year since 1960. Moreover, the establishment of strong and effective cooperation schemes must involve a surrendering of national sovereignty and a willingness to accept the decision of supranational economic organizations. Third World governments have been very jealous guardians of national sovereignty and this has seriously damaged the prospects for economic cooperation at both the regional and the Third World level. The reluctance to 'pool' sovereignties has severely restricted the ability to take advantage of their increased power in world financial markets and no 'debtors' union' has emerged to challenge the imposition of deflationary and restructionist policies at the international level.

Nevertheless some progress has been made and South–South economic transactions have increased. Today virtually every LDC is involved in some form of institutionalized cooperation with its neighbours – often in the context of a regional integration scheme.[51] There is general enthusiasm for the establishment of UNCTAD's Global System of Trade Preferences (GTSP) but negotiations are not at a particularly advanced stage. In the following paragraphs we review the problems associated with the operation of regional integration schemes in the Third World on the one hand and with the growth of countertrade on the other.

Countertrade: Latin American experiences[52]

Countertrade operations may be defined as operations in which an export (or import) commitment is one of the prerequisites for the conclusion of an import (or, conversely, export) transaction. The parties to the transactions in each direction need not be the same, but there must be a conditional link between the two transactions, so that one of them cannot be carried out without the other.

Generally speaking, there is said to be a certain degree of coercion in countertrade, in the sense that at least one of the parties decides to participate in the import or export transaction concerned after reaching the conclusion that, if it had refused to accept the link between the two, it would have been excluded from the operation. The element of coercion may be prompted by very diverse factors (national provisions, international agreements, exchange market characteristics, etc); however, this is not an essential characteristic of countertrade, although it is apparent in most cases.

In recent years a resurgence of interest in countertrade has become apparent in many Latin American countries. Several countries in the region – including Bolivia, Colombia, Costa Rica, the Dominican Republic, Ecuador, Guatemala and Nicaragua – have adopted specific provisions on countertrade or amended their regulations on implementation since 1982. Other countries, such as Brazil, Jamaica and Uruguay, have been using this instrument since the beginning of the 1980s. In Uruguay, 12.5 per cent of total external trade was accounted for by countertrade transactions during 1983–4. In Brazil (which alone accounts for about 60 per cent of countertrade undertaken by the Latin American countries), this share was 5.5 per cent.[53]

A recent detailed study of countertrade in Argentina, Brazil and Uruguay[54] has shown that in the early 1980s countertrade linked with oil imports represented 54 per cent of the total countertrade recorded (2.6 per cent of their total foreign trade). Bilateral clearing arrangements with East European socialist countries accounted for 29 per cent of the group's countertrade (1.4 per cent of their total trade). Countertrade deals concerning non-oil government imports (essentially of capital goods) represented some 7 per cent of the total countertrade (0.4 per cent of total trade). Countertrade under the existing arrangements for the motor vehicle industry represented some 6 per cent of total countertrade.

Practically all the countertrade, with the exception of trade conducted under bilateral clearing arrangements with East European countries, seems to have taken the form of counter-purchase. No barter or buy-back deals have been noted. Imports by public agencies are involved in at least 60 per cent of the countertrade observed.

Regarding the products that are included in countertrade exports, there appears generally to be a trend towards exclusion of traditional export items. This is believed to be due to considerations relating to their past competitiveness, the interest in concentrating promotional efforts on the diversification of non-traditional products and the difficulty in preventing undesirable re-exports that would involve additional competition on already established markets. However, on some occasions various circumstances have made it necessary to accept the inclusion of traditional products among countertrade exports.

No attempt has been made by authorities in the Latin American countries to estimate the extent to which countertrade exports are genuinely additional to exports that would have taken place in the absence of countertrade agreements or to calculate the price distortions that might be associated with countertrade deals. There have been no recorded cases of purchase involving two bids by each party – one taking into account countertrade requirements and the other not doing so. This concept is being examined in Brazil, and could provide interesting elements for determining the costs associated with use of this instrument.

It has been widely recognized that, despite the obvious advantage of economizing the use of foreign exchange resources, countertrade may involve many substantial costs.

One of the most obvious disadvantages of countertrade by comparison with conventional trade is the greater cost of transactions. Whereas conventional trade simply requires the coincidence of needs, countertrade requires that a dual coincidence of needs should be met in a single transaction. In practice this is more difficult to achieve. Diversion of one of the two flows to third parties introduces flexibility into the requirement of dual coincidence, but it may further increase costs. The identification and negotiation of viable pairs for transactions is a costly process in which one or both parties have invested real resources, frequently with uncertain results.

139

There is a particularly low return on countertrade in terms of effectively completed deals as a percentage of planned deals. The cost of the administrative and legal structures used in the identification and negotiation of non-completed countertrade transactions should be added to the cost of the much fewer transactions that are actually completed.

Countertrade may cause distortions in the domestic economy of the country engaging in it. First, the rest of the economy not directly involved in countertrade transactions may be affected by the price distortions that normally accompany this type of trade, when they transmit inaccurate indications for the appropriate allocation of resources. In this connection it should be noted that even if such distortions are not transmitted directly to the rest of the economy – for example, if they are absorbed by the state budget under an administered pricing policy – they may in any event influence the economic calculation for development projects that utilize inputs of capital goods purchased at prices that are distorted by the use of countertrade. Such projects may appear to be less viable than they really are – or even unfeasible owing to such distortions, when in actual fact they would clearly have been viable in the absence of countertrade requirements. Secondly, when countertrade schemes result in practice in a simulation of the effects of a selective devaluation, the resultant pattern of multiple exchange rates may involve effective differential export incentives that distort and are even openly at variance with those that have been decided on in accordance with government policy. Lastly, the price distortions in countertrade operations that involve imports of very widely used products in exchange for exports produced by a relatively small sector of the economy may involve regressive transfers of earnings. In these cases, one of the by-products of countertrade may be a virtual tax on the relatively large number of users of the imported product, a tax the proceeds of which accrue to the smaller group of producers of the goods exported.

It is clear, therefore, that countertrade deals must be worked out carefully and are likely to be most beneficial in the context of regional integration schemes when detailed knowledge of cost and production conditions are easier to acquire. It is encouraging to note therefore that several Latin American regional groupings are currently studying the potential of countertrade deals as a means for stimulating regional trade, and the Latin American Integration Association has actually developed appropriate instruments for the organization and regulation of countertrade among its members.[55]

Regional integration in the Third World: a case study

Development programmes within the LDCs are severely constrained in both supply and demand conditions. On the supply side, there is a general scarcity of capital, managerial ability, technical know-how and skilled labour. On the demand side, the smallness of the domestic market thwarts growth and expansion. The size of the market is primarily determined by income levels and on this count even such large countries as India, Pakistan and Bangladesh have significant demand constraints on economic expansion.

One possible solution to the problem of market size is offered by the establishment of common markets and economic integration. The forging of strong regional economic ties is, however, no easy task, because at present the national entities of the developing world seldom have strong economic links. They buy from the rich countries and sell to the rich countries: about 70 per cent of the LDCs' trade is with the rich countries. Thus, regional economic integration among developing countries implies the necessity of developing new economic relations between them, which is bound to be a long drawn out process. Conventional customs union theory, with its emphasis on the overall benefits of economic integration, tends to ignore the problem of assessing the 'durability' of a particular regional integration scheme. A regional union among developing countries is discussed below, attention being focused on the question: to what extent are these unions successful in establishing new economic relationships between their members with the gradual reduction of their dependence on the metropolitan country in whose periphery they at present are? The case examined is that of the Latin American Integration Association.

LATIN AMERICAN INTEGRATION ASSOCIATION (LAIA)[56]

The Latin American Integration Association (LAIA) was established in 1980 as a replacement for the generally unsuccessful Latin American Free Trade Association (LAFTA) created in 1961. LAF-TA's founder members were Argentina, Bolivia, Brazil, Chile,

Colombia, Ecuador, Mexico, Paraguay, Peru, Uruguay and Venezuela. The Montevideo Treaty, signed in 1960, which led to the formation of LAFTA, considered the establishment of a free trade area to be a first step in the evolution of a Latin American economic community, and it provided that within twelve years the members of LAFTA would abolish virtually all restrictions on trade within the area. In order to attain this objective, periodic negotiations were to be arranged between the member countries on both a bilateral and multilateral level. Special arrangements were agreed upon to discriminate in favour of Bolivia, Ecuador, Paraguay and Uruguay – the relatively poorer members. The agreement also envisaged that the member countries would attempt to coordinate their industrialization policies and would develop complementary lines of industrial production.

A number of negotiation 'rounds' have been held under the Treaty, and a large number of minor tariff and trade concessions have been granted. There has, however, been a noticeable decline in the success of negotiations as the years have passed, many more concessions being granted in the earlier years. Semi-manufactured goods have been favourably treated, but very few concessions have been granted for new industrial products. Negotiations with regard to changes in the Common Schedule (which lists the products whose duties are to be eventually abolished) have generally been difficult, and little seems to have been achieved in this area. Hence investors in new products generally have no guarantee that they will have access to the regional market. Attempts to regulate trade in agricultural goods have also sometimes run into difficulties. All this led to a modification of the original LAFTA treaty. In early 1969 it was decided at Caracas that the end of the liberalization programme was to be postponed from 1973 to 1980, and that new regulations were to be drawn up for the compilation of the Common Schedule. The annual tariff reduction that the member countries were required to make was reduced from 8 per cent of the (weighted) average import duties (to non-member countries) to only 2.9 per cent.

The limitations to the success of LAFTA emanated chiefly from two main sources: its organizational defects and the economic conditions of its member countries. With regard to the first group of factors, it was quite obvious that the methods used and the institutions established by LAFTA were by their nature rather

inadequate for the comprehensive integration of the national economies of the region. The extraordinarily cumbersome method of
annual item-by-item negotiation was not suitable for the achievement of economic coordination between countries at that level
of development, partly because it was quite incapable of taking
into account new products. Agricultural imports were also treated as
special exceptions. Indeed, the whole emphasis seemed to be on
reaching arbitrary compromises without reference to a common set
of procedures. This lack of procedures for the automatic elimination
of tariffs prevented policy harmonization, restricted regional investment and increased the problem of the distribution of benefits from
free trade. The LAFTA agreement did not provide for the implementation of a regional investment policy and did not lay down the
procedures by which the fiscal and monetary policies of the member
countries were to be brought together. It also failed to take into
account differences in the levels of development of the member
countries. All these factors reduced the usefulness and effectiveness
of LAFTA.

The 1980 Montevideo Treaty, ratified by all eleven LAFTA
members in March 1981, signalled the official demise of LAFTA.
LAIA downplays the concept of a free trade area embodied in
LAFTA's system of regional trade concessions and favours 'partial
accords', which may be signed by two or more members. Within the
framework of LAIA a preferential treatment scheme has been
adopted to favour the less developed countries and stimulate their
exports to the rest of the region. The seventh extraordinary
evaluation conference held in Sptember 1984 approved the first
expansion of the market openings lists in favour of Bolivia, Ecuador
and Paraguay.

LAIA provides the basis for granting special treatment according
to each country's comparative level of economic development. In
the area of bilateral accords, differential treatment operates; if a
member grants a less developed state a certain margin of tariff
preference on an item, it may not award the same degree of
preference on that product to a more advanced country.

LAIA is calling for significant reductions in tariff rates for member
nation imports as part of a broader thrust toward regional import
substitution. Delegates from four entrepreneurial groups (food,
glass, metal and non-ferrous minerals, and refractory material

industries) within LAIA have formulated tariff reduction, communication and integration recommendations at recent meetings during 1986. Food industry delegates from eight countries recently agreed to substitute foodstuff purchases from third countries with regionally sourced ones, to establish countertrade mechanisms aimed at helping food processors, and to turn current purchasing policies by LAIA and state-owned enterprises toward the acquisition of zonal-sourced products. Glass industry representatives are currently evaluating the existing agreements in favour of import substitution. Tariff reductions pertaining to metals and non-ferrous minerals and refractory materials are under way to promote intra-regional trade. LAIA members agreed to submit by October 1986 a list of goods for which regional import substitution possibilities exist.

A first series of cuts affects tariffs on goods currently purchased from third nations but that are available locally. Duty reductions will range between 40 per cent and 80 per cent, with the highest rates applied to imports from LAIA's less developed members. In the sphere of the preferential tariff system, duties on goods not included in any other LAIA agreement appear to be cut by 10 per cent for imports from Argentina, Brazil and Mexico; 14 per cent for goods from Uruguay, Peru, Colombia, Venezuela and Chile; and 20 per cent for goods from Bolivia, Ecuador and Paraguay. These measures were expected to boost regional trade by at least 40 per cent during 1987–8. The achievement of this ambitious target will depend on how fast individual countries adopt these measures.

The Impact of UNCTAD[57]

The United Nations Conference on Trade and Development was established in 1964, with the main purpose of coordinating international effort in order to promote the development of the poor countries, who felt that the United Nations was the right place for negotiating economic arrangements with the rich countries. UNCTAD has provided a forum for the poor countries to express their views on international trading arrangements and on the economic policies of the rich countries in general. However, UNCTAD's achievements have not been as spectacular as the optimists expected. In the field of international trade its main contribution has been the pioneering in 1971 of the General System of Preferences (GSP), already mentioned, which was designed to cover the manufacturing exports of the poor countries. Other major policy initiatives have included the establishment of a 1 per cent aid to GNP target, the creation of a link between aid and the issue of SDRs,[58] and the emergence of the Common Fund. Seven triannual conferences have been held (in 1964, 1968, 1972, 1976, 1979, 1983, 1987) at which many other resolutions have been passed on the issues of protectionism, commodities, transfer of technology, financial flows, economic cooperation among LDCs and the establishment of New International Economic Order (NIEO). These resolutions are, however, ambiguous and commit nobody to any specific action. Thus the 'transfer of technology' resolutions adopted at the 1972 Santiago session call for the promotion of technology transfer from the rich to the poor countries and ask the rich to participate actively in the identification of restrictive business practices that affect the transfer of technology, but they do not specify the methods by which these aims are to be achieved. They do not create any permanent machinery that can administer and coordinate the implementation of the resolutions.

Other resolutions have been equally ambiguous. The Common Fund that has emerged is a far cry from the original proposals contained in the International Commodity Programme.[59] Similarly the UNCTAD V (1979) resolutions on economic cooperation among LDCs and on protectionism do not commit UNCTAD's members to take specific and concrete substantive initiatives in their areas. Hence UNCTAD rarely leads to action or any significant changes in international economic policies. Although the developed countries generally accept the need for greater LDC participation in world commodity and factor markets, they do not agree that new international machinery is necessary to achieve this aim. Existing institutions, laws and agreements could be gradually reformed to meet the needs of the poor countries. The developing countries have refused to accept this view and the gap between the two groups on the institutional question has tended to widen.

The limited and disappointing results of the conferences have created a great deal of disillusionment about UNCTAD. The Group of 77 (actually comprising 120 poor countries) and Group B (consisting of the rich western countries) have both become

145

increasingly disheartened. The rich countries believe that the demands of the poor are 'unbalanced' and 'unrealistic', while the poor countries view the stand taken by the rich as niggardly and overcautious. The rich and poor countries carry on a dialogue that tends to become purposeless and devoid of substance.

UNCTAD must share some of the blame for the North–South stalemate. It has a strong in-built Third World voting majority, unlike other international economic organizations such as GATT, the IMF or the World Bank group. LDCs have continued to press for task expansion but, particularly during the 1980s, UNCTAD has been pushed to the sidelines. Why has the UNCTAD secretariat failed to sustain the momentum of the North–South dialogue generated in the early days of the NIEO negotiations?

Three major factors may be identified as crucial in this respect. First the decision-making process in UNCTAD proved to be inadequate for negotiating concrete deals. The negotiators came from the foreign ministries and permanent diplomatic missions – rather than from the ministries of commerce and trade. This was true of the delegations of both rich and poor countries at the UNCTAD conferences and associated Trade and Development Board meetings.[60] It is natural that such delegations were principally interested in scoring diplomatic points. Often they lacked the necessary technical expertise to negotiate complicated trade deals.

Secondly, the negotiation of such deals was impeded by the inability of the Third World countries to agree among themselves rules and procedures for the effective sharing of costs and benefits of deals negotiated in UNCTAD. The Group of 77 thus usually adopted the 'maximum common denominator' approach – lumping all interests and demands together – in formulating its negotiating position. It was relatively easy for the OECD to dismiss such demands as unrealistic and to play off one LDC sub-group against another to prevent effective implementation of reform. The Group system proved an effective means for interest articulation by the LDCs but it did not in general facilitate the striking and implementation of concrete economic deals between North and South.

The striking of such deals and the establishment of viable international institutional mechanisms for the sharing of associated costs and benefits were severely constrained by the unwillingness of Third World governments to accept restrictions on national sovereignty and to delegate power to regional and trans Third World international organizations. However, as pointed out above, an increase in the bargaining power of the Third World simply cannot occur without such a 'pooling' of national sovereignties, and UNCTAD has failed to provide the necessary institutional focus. Third World unity has been essentially symbolic in nature and its potential for transforming international economic relations has remained largely unrealized. This is demonstrated by the inability of the Third World to institutionalize 'commodity power'[61] during the 1970s, exercise 'debtors' power' in the 1980s and prevent a general collapse of the North–South dialogue.

UNCTAD has failed to sustain momentum for this dialogue in the West because it has developed few links with those interest groups – transnationals, consumer associations, trade unions, religious and humanitarian bodies – that are affected by the growth of North–South economic transactions. These interest groups are potential supporters of the expansion of such transactions and of improvements in the terms on which these transactions are conducted. Yet UNCTAD has remained content with issuing macroeconomic studies that demonstrate the general desirability of proposed policy changes on grounds legitimized by conventional welfare economic analysis. But policy-making and implementation in western societies is a complex process. Policies are adopted not merely because they are shown to have positive welfare effects but because interest groups committed to their implementation strike political and economic bargains within markets, within political parties and within the administrative structures of the state. The collapse of the NIEO dialogue shows that a viable and politically effective coalition of interest groups to press for a widening and deepening of North–South economic transactions has not been constructed. UNCTAD – and other international economic organizations in which the LDCs have a majority – has missed an important opportunity in this respect.[62]

A Trade Policy for the Third World[63]

The Third World countries have, with very few exceptions, been strongly influenced by developments in world markets. Attitudes to international trade as a mechanism for accelerating development have, however, changed over the years. Over the 1940s and 1950s many LDCs favoured an import substitution strategy, which promised to 'de-link' them from international markets.[64] In the 1960s and 1970s, trade liberalization was back in fashion and some leading LDCs – particularly in East Asia – experienced spectacular levels of export growth. In the 1980s there has been a shift back towards 'favouring the domestic market' and the 'avoidance of domestic inequalities', particularly in South America which has suffered more in the recession and is more threatened by the debt crisis than Asia. There is particular emphasis on the 'multiple distortions' of international markets – with the implication that concentration on the removal of one or two key distortions (e.g. exchange rates or subsidies) may well increase rather than diminish overall distortions and the difficulties of reaching an optimum solution.

At the same time, there is also emphasis on avoiding the errors of the past. Both the old ISI and the more recently attempted EOI have proved to be flawed. Paradoxically, they both resulted in an inefficient industrial structure, with insufficient vertical integration and horizontal linkages. Any new domestically oriented industrialization strategy must pay more attention to monetary, price and balance-of-trade and balance-of-payments implications than the old ISI did. It must also encourage exports more. In other words, it must be more a move forward to something new than a return to the old. In this sense also, the debate between the proposals of ISI and EOI as exclusive alternatives is dangerously misleading. We need a strategy that combines the best elements of both and utilizes their complementarities. It must also pay more attention to the structure and quality of industrialization as distinct from its simple volume and simple industrialization ratios.

In fact, an ISI that fails to develop an industrial structure capable of paying its way in international markets fails in the purpose of ISI, which was put forward as a natural escape out of primary commodities with their unfavourable price trends. The terms of trade of the 'old' industrial consumer products versus the 'new' and capital goods may be no more favourable than those of primary commodities; hence old-style ISI often proved a dead-end way out of 'unequal exchange'. The watchword of the new synthesis must be 'integrated industrialization'.

148

This implies that the new industrial strategy must be less dualistic than either ISI or EOI, both of which have shown themselves capable of creating pockets of modernity, with more links abroad than domestically and many of the inputs imported, while leaving the poorer section to survive with a capital-starved and discouraged 'informal sector'. The new synthesis should blend the two technologies into an intermediate technology, or blend them purposefully together in both inter-firm and intra-firm linked structures. New technological advances have created opportunities in this direction, and their exploration in the framework of the new industrial strategies now widely grasped for in Latin America and elsewhere opens up a big new agenda.[65]

What is suggested here is not so much a development strategy that is 'neutral' between IS and EO (this is the formulation favoured by, among others, the World Bank). Rather, what is suggested is a systematic combination of IS and EO, with a different emphasis on IS and EO at different periods and for different sectors. In the nature of things in developing countries, the sequence from IS to EO will be more frequent than the reverse, both in time and for given sectors. But EO itself will also lead to new opportunities for IS to reduce the import content of exports and increase linkages from the export sector to the rest of the economy, thus preventing dualism.

The strategy advocated here accepts the need for pursuing protectionist policies in the Third World. But such policies must be selected with care and executed with flexibility and skill. Obviously the policies of different countries will differ. The size of the domestic markets, the geographic position of the country, its relationship with foreign countries and its resource endowment will be important factors in determining its protectionist policies. But a few general conclusions may be drawn about the nature of the protectionist policy that is most likely to be conducive to development, given the general economic characteristics of most developing countries.

To begin with, the LDCs must pursue a consistent protectionist policy. This is a point that has to be stressed, because in most LDCs the system of protection has evolved in a very haphazard way. Tariffs and taxes have been imposed, modified and withdrawn at different times in response to the pressure of circumstances and of individual investors, and the effect of these sporadic measures on the different industries has been very varied. The standard deviation (i.e. the average variability) of the ERP among industries is very large in most LDCs.

Protectionist policies must also aim at providing incentives for the growth of the technological resource potential of the poor country. It is important to realize that, unless the technological backwardness of the developing world is eliminated, the poor countries will find it impossible to tackle the problems of low productivity levels, economic inefficiency and high unemployment rates. An overriding aim of policy in developing countries should be to promote the development and use of local resources (including labour resources) and the development and import of suitable technological capacity. These considerations apply with equal force to both rich and poor developing countries.

Beyond this, it would be difficult to specify an 'ideal protectionist' policy for the whole developing world. Currently, many western economists advocate trade liberalization and specialization in accordance with international comparative advantages. Developing countries are being advised to reduce their protection of manufactured products to emphasize production for export (as against import substitution) and to explore the development of world markets for non-traditional primary commodities. They are being asked to refrain from setting up producer cartels or debtor clubs. It is difficult to be enthusiastic about these recommendations. For one thing, the rich countries seem reluctant to ensure the stabilization of commodity prices and their linkage to the prices of manufactured products. For another, the acceptance of these policies would leave unchanged the nature of the relationship between the rich and poor countries. The type of international economic integration that is envisaged by the authors of these policies would tend to perpetuate the economic and technological dependence of the LDCs on the industrial countries and would increase the gap between the haves and have-nots on both a national and an international level. It is therefore not surprising that many LDCs have sought to improve their bargaining position in world markets by first developing domestic demand oriented industries. Those that have penetrated world markets are confronted with the New Protectionism, and are therefore seriously questioning the continued viability of a liberal trade strategy.

150

Trade policy can be effective if monetary, fiscal and general planning measures are used to support it. Unfortunately, most LDCs have tended to use conflicting domestic and external economic policies and have only rarely attempted to rationalize these policies in accordance with the economic objectives laid down in their national development plans. The impact of trade policy measures has thus been reduced.

The overall economic dependence of the poor countries on the developed world is the most significant reason for the ineffectiveness of their own trade policies. The greater this dependence, the lower the ability of the LDCs to undertake comprehensive programmes of economic reform and reorientation unilaterally. Lowering this dependence would necessarily involve a substantial net transfer of real and financial resources from the rich countries to the Third World. Part III of this book addresses this question in some detail.

Appendix: The Rate of Effective Protection in the LDCs

The concept of the effective rate of protection (ERP) has been discussed in this chapter. The ERP is usually calculated by the use of input/output coefficients. Effective protection is the protection that is accorded to a particular economic activity as a result of the protection of all the different stages of the manufacturing process. It is evident that protection might raise the prices of both the inputs and output of an industry. The ERP estimates the amount by which value-added in a particular activity is raised by protection. A number of methods for measuring ERP have been given; Corden's method is the most frequently used.[66] It is given by the formula:

$$g_j = \frac{t_j - \sum_{i=1}^{n} a_{ij} t_i}{1 - \sum_{i=1}^{n} a_{ij}},$$

where g_j = effective protection rate for activity j
a_{ij} = share of i in cost of j in absence of tariffs
t_i = tariff rate on i
t_j = tariff rate on j.

151

Therefore the effective protection rate depends not only on the protection of industry *j* but also on the input coefficients and the level of protection of the inputs of industry *j*. The effective protection rate is the percentage change in value-added per unit in industry *j* made possible by the existence of a protection structure relative to a 'no tariff' situation but with the same exchange rate.

It is evident that the concept of ERP is not without its ambiguities.[67] Economists have differed on the ways in which non-traded goods should be treated in measuring ERP for a particular activity. Doubt has also been expressed about the ERP as an indicator of the attractiveness of different industries from the point of view of the investors. Why should the percentage increase in value-added be a measure of this? Some may suggest that the percentage by which net profits would be raised would be the right measure. It has also been argued that ERP should be measured relative to a 'realistic' or 'equilibrium' foreign exchange rate rather than the official exchange rates of the LDCs.

The debate on these issues has by no means proved conclusive, and most of the refinements that have emerged from it seem to be too ambitious for incorporation into the actual empirical work that is undertaken on the basis of the data produced by the LDCs. Hence the ERP is still measured in a fairly straightforward, or even crude, way. Despite its shortcomings, it represents the best available, relatively simple measure of the structure of protection of a country.

Notes

1 This strategy is described in detail in I. M. D. Little, T. Scitovsky and M. Scott, *Industry and Trade in Developing Countries* (Paris: OECD Development Centre, 1970) and J. Bhagwati, *Anatomy and Consequences of Exchange Regimes*, Vol. 9 of J. Bhagwati and A. Krueger (eds), *Foreign Trade Regimes and Economic Development* (Cambridge, MA: National Bureau for Economic Research and Ballinger, 1978).

2 This argument is developed at length in Chapters 2 and 4.

3 Little *et al.* (n.1).

4 B. Balassa, *Development Strategies in Semi-industrialized Economies* (Baltimore, Md: Johns Hopkins University Press, 1982).

5 Bhagwati and Krueger (n.1).

6 D. Evans and P. Alisadeh, 'Trade industralisation and the visible hand', *Journal of Development Studies*, 1984, pp. 75–96.

7   H. W. Singer, 'The terms of trade controversy and the evolution of soft financing', in G. Meier and D. Seers (eds), *Pioneers in Development* (London: Oxford University Press, 1984), p. 16.

8   B. Balassa, *The Newly Industrialising Countries in the World Economy* (Oxford: Pergamon Press, 1981), p. 15.

9   M. R. Datta Chaudhuri, 'Industrialisation and foreign trade: The development strategies of South Korea and the Philippines', in E. Let (ed.), *Export Led Industrialisation and Development* (Geneva: ILO, 1981), pp. 47–79.

10 J. A. Ansari, R. Ballance and H. W. Singer, *The International Economy and Industrial Development* (Brighton: Wheatsheaf, 1982), ch. 1.

11 See S. R. Lewis, *Economic Policy and Industrial Growth in Pakistan* (London: Allen & Unwin, 1969).

12 The 'vent for surplus' argument was first presented by Adam Smith and is elaborated in M. Todaro, *Economic Development of the Third World* (London: Longman, 1985), pp. 233–5.

13 W. R. Cline, 'Can the East Asian model of development be generalised', *World Development*, 10(2), 1982, pp. 81–90.

14 ibid., p. 89.

15 For evidence on protectionism in the West see Chapter 5.

16 On this see pp. 135–44 above.

17 H. W. Singer, 'North–South multipliers', *World Development* 11(5), 1983, pp. 451–4.

18 UNCTAD, *Trade and Development Report 1985* (New York: UN, 1985), pp. 17–18.

19 R. M. Kavoussi, 'International trade and economic development: The recent experience of developing countries', *The Journal of Developing Areas*, 19(3), April 1985, p. 391.

20 G. D. Guryer, 'Perennial Crop Supply Response: the Case of Tanzanian Sisal' (Wye College, University of London, 1971), mimeo.

21 The Iraq–Iran war is now (1987) in its eighth year.

22 The First International Tin Agreement came into force in 1956.

23 UNCTAD, *Monthly Bulletin*, June/July 1985.

24 As of July 1986, contributions to the official subscription of the fund stand at $271 million. Total official contributions have been fixed at $470 million – 66 per cent of which must be received before the fund can commence its operations. The USA's contribution has been fixed at 15.71 per cent of the total and that of the USSR and its Group D allies at 10.21 per cent. Thus the US and the USSR are primarily responsible for the continued stalemate in the negotiations to establish the fund. The full story of these negotiations is told in J. A. Ansari, *The Political Economy of International Economic Organisations* (Brighton: Wheatsheaf, 1986), Ch. 8.

25 For a review of this literature and the most comprehensive presentation of the neo-classical arguments in this area see D. Newberry and J. Stiglitz, *The Theory of Commodity Price Stabilisation: A Study in the Economics of Risk* (Oxford: Oxford University Press, 1981).

26 A. Thirlwall, 'Keynes' economic development and the developing
countries', Paper presented at seventh Keynes Seminar, University of
Kent at Canterbury, November 1985, pp. 40–1.

27 Discussion in Thirlwall, ibid., pp. 23–31.

28 N. Kaldor, 'Inflation and recession in the world economy', *Economic
Journal*, 1976, pp. 134–63.

29 Thirlwall (n.26), pp. 23–4.

30 Keynes' proposals are to be found in G. Moggridge (ed.), *The Collected
Works of John Maynard Keynes*, vol. 26 (London: Macmillan, 1980).
Keynes also proposed that the value of the new international currency (to be known as Bancor) should be linked to the prices of a
bundle of key commodities. On this see the discussion in Chapters 9
and 11.

31 A description of the evolution of the CFF is presented in R. Kaibrui,
'Evolution of the Compensatory Financing Facility', *Finance and
Development*, 23(2), June 1986, pp. 24–7.

32 This provision was made initially for a period of four years, but has
now been extended to 1989.

33 Trend calculations for export shortfalls are presently made on the basis
of a geometric average (defined as the fifth root of the export values for
the five years), where calculation for the excess payments to cover
cereal imports are made on the basis of an arithmetical average (defined
as the sum of the payments for the five years divided by five). For details
see Kaibrui (n.31), p. 25.

34 I. Gruhn, 'Lomé convention renegotiations', in R. Boardman *et al.*
(eds), *Europe, Africa and Lomé III* (London: Dalhousie University,
Centre for African Studies, 1985), p. 17. This criticism may also be
levelled at the CFS of the IMF.

35 The STABEX scheme is discussed in detail in J. Ravenhill, 'Europe and
Africa: an essential continuity', in Boardman (n. 34), pp. 46–9.

36 ibid., p. 47.

37 ibid., p. 49.

38 M. Blackwell, 'Lomé III: The search for greater effectiveness', *Finance
and Development*, 22(3), 1985, pp. 31–4.

39 Brazil – SDR 1.1 billion; Mexico – SDR 0.9 billion; Malawi – SDR 10
million. IMF, *Annual Report* (Washington, DC, 1986), p. 73.

40 Cumulative borrowings should not exceed 450 per cent of quotas.
These limits were agreed in November 1984 and are subject to periodic
revision. IMF, *Annual Report* (Washington, DC, 1985), p. 73.

41 Although no formal links had existed prior to this, in fact the structural
adjustment assistance of the Bank had since 1978 been conditional on
prior agreement between the country concerned and the IMF on
stabilization measures considered appropriate by the latter.

42 See 'Structural adjustment facility', *Finance and Development*, June 1986,
p. 39.

43 B. Gosovic, *UNCTAD: Conflict and Compromise* (Leiden: Sijthoff,
1972), pp. 91–2.

44   A large literature has grown up in recent years evaluating the GSP. See in particular T. Murray, 'How helpful is the GSP', *Economic Journal*, 83(2), June 1973; R. Longhammer and A. Sapir, *Economic Impact of Trade Preferences* (London: Trade Policy Research Centre, 1984); United Nations, *Operations and Effects of the GSP* (New York: UN, 1983), Sales No. E81.2.D.6.
45   Details of individual schemes are given in UNCTAD, 'Review of the Implementation of the GSP' TD/BC/C.5/105, February 1986 (unpublished).
46   For discussion of the impact of the Tokyo Round cuts on the GSP benefits of the LDCs see Chapter 5.
47   Oil imports are also an exception, but this is explained simply by the fact that the developed countries are not major oil exporters.
48   Calculated from UNCTAD, *Handbook of International Trade and Development Statistics 1985* (New York: UN, 1985), pp. 70, 74, 90, 94.
49   UNCTAD, *Strengthening the Weakest Link* (New York: UN, 1986), p. 6.
50   W. Arthur Lewis, 'The slowing down of the engine of growth', *American Economic Review*, September 1980, pp. 555–64.
51   In 1987 the number of economic integration schemes within the Third World was forty-three – with almost half of them being in Africa. UNCTAD (n. 49), p. 20.
52   There exists a sizeable literature on countertrade. See e.g. G. Banks, 'The economics and politics of foreign trade', *The World Economy*, 6(2), 1983, pp. 159–82; R. E. Caves, 'The economics of reciprocity: theory and evidence on bilateral trading arrangements', in W. Sellekaerts, *International Trade and Finance: Essays in Honour of Jan Tinbergen* (London: Macmillan, 1976), pp. 17–50; H. Leibman, 'GATT and countertrade regulation', *Journal of World Trade Law*, 1986, pp. 252–61; and I. Hodara, 'Countertrade: experiences of some Latin American Countries', UNCTAD/SN/ECDC/27, 1985, mimeo.
53   Hodara (n. 52), p. 45.
54   ibid.
55   Reviewed in Hodara (n. 52), pp. 10–14.
56   This section was written by Jabamalai Arachi of the Centre for Research on the New International Economic Order, Madras, India.
57   This section draws heavily on Ansari (n. 24), Ch. 8.
58   Both of these are discussed in Chapter 8 below.
59   See above, pp. 123–5.
60   The Trade and Development Board is UNCTAD's executive body.
61   Sometimes referred to as 'producers' power'.
62   No doubt this is partly explained by the LDC governments' excessive concern with national sovereignty. They show little enthusiasm for the transformation of EIOs from intergovernmental bodies to organizations with strong links with non-governmental economic, political and social groups.

63 This section is based on H. W. Singer and P. Alizadeh, 'Import substitution revisited' (Brighton: Institute of Development Studies, 1986), mimeo.
64 This promise was, of course, not kept; see pp. 104–9 above.
65 G. Boon, 'Dualism and technological harmony for balanced development', *Industry and Development*, No. 9, 1983.
66 W. M. Corden, 'The structures of a tariff system and the effective rate of protection', *Journal of Political Economy*, June 1960.
67 Discussion at length in B. Balassa *et al.*, *The Structure of Protection in Developing Countries* (Baltimore, Md: IBRD, 1971), pp. 315–34.

PART III

International Finance

7   Aid and Development

Aid, Trade and the Widening Gap

A central aspect of international development that we ought perpetually to keep in mind is the fact that it can safely be predicted that the gap between the richer and poorer countries is bound to grow in both absolute and relative terms in the foreseeable future. The specialists may quibble about the exact magnitude of the different variables and their growth rates, but intellectual sophistry of this sort cannot conceal the hard fact that the average Bangladeshi or Tanzanian will in the year 2000 have a much lower standard of living *in comparison* to the standard of living enjoyed by the average British, American or USSR citizen.

In the course of the next thirty years the gap between the rich and poor countries may widen by between three and four times, and the consequences both political and economic of this colossal growth in inequality are likely to be immense. Indeed, it goes without saying that the stability of the world order as we know it depends crucially on the way in which this problem of the ever-widening gap between nations is handled by the international community. Two-thirds of the world's population will not reconcile itself to a level of living that is permanently diminishing in comparison to the standards enjoyed by the privileged citizens of Northern America, Europe and the oil-rich countries. A crisis in international relations is almost inevitable if the rich countries complacently accept their lead and advantages as a fact of life. If the international economic system is incapable of providing the wherewithal for an effective reduction of inequality within the community of nations, the LDCs will feel justified in their attempts to destroy the political and economic system that perpetuates international inequalities.

A realization of the seriousness of this problem was fundamental

159

to the first Brandt Report.[1] Published in March 1980, the report recommended a 'massive transfer of resources' as one of the main instruments (but by no means the only instrument) for reducing the inequalities of income distribution between rich and poor countries, and for releasing at the same time the world economy, including especially the rich countries, from the deadlock of world depression and 'stagflation'. Within this massive transfer of resources, in turn, the increase and improvement of aid or official development assistance (ODA) was to play a key role. In this, the Brandt Commission echoed some of the proposals made over a decade earlier (1969) by its predecessor, the Commission on International Development, headed by the former Canadian Prime Minister, Lester B. Pearson. The Pearson Report at the time failed to have an impact, because shortly after its publication the Bretton Woods system began to come apart, the industrial countries became preoccupied with their own troubles, and a little later the oil crisis of 1973 changed the context of international discussion.

Regarding the *quantity* of ODA, the Brandt Commission once again recommended an early achievement of the old UN target of 0.7 per cent of GNP of richer countries. This was optimistically to be achieved by 1985, as part of a 1980–85 Emergency Programme. It would more than double the flow which had shown no signs of moving towards the UN target since 1969 when the Pearson Commission recommended its achievement 'by 1975'. After 1985, ODA was to increase to 1 per cent of GNP 'before the end of the century'. This increase in the quantity of ODA was to be assisted by more active participation of the East European countries, whose aid flow is not minimal, OPEC countries and the newly industrializing countries, such as Brazil, Mexico or Korea. In fact, all 'except the poorest countries' would participate, but the poorer among the donor countries would be assisted by a sliding scale related to national income; no specific scale was suggested (see Chapter 8).

Another way in which new sources of ODA would be developed was through a system of international levies, which could include levies on international trade, arms production and/or arms exports, international travel, and the profits from the exploitation of sea-bed minerals or other uses of the 'global commons'. This development of a system of international taxation was one of the striking proposals of the Brandt Report. Apart from increasing the quantity of ODA, the proposal was designed also to improve it qualitatively at the same time, by making it more automatic, more predictable and more capable of long-term commitments.

Other new sources to help in the expansion of ODA recommended by the Brandt Report included the profits obtainable by the International Monetary Fund (IMF) from the sale of its gold reserves and their replacement or partial replacement by specially created world currency reserves – the Special Drawing Rights (SDRs) – or by using the gold reserves as collateral for raising funds for ODA to developing countries. The lending capacity of the World Bank was to be quadrupled (in money terms) by doubling its capital and at the same time doubling the borrowing/capital gearing ratio. Finally, the resources of the Regional Development Banks – the Asian Development Bank in Manila, the African Development Bank in Abidjan and the Inter-American Development in Washington – were to be greatly increased. All these proposals also had the dual purpose of increasing the quantity of ODA and improving its quality – or at least its acceptability – by increasing the multilateral share in ODA (an objective also shared with the Pearson Report, and in that case fairly successfully achieved in the intervening decade).

To play its proper role as a development agent in the context of a massive resource transfer, it was necessary, in the view of the Brandt Commission, to increase the 'absorptive capacity' of poorer countries for ODA. Their limited absorptive capacity was attributed mainly to unduly restrictive conditions imposed by the donors: political conditions of bilateral donors; tying of bilateral ODA to capital goods and other supplies from the donor country; the 'conditionality' of the IMF, that is, the imposition of strict policy conditions with a deflationary/monetarist bias for much of the IMF support; the tying of World Bank funding to specific projects with a high standard of project analysis and project preparation expected; the limitation of practically all ODA to covering only external (import) requirements to the exclusion of local cost financing, etc.

To increase absorptive capacity for ODA, therefore, it would be necessary to abolish or modify all these restrictions. Here, again, the Pearson and Brandt Commissions had made corresponding proposals, especially on the untying of ODA, to very little effect. Most economic analysts would support the need for a broader and less restrictive ODA. (The issue is discussed in more detail later on in this chapter.)

Among those liberalizations designed to increase absorptive capacity for ODA, the Brandt Report placed particular emphasis on a greater share for programme lending, that is, flexibly usable funds that are not tied to specific investment projects. The lack of such programme lending was described as 'the most serious gap' in the current system of ODA. Without going into the details of the advantages and disadvantages of project and programme lending, respectively, which are also discussed later in this chapter, we may look a little more closely at the assumption of the Brandt Report that a transition to programme lending would increase absorptive capacity for ODA. Such a closer look will raise some doubts.

The Brandt Report expected programme lending to be 'related to well-conceived, clearly-defined development programmes' and might also be severely limited – perhaps more so than the capacity to draw up specific projects, especially if the projects were researched and developed with the active assistance of donors such as the World Bank. Of course, the poorer countries could also get technical assistance, for example, through the UN Development Programme (UNDP), in drawing up 'well-conceived, clearly-defined development programmes', but such a precondition for making programme lending effective in increasing absorptive capacity should surely have been specified and made the subject of specific recommendations.

The second condition that the fulfilment of the development programmes must be 'monitored', presumably by the donors or on behalf of the donors, or at any rate in ways acceptable to the donors so as to continue to give programme aid, also provides some food for thought. Would such 'monitoring' of programme aid be politically acceptable to the poorer countries? Is it compatible with self-reliance? How could or should it be organized? Could it be done by the poorer countries themselves, and yet be acceptable to donors? Once again, the report did not answer such questions or provide any details of how 'monitoring' was to be implemented.

For aid to be an 'agent of development', it is necessary that it should be given in such a way that it attacks certain key steps towards the achievement of structural change in the world economy, such as the increased processing of primary commodities in the poorer

countries, increased mineral (including fuel) exploration and development in poorer countries, buffer stocks and other measures to
stabilize and improve primary commodity prices, increased food
production and rural development, strengthening of technological
capacities, etc. In all these respects, the Brandt Report made
important suggestions.

A primary objective of aid allocation policy must be the reduction
of the ever-widening international gap. Aid must not be seen as a
temporary self-liquidating, stop-gap measure. Instead, it must be
frankly recognized that aid, as we know it, ought to be the first step
that has been taken towards the evolution of a progressive international taxation structure based on the principle: 'From each according to his ability; to each according to his need.' In other words, the
fact must be faced that aid is a *permanent* feature of the process of
international resource allocation. The extent to which it is distributed in accordance with the true principles of equity and efficiency
reflects the contribution of the well-to-do members of the international community towards eliminating the imbalances and inequalities within the world economic system. Indeed, international
assistance that is given without regard to the relative needs of the
recipients is self-defeating, in that its contribution to the development of the recipient country is highly unlikely to be very fruitful.
The contribution of the rich economies towards the development
requirements of the poor nations will thus have to be geared to the
development needs of the latter and not to the interests, both
political and economic, of the rich countries themselves. This is a
feature of central importance. If aid is to be used as an agent of
development we will have to move towards the creation of an
international institutional aid allocation mechanism that minimizes
the political control of the aid donors and allocates assistance strictly
in accordance with development criteria. The sceptics say that it is
foolish to think that such a system can be evolved: the richer nations
could never be induced to put their national interests in the
background. If this is true, it is inevitable that we are moving rapidly
towards an international catastrophic holocaust in which civilization
as we know it may well be destroyed.

In the 1960s and 1970s there was a renewed interest in the
aid versus trade debate. Economists tried to identify the extent to
which aid and trade can supplement each other, and there was

also some concern with the effects of aid and trade restrictions.[2]

Quantitatively, aid is still very much the junior partner to trade. In recent years official assistance has been equivalent to about one-fifth of foreign exchange earned through merchandise exported by developing countries. A reduction of exports would therefore hit developing countries much more severely than a proportionate reduction of aid.[3] The lesser average quantitative role of aid does not, of course, imply a lesser marginal role. There is no *a priori* generalization to be made concerning the relative worth of an extra dollar of aid versus that of an extra dollar earned through trade. Also, aggregate figures can be highly misleading in this case, for, while some countries obtain almost their entire foreign exchange through exports, others are highly dependent on external assistance. Aid programmes are not spread evenly across the board; rather, national programmes concentrate on a very small number of countries, though different donor countries have different geographical areas of aid interest.

The availability of foreign exchange, or, more broadly, of foreign resources, can of course be increased by export expansion as well as by additional transfers in the form of aid. To this extent at least, trade and aid are exactly equivalent – both provide foreign resources. Once this level of generality is abandoned, however, serious arguments have been brought forward to support a preference of trade over aid or vice versa.[4]

On a theoretical level, while both trade and aid allow a country to avoid the need for the inefficient domestic production of necessary foreign inputs, aid also provides additional real resources. Aid would therefore seem preferable on this account. The argument, of course, implies that the opportunity cost of resources used in the production of additional exports is greater than zero; this will almost always be the case. However, opportunity costs may often be considerably lower than nominal costs if the resources used in export production are specific to it and/or if, for any reason, they would not actually be used unless exports were increased. Even with this qualification in mind, aid will increase *total* resources available to the country, while the contribution of trade will be limited to avoiding the income losses of transforming domestic into foreign resources.

Trade, on the other hand, gets the nod on the basis of another general consideration. Trade has traditionally been considered the engine of growth, in addition to having its classical welfare-increasing role. The competitive stimulus of expanded trade relations, the push to modernization as the only path to industrial survival, the elimination of the grosser inefficiencies of import substitution pushed to the limit – all have traditionally been viewed as powerful points in favour of the trade expansion route.

It has also been argued[5] that, even though the yield of investment of foreign aid may initially be greater than that of investment in additional exports or in the least inefficient import substitutes, the economic policies of developing countries (especially aversion to devaluation, combined with weak monetary and fiscal policies and with overambitious development plans) tend in time to push import substitution (financed through foreign aid) to the point where the yield of investing aid falls below that of investing in new exports, in expansion of traditional exports and in least inefficient import substitutes. While the conclusion is a valid one, the reasoning behind it is rather misleading, mainly because the argument draws a developmental conclusion from what are essentially efficiency considerations. It is perfectly true that freely fluctuating foreign exchange rates, or frequent devaluation of fixed rates, would restore balance-of-payments equilibrium, but naturally they would do so partly by reducing imports. To the extent that substitutability of domestic for imported capital and intermediate goods is low, external balance is then reached at a high cost in terms of growth. In developing countries, and in the context of structural transformation needs, a large proportion of imports do not really carry a minus sign – as in conventional income-determination analysis – because without those imports the welfare loss is dwarfed by the possible impairment of future growth prospects. Equilibrium accompanied by stagnation is hardly a desirable solution. The foreign exchange constraint would indeed be alleviated by this strategy, not so much by increasing foreign exchange availability, but rather by the reduction of foreign exchange needs attendant upon slower growth.

At a practical level of discussion, several points have emerged concerning the relative desirability of trade and aid. At this level it is useful to make a distinction between the points of view of the developed and developing countries.[6] Some of the more relevant among the several possible arguments are the following:

1. Additional trade has the advantage that it does not add to developing countries' indebtedness; neither, however, does aid in the form of grants. Besides, some forms of trade (e.g. bilateral arrangements) do imply a kind of indebtedness, in the form of import obligations.

2. Additional trade has no strings attached to it, whereas aid normally is conditioned in some respect or another. However, some trade expansion may also have to be bought with political or economic concessions. From the developed country's viewpoint, conditionality is, of course, an advantage of aid, for it allows a degree of influence over the recipient country, which can be used for either economic or political objectives, or both. Also, there may be an honest desire to influence the use of external resources for the recipient country's own benefit, in the belief that allocative decisions can be more efficiently made from the outside than if they are left to a presumably inefficient developing country's government. A special subadvantage (in reality of tremendous importance) for donor countries is the possibility offered by aid programmes, directly or indirectly, to promote the donor country's ideology. An increasing degree of pragmatism of donor countries has, however, crept into the scene, and at the same time more and more developing countries are quite aware of the possibility of such ideological interference and have found ways to resist it.

3. From both the developed and developing countries' viewpoints, aid administration procedures are costly and time-consuming. Although improvements are possible, procedures are to some extent dependent on the very same motives that govern the granting and acceptance of aid in the first place. The results that an aid programme is supposed to achieve are so many and so complex that its administration is necessarily costly and complicated; it has to consider the donors' desires for channelling the aid in certain directions and for certain purposes, as well as the recipients' preoccupation with avoiding excessive interference with their economic policies.

4. An important advantage of aid over trade, from the developed countries' viewpoint, is the avoidance of direct losses to domestic producers. While the political capacity of the developed countries to give aid and alter its magnitude is limited

166

by the *general* attitude of their citizens towards international development, their political capacity to grant trade concessions (in the sense of preferential treatment of the developing countries' exports or at least of removal of implicit discrimination against them) is limited, probably more severely, by the political strength of the domestic manufacturers who would stand to lose from such concessions. To paraphrase an old economic maxim: while aid costs everyone a little, trade preferences cost a few people a lot. Thus, while the general resistance to transferring budgetary funds to poor countries is the aggregate result of minimal individual economic losses, the particular resistance to granting trade concessions may be the very powerful one resulting from clear and present danger to the economic interests of a specific group.

5. Aid may be thought to be more or less uncertain than trade. Thus, the cost of aid to the developed countries is more clearly identifiable and measurable than the *total* cost of trade concessions. For the developing countries, depending on the circumstances, future aid inflows may be seen as more or less uncertain than future export earnings. On the other hand, the uncertainty attached to new export markets is undoubtedly an important factor limiting the willingness of the developing countries to seek increased foreign resources through export expansion. Also, satisfactory export performance may have the perverse result of reducing aid transfers to the country. Conversely, if export performance is a positive criterion for the granting of aid, the rewards of successful export expansion would be reinforced by an increase in external assistance.

6. Finally, both the developed and developing countries may have a preference for earned income over handouts; in fact, they certainly do, but whether this general preference in practice plays a significant role is highly questionable, in the face of down-to-earth considerations.

The variety and complexity of arguments for and against trade or aid should make it clear at this point that any generalization is at best very doubtful. It is sufficient to note the considerable differences in the attitudes of different countries, both developed and developing, towards aid programmes and trade concessions. At any rate, the conflict (which is only apparent) disappears if the more general question is formulated, i.e. the question of maximizing the net real flow of external resources to the developing countries and the efficiency of their utilization, while keeping the costs to the developed countries down to a politically acceptable minimum.

Neither 'Trade not Aid', then, nor 'Aid not Trade', but obviously 'Trade and Aid' is the answer; innumerable concrete circumstances will determine the proper weight of each, at different points in time. We fully concur with Pincus's conclusion on this point: 'There can be no clear-cut generalization about the absolute merits of aid and trade. The viewpoint of each party and the conditions under which aid and trade are conducted will determine the preference of each.'[7]

The very distinction between trade and aid loses clarity and operational meaning if the interactions between the two are taken into consideration. (Linking aid to trade should not necessarily have the effect of obscuring the consequences of each, if some care is exercised to isolate conceptually the subsidy element from the commercial element.) In addition to being a useful concept for policy purposes, this link-up is inevitable; one would be hard put to visualize an international subsidy that did not have a significant influence on trade patterns between the parties involved, or a trade concession that did not contain an element of transfer. It would appear then that the proper question is how to link aid to trade in an efficient and politically realistic way. Again, concrete steps would have to be taken in the light of current conditions. A few general possibilities can, however, be briefly mentioned here.

One clear link of aid with trade is embodied in the various supplementary financing schemes (see Chapter 6). Another major step would be for aid to be given in the form of a subsidy on imports from developing countries greater than the tariff on those imports (i.e. a negative tariff). This is a more generalized version of the tariff preferences proposed by UNCTAD. It would be much more effective since the subsidy would give preference over the local producer as well as over the rival exporter from the competing developed countries, but for this very reason it would be politically more difficult. There may be some ground for very qualified optimism in this respect as, not only is there a parallel situation in the negative income tax proposal in the United States, which is enjoying increased acceptability, but also the damage that negative tariffs

168

would imply for the larger producers in the developed countries (in the short run), given the modest possibilities for increased production of manufactured exportables by the developing countries, would be very modest. A negative tariff can be viewed as equivalent to an agreed partial devaluation of the currencies of the aid recipients, without their having to pay the penalities on import prices (i.e. as an internationally agreed dual exchange rate system).

Apart from supplementary financing and from negative tariffs, aid can be used to stimulate trade. Among aid-financed projects, those with an export potential could be specially emphasized, technical assistance on export promotion could be given,[8] and donor countries could prevail upon their private firms establishing branches or subsidiaries in developing countries, or licensing production there, to permit exports of new production more freely. Also, aid could be given more on a regional basis and for multinational projects or groups of projects, thus encouraging the developing countries' trade with one another; this could be associated with the use of regional banks (e.g. the African and Asian Development Banks). Yet, one still feels that a policy by aid donors of using aid to help trade (that is, the recipient's trade, not the donor's!) would be meaningless unless accompanied by a trade policy giving easier access to the donor's markets and reducing the current discrimination against processing and fabrication inherent in (and often concealed by) tariff structures. Only in this sense would aid be truly supplementary to trade.

We must also note that aid is of less value to the advanced LDCs: the oil-rich LDCs clearly have no need for aid; the intermediate LDCs (e.g. Argentina, Turkey and Spain) would benefit more from expanded export opportunities and foreign investment than from aid. But Chad, Niger, Laos and Bangladesh need aid desperately. However, even the poorest of the LDCs see aid as linked to a reform of the whole international trade and monetary system. This is clearly seen in the UN resolutions on the New International Economic Order.

Aid Defined and Measured

Granted the importance of aid in international development, we may next turn to the problem of defining it in a precise way. What is meant by aid? Aid implies the idea of a gift, of assistance rendered, of unilateral transfer, of a *quid sine quo*. This means that not everything that results in a transfer of resources, and that is often loosely referred to as aid, is in fact included in our definition. For instance, private foreign investment, export credits, and public loans at commercial rates of interest do not represent aid, even though they may be useful to the recipient, since there is a *quid pro quo* – in fact, sometimes the *quo* is a lot bigger than the *quid*!

The fact that aid has become a global process in which all the richer countries are involved itself set in motion processes that led as a by-product to a better definition of aid; the global nature of aid gave rise to the evolution of the concept of burden-sharing among donors. Burden-sharing means that the burden of aid should be shouldered by the various donor countries in some sort of agreed ratio related to their respective economic or financial aid-giving capacities. The attempt to work out agreed formulas for burden-sharing immediately raised the question of what should or should not be counted as aid within the meaning of the agreed formula. Discussion on this question among the donors took place mainly in the Development Assistance Committee (DAC) of the OECD. In the Pearson Report this led to a clear distinction between the total flow of financial resources from richer countries to poorer countries on the one hand, and public aid on the other hand, with separate specific targets for the two categories (1 per cent of GNP for total flows and 0.7 per cent of GNP for public aid). Even this distinction, however, was clearly in need of further subdivision, since public aid could be anything from a straight grant or gift to a loan at 5, 6 or 7 per cent interest payable in hard currency. This led to such further refinements as the definition of the grant element in aid and the evolution of agreed standards regarding the terms of loans within the DAC, including rate of interest, duration, grace periods, etc. the target of 0.7 per cent of GNP for public aid, if it were really implemented as well as accepted on paper, would amount to a considerable expansion; the present flow of public aid is little more than half of this target figure, and considerably less than half if the grant element alone is considered. The percentages thus obtained are further reduced if the eastern donor countries of the Council for Mutual Economic Assistance (Comecon) as well as the western donors of the OECD are included.

The idea of an international 'target' for aid to the LDCs in terms of the available resources of the richer or donor countries originally formed part of the proposals for the First UN Development Decade of the 1960s. The idea has historical roots further back into the 1950s. It had a counterpart in a similar 'target' of a 5 per cent growth rate for the national income of the LDCs or recipient countries themselves.

Neither of these targets was very clearly defined; nor was there any specific consistency model developed at the time to link those two targets. Both targets initially had little more than declamatory value; neither represented any binding or legal commitment. The unanimous acceptance of the 1 per cent target by the donor countries did not therefore amount to more than a statement of good intention to follow policies – presumably more direct policies in the case of public aid than in that of private investment – that would move total 'aid' (as defined for inclusion in the 1 per cent target) towards this target figure. From the beginning it became clear that to have any 'potency of life' the 1 per cent target would require some kind of definition of 'aid'. A need arose to distinguish between the different forms of resource transfers to LDCs: grants, loans, private investment, etc.

The second form taken by the distinction between real aid and the flow of financial resources was the elaboration of a series of subtargets, within the 1 per cent overall target, regarding the *terms* on which aid was to be given. Thus, in its 1965 Terms Recommendations, the OECD enjoined upon its member countries that at least 81 per cent of all public aid should be given at less than 3 per cent rate of interest, with a minimum loan duration of twenty-five years for 82 per cent of all loan commitments, and a weighted average grace period of 7 per cent or more (these targets are continually raised). The DAC annually calculates comparative 'terms performance' of its member countries.

In fact, these subtargets have become extremely complicated since various alternative combinations, indicating a certain 'softness' of the flow of public financial resources, are optionally given to the member countries. While these subtargets defining a degree of softness and hence the presence of real aid also have a rather vague status and cannot be considered as more than a declaration of good intentions, they too have had a considerable effect in softening the terms of transfers of public capital to poorer countries. There is

171

perhaps a tendency for this influence to be more marked in countries where there was in the first place an intention to increase real aid and to soften terms and perhaps less effect in bringing sinners into line. In that sense it is legitimate to question the real effectiveness of the subtargets.

The original target, 1 per cent of national income of donor countries, was subsequently raised to 1 per cent of GNP at market prices. This effectively amounted to raising the target by about 20 per cent. The question arises: why not maintain the old basis of national income and raise the 1 per cent target to, say, 1.25 per cent? Presumably the answer is the beautiful simplicity and symbolic value of 1 per cent. Just possibly it could also be argued that the GNP is conceptually preferable to net national income as a basis for determining aid-giving capacity, since the GNP measures resources that either could be channelled back into the replacement, mainte-nance and repair of capital used up in production – thus bringing us back to the lower national income figure – or else could be used for giving aid to poorer countries. This, however, is not a particularly convincing line of reasoning. 'It must be assumed that the replace-ment of their own domestic capital basis is considered by donor countries as a prior charge on total resources and that the relative priorities of foreign aid in relation to other claims are considered only in respect of resources left over after replacing capital (i.e. in relation to national income). To this extent, it may have been more direct and honest to keep the national income basis and raise the target percentage instead. The raising of the target at the second UNCTAD conference (two-thirds of the way through the develop-ment decade) can perhaps be best considered as a recognition of the fact that, under the old accounting system of 1 per cent of national income, many more items had come to be included within the 1 per cent target than had been dreamed of by President Kennedy and his economic advisers (who had been thinking of real *aid*). Of course, if this was the motive, the changeover from 1 per cent of national income to 1 per cent of GNP was a very indirect and rough-and-ready way of dealing with this, as compared with the approach through the grant element or through subtargets relating to softness of aid.

The culmination of this effort to disentangle real aid from the flow of financial resources is the recommendation to establish as a subtarget, within the 1 per cent overall target, 0.7 per cent of GNP in the flow of *public* (government) aid. This can, of course, be justified on two grounds: (1) it is only in connection with public capital transfers that the question of aid in the sense of a *quid* without a *quo* really arises; and (2) it is only *public* aid that it is more directly within the power and control of governments to determine. It is perhaps interesting to speculate that 0.7 per cent of GNP is not too different from 1 per cent of national income; thus we are back to the old Kennedy idea that 1 per cent of national income should be given in real aid. On top of this there is now the implicit additional target of 0.3 per cent of GNP in terms of private investment, export credits, etc. This must remain largely non–operational since the flow of private investment is not really in the power of governments except very indirectly. Further, as we have seen, the Brandt Commission recommended that ODA should constitute 1 per cent of GNP by the end of the century, and a universal system of revenue mobilization should be adopted that should include both OECD, Comecon and the better-off less developed countries.

This is not the place to discuss and develop upon the implications of meeting the 1 per cent target. One salient fact, however, stands out. During the 1960s, the 1 per cent aid target was certainly not achieved, even if the total flow of financial resources from the rich countries to the LDCs as a group is taken into account. However, the target had been reached by a number of DCs in the 1970s and 1980s. The very large increase in financial aid that the Brandt Commission had called for cannot be achieved, however, without a major change in political attitudes and in international economic policy.

A definition of aid that is acceptable to most economists is one that dramatically shows up the inefficiencies of the existing concepts that underlie resource transfers to the LDCs. Resource transfers, the cost of which exceeds their contribution to the development process of the recipient country, cannot be classified as economic assistance. It is necessary that the donors restructure their aid administration set-up in order to provide the financial resources that are most needed and can be most effectively used by the poor country concerned.

Aid Allocation Criteria

At least in a short- and medium-run sense, aid allocation must be determined by the requirements of the recipient countries. In other words, if aid is to have any economic meaning at all it must be related to the development process of the LDCs. The necessity for unilateral resource transfers from the rich to the poor countries has arisen because of the widening gap that separates these two groups of economies. The ultimate aim of economic assistance must be to bridge this gap.

As a result of the impact of aid upon development and the interest shown by economists in devising economic criteria for aid allocation, there is now available a theoretical framework based on the famous 'two-gap models'. This arises from the dual nature of the aid resources transferred to the LDCs:

1. Aid adds to the total resources, or savings, of the LDC available for investment (at any rate it does so if it is assumed that aid resources go into investment, rather than consumption, in a 1 : 1 relationship).
2. In addition to adding to total resources and investment, aid specifically adds to the foreign exchange resources.

The models have been extensively used by development economists in order to project the aggregate requirements of both domestic saving and foreign capital of the LDCs. A number of LDCs have explicitly based their economic plans on projections that have been derived from the two-gap models.

A two-gap model in its simplest formulation assumes that there are two constraints on development: the availability of domestic saving and the availability of foreign capital. It is assumed that labour is in abundant supply and is (disguisedly?) unemployed, and that expansion in the capital input will automatically call forth the required labour. This assumption allows the theorists to characterize the economy they are studying by a Leonteiff production function. McKinnon has shown that *the same amount of foreign assistance will be more effective in a country that is faced with a balance-of-payments constraint rather than a savings constraint.*[9] It was thus usually held that aid should be allocated to those countries that demonstrated a capability to generate domestic (public or private) savings but were finding it increasingly difficult to meet their import needs.

Strictly speaking, there is no reason why the analysis should remain limited to two gaps. It could be argued that some forms of aid, especially technical assistance, remove barriers other than foreign exchange or savings (e.g. availability of local skills). This could further enhance the contribution of aid to GNP growth beyond that which the simple neo-classical analysis would suggest.

The gap models have been subjected to extensive criticisms. It is pointed out that the gaps can be identified only in an *ex ante* sense; *ex post* they have no significance. The size of the dominant gap depends crucially on the growth rate. A country may have a savings constraint at a higher growth rate but a balance-of-payments constraint at a lower growth rate, or vice versa. If savings or export earnings do not increase at the rate required by the target growth rate, the growth rate of income will itself fall short of the target and no resource gap will appear.

Moreover, it is difficult – some would argue impossible – to estimate with a reasonable degree of accuracy the existence of the dominant gap from historical data that reflect definitional identities, not behaviouristic patterns. The gap models have, however, served some very useful purposes. They have drawn attention to the fundamental problem of estimating the elasticity of factor substitution in the different production activities undertaken in the LDCs. This elasticity is neither zero nor unity. It varies from activity to activity, and the specific needs of the LCDs can be taken into account only within the context of an analytical framework that allows the planners to evaluate the changes that are taking place in the elasticity of factor substitution in the different economic activities as a result of development. The needs change as the input coefficients change in the inter-industrial production matrix.[10]

The second UNCTAD conference tried to estimate the size of the resource gaps of a number of LDCs in 1968. It came to the conclusion that most of the LDCs either had a dominant trade gap or would generate one if the growth rate were raised to 6 per cent per annum. It was thus suggested that, if the criteria for foreign aid allocation were those implied by the gap analysis, there was considerable scope for expansion in the flows of resource transfer from the developed countries to the developing countries.

The gap analysis suggests one set of economic criteria that should be applied when aid is being apportioned among recipient nations. Other economic criteria have also been recommended, and some of the more important among them are:

- to eliminate poverty in the poorest countries; this is identified as the 'welfare' objective of foreign aid;
- to discriminate in favour of countries that have effective aid administration set-ups;
- to discriminate in favour of countries where the *future* marginal efficiency of aid is highest.

These objectives are rarely consistently pursued in the aid programmes of any of the major aid donors. Partly, as a number of economists have pointed out, this is owing to the multiplicity of the economic objectives that the donors of foreign aid have in mind. A given programme of foreign aid has to balance the 'development' objective against the 'welfare' objective. In a short-run sense it is certainly true that these objectives may be irreconcilable. The aid package that is finally decided upon reflects the compromise that has emerged when the aid administrators have sought to reconcile the different objectives.

If this is so, the operationally important question is: what weight have the donors applied to the various objectives in determining the mix of a given aid programme? An inability to quantify, if only in an approximate sense, the allocations that are made in response to specific criteria has reduced the usefulness of this type of approach. Moreover, analysis of this type is incapable of taking into cognizance the institutional and historical factors influencing aid allocation.

Furthermore, the criteria enumerated above are not 'value-free'. They require international comparisons based on how the donors view the policies being pursued by the recipients. Hence it may be questioned whether *any* objective criteria for aid allocation can ever be evolved. What is 'development' from the point of view of the recipients may not be 'development' from the point of view of the donors. Indeed, if, as the radicals among us maintain, aid is being given by the donors in order to attain their own economic interests and relentlessly to exploit the poor countries, it would be futile to expect to be able to explain aid allocation patterns by their effect on the development of the LDCs. However, such a view ignores the fundamental complementarity of the interests of the different components of the international economy. It is precisely because the economic interests of all the countries are, at least in a long-run sense, coincidental that we have advocated a transfer of resources from the rich to the poor countries and hence are justified in expecting the evolution of an aid rationale, as it were, that specifically takes into account the development needs of the LDCs. This means that there need be no ambiguity in the allocation criteria that *should* be used for aid distribution. The criteria should provide an index that measures the contribution of the rich countries towards the effective reduction of the widening gap between the rich and poor countries. The value judgements implied by aid allocation based on criteria of this sort reflect merely an extension of the concept of the welfare state from the national to the international level.

Scope of Aid

We have seen that the flow of resources to LDCs is at the same time wider and less wide than true aid. It is wider than aid because it includes a number of transactions that are strictly commercial and in which there is no presumption that there is a unilateral advantage to the recipient of the flows. These include private investment abroad, which by definition cannot be aid because it is strictly commercial.[11] They also include such things as export credits, or loans made by governments or international organizations (e.g. the World Bank), at more or less commercial rates of interest (e.g. 8 per cent per annum) without grace periods and repayable as a firm commitment in hard currency. Such a loan would not be called aid, the 'grant element' in the loan being zero or close to zero.

In recognition of this fact, the UN target has been subdivided to specify that at least 70 per cent of this total flow of resources must be aid, i.e. 0.7 per cent of GNP of the donor countries. Thus it would be more justified to speak of a '0.7 per cent aid target'. But even this concept of aid is still much too broad. Even if private and other obviously commercially oriented transactions are ruled out, the remaining transactions, which are largely flows from non-commercial organizations (e.g. governments, the Rockefeller Foundation, Oxfam, personal charities, etc.), still include a great variety of forms of aid. The troubling point is that the true aid element in these various transactions is very different. At one extreme may be placed the government loan at 8 per cent repayable in hard currency, which, as already mentioned, has a zero or negligible 'grant element'. At the other extreme may be placed the unconditional gift by a rich government or Oxfam to the government or people of an LDC without any obligation or strings attached; in this transaction the true aid element, or 'grant element', is close to 100 per cent.

Between these two extremes is a continuum of many forms of aid, too numerous to mention. There is the 'soft loan', e.g. a loan at 2½ per cent interest, repayable over a long period of thirty years, with an initial grace period[12] of seven years, possibly with a provision that repayment can be postponed if the recipient country is in difficulty, etc. Another type of intermediate transaction, neither fully commercial nor wholly aid, is a grant or gift that, however, can be used by the recipient only for the import of specified capital goods from the donor country. If the recipient country could otherwise have obtained these goods more cheaply or better elsewhere, or possibly even domestically, obviously part of the value of this gift in effect represents a subsidy to the capital goods producers of the donor country and that part should not be considered as aid to the recipient. In other words, if 'trade' and other commercial transactions can be defined as a *quid pro quo*, while 'aid' is defined as a *quid sine quo*, the difficulty is that in real life many transactions are somewhere in between: a *quid pro 'half a quo'*.

Economists and aid statisticians have not been at a loss in dealing with this particular difficulty. The answer has been to disaggregate these in-between transactions into two separate transactions: the part of the transaction that can be called 'fully commercial', and the part representing the 'grant element', which can be called 'fully aid'. For instance, in the case of the soft loan mentioned above, the present discounted value of the repayment obligation involved in this transaction can be calculated. If the total soft loan was £1 million while the present discounted value of the repayment obligation involved was £400,000, we would say that the 'grant element' in this transaction was 40 per cent; then £400,000 out of this £1 million would be counted as aid while the rest would be counted as a commercial flow.

Ingenious as this device of disaggregation and calculation of the grant element is, it still leaves a number of loopholes for measurement and definition. An obvious one is the selection of the poorer discount rate for the purpose of calculating the present discounted value. This can make a considerable difference in the case of long-term transactions. Another deficiency is the failure of the calculation of the grant element to take into account other restrictions attached to the use of the loan or grant. A loan or grant at the free disposal of the recipient to cover budget deficits or balance-of-payments deficits, or to support the general development plan of the country, is obviously much more valuable to the recipient than a similar loan or grant hedged around with very restrictive conditions, or perhaps limited to a project that would not be within the recipient's priority scheme without the loan or grant. It can be seen that the device of the grant element is more useful in measuring the cost of aid to the donor – and it was essentially developed for this purpose, especially for comparing the relative aid burden carried by different donors – than in measuring the value of aid to the recipient. For this purpose, in fact, an entirely different set of concepts and measurements would have to be developed.

There is another reason why even the non-commercial flow of resources – the 0.7 per cent UN aid target – is still too wide a definition of what should be called aid. A rich country will allocate resources to a poor country for a great variety of reasons. The purely commercial motive and purely humanitarian aid motive are only two possible motives among a variety of others. An obvious example is the military motive. You make grants or supply equipment free of charge or on soft terms to a military ally or to a country that you expect to become either a military ally or an enemy of your enemy – it is non-commercial, but is it aid? The UN definition would exclude military aid, but in practice this is not easily disentangled from development aid. The Americans have the concept of 'military support aid'; this means that you strengthen an ally, not only by direct military aid, but also by economic aid that enables him to carry the recurrent cost of the economic burden of a larger military establishment than would otherwise be the case. Is this military aid or economic aid?

Then there is aid that is perhaps not strictly military but that is closely linked with diplomatic support. A rich country may give aid to a poor country in order to buy its vote at a crucial UN discussion, to keep a tottering government in power, to 'cement the Commonwealth ties' (in the case of the United Kingdom), to promote the teaching of the French language in Africa (in the case of France), to counteract Chinese or American influence (in the case of the USSR), or to keep Cuba isolated within the Latin America (in the case of the United States). What of all this is true aid and what is not? In general, in these cases, the underlying motive of the donor – honourable or dishonourable according to one's judgement – should not enter into the measurement. As long as the flow is non-commercial and meant to be devoted to development, it should be included as aid whatever the motive. Among the above examples, aid to promote the teaching of the French language in Francophone Africa would be only doubtfully called aid since the intended use is not clearly related to development (though this is arguable and shows that our definition of aid may call up the equally difficult problem of defining development). Military aid would be more clearly excluded because it is not considered as part of a 'development', but even this is far from clear. The establishment of an aircraft industry in a LDC can be both a military proposition and a part of the industrialization of the country; swords can be beaten into ploughshares, and tractors and tanks have obvious similarities.

Wider Aid Concepts

It is time now to look at the reverse side of the coin. We have previously said that true aid can be larger than is indicated by the flow of financial resources, even when this is limited to the unilateral flow and to the case of aid destined to development purposes only. The flow of financial resources and the part of it that is normally called aid is only a part – and a comparatively small part at that – of the total relations between rich and poor countries.

It follows that effective and true aid can be given by a rich country to a poor country by the rich country's opening its markets wider to exports from the LDC or by its offering imports to the LDC at a lower price. Vice versa, aid can be nullified by the rich countries' operating restrictive policies to limit exports from the LDCs, also by their worsening the terms of trade of the LDCs, lowering the prices obtained for their exports and/or raising the prices that they have to pay for their imports. Thus the reader of this book should realize that the matter discussed in this chapter under the heading of 'aid' should be seen in close relation to the matters previously discussed under the heading of 'trade'. Most LDCs, if given the choice, would prefer, not an expansion of aid, but rather trade concessions – e.g. the conclusion of international commodity agreements raising and stabilizing the prices of major export commodities, or revisions of the tariff structure of the richer countries to enable them to export more, say, labour-intensive manufactures.

In addition to export proceeds, there are such non-aid relationships between the rich and poor countries as tourism, shipping, insurance, transference of technology and others. All these do not come under the heading of 'flows of financial resources', yet concessions in these fields could be as valuable – or even more valuable – to the LDCs as increased aid. It will be clear that the questions of aid performance of different donor countries, as published annually by the DAC of the OECD,[13] are a very doubtful exercise if taken by themselves. The behaviour of a rich country in relation to the LDCs must be seen in the round; to concentrate only on the small segment of it entitled 'flow of financial resources' can give a very misleading picture.

The extreme case of a trade concession is where a rich country sends its exports to the poor country free of charge. In this extreme case, the commercial element is so clearly non-existent and the aid element is so dominant that this type of 'trade' is always included in aid, as the special form of commodity aid. The best-known type of commodity aid is food aid, such as has been given by the United States under the Food for Peace programme – more technically known as Public Law 480. On occasion, however, commodity aid has also consisted of other essential supplies. There is also a multilateral commodity aid programme: the UN World Food Programme, jointly administered by the United Nations and the FAO in Rome. The 1974 Rome Food Conference envisaged substantial expansion of this form of aid.

Commodity aid illustrates some of the difficulties of measuring and defining aid, particularly for the purpose of comparing the aid 'burden' carried by different donor countries. This problem is far from being theoretical, since a considerable share of the aid programme of the largest aid donor, the United States, consists of precisely such commodity aid. How is such aid to be measured and valued? The United States, not unnaturally, measures the value of the aid at the artificially high domestic support price of the wheat, maize, rice, etc. delivered under this programme, since this is the cost of buying up the food to the government agency[14] charged with securing this food for the US aid programme.

However, it could well be argued that this food should be valued at the world market price, which may be considerably lower. Or it could be argued that the food should be valued at what the world market price would be if this US surplus food were not artificially removed from the commercial market by being supplied under US aid programmes but were instead added to commercial supplies; that price would, of course, be hypothetical, but it could be a great deal lower again than the actual world market price. Going even further, it could be argued that the food is surplus to the requirements of the US economy – i.e. is the result of policies designed to help American farmers, not to aid the LDCs – and therefore that its opportunity cost to the US is zero or close to zero. Any of these positions would be defensible and appropriate for measuring the value of the food aid for different purposes.

It is clear that the apparent simplicity of valuing such aid immediately resolves into a great many complexities when the problem is more closely scrutinized. Nor is this the end of the complications. Quite often the food aid, while essentially a grant, is hedged around with certain conditions. For instance, the recipient country may be committed, out of sales proceeds of the food delivered as food aid, to provide a certain proportion of local currency for the expenses of the US embassy or for scholarships under US programmes, etc. Should this repayment be deducted from the grant element? And if so, how should it be valued? Again, many different answers are possible depending on the purpose of the measurement.[15]

The problems of defining and measuring aid, which have been briefly illustrated above for the case of food aid, all have their equivalent for many other forms of aid. Even if the loan or grant is defined in terms of money, its real value to the recipient may be less than the normal cost to the donor, for example if the use of the money is tied to specific commodities, projects, sources of supply, etc. The important part of aid that appears as 'technical assistance', as distinct from 'financial aid', is by its very nature similar to commodity aid; the donor country provides an adviser, and the value of the aid is measured by the salary that the donor country pays to the adviser. Yet if the recipient country had been given a free grant of money to recruit its own consultants, it might have been able to obtain the necessary advice more cheaply from a different country or through a consulting service.

On other occasions there may be undervaluation of the technical assistance rather than overvaluation. For instance, if the United Kingdom makes a technical assistance grant in the form of a fellowship to enable a Kenyan to undertake graduate studies of economics or chemistry in a UK university, the value of the fellowship is measured – apart from living expenses – by fees that have to be paid to the university; however, these fees may be very much less than the true cost of the facilities to the UK taxpayer, university fees being heavily subsidized. Perhaps enough has been said to indicate that the question of measuring and valuing aid is not without its pitfalls, and that not too much should be read into the comparative data on the total flow of financial aid to the developing countries.

Bilateral versus Multilateral Aid

The distinction between bilateral and multilateral aid may at first seem clear, but like many other 'clear' distinctions it becomes blurred on subsequent analysis. The 'pure' case of bilateral aid is where one single donor, normally a donor government, deals directly with one single recipient, also normally a government. The 'pure' case of multilateral aid is represented by a global or world agency, normally part of the UN system, dealing directly with a recipient government or group of governments. However, there are many intermediate forms of aid between these extreme forms of bilateralism and multilateralism.

To begin with, much of such-called bilateral aid is given in a multilateral framework. For instance, aid to India and many other important countries is channelled through an aid 'consortium'. In this aid consortium, all the donors or major donors are represented and discuss the respective amounts of aid that they plan to extend to India in the coming year, the type of projects that each of them proposes to support, the amounts to be financed by hard loans, soft loans, grants, etc., and other aspects of their respective aid programmes. The consortium is chaired by the World Bank, which has previously prepared an independent report on the aid requirements of India, Indian development policies, priority projects to be supported, etc. The Indian government is, of course, also represented and submits its own report and estimates of aid requirements. The discussion in the aid consortium is then followed by a pledging conference, at which the various donors represented commit themselves to extend aid in the light of what the other donors in their turn are willing to pledge.

The aid recipients, as well as the aid donors, have shown an increasing preference for placing bilateral aid in such a multilateral framework. The advantages to both sides are fairly obvious, though some recipients may feel that this is a method where the donors have an opportunity of ganging up against them. Such bilateral aid comes within the statistical definition of 'bilateral', rather than under 'multilateral', but this is clearly a matter of arbitrary definition.

In other cases, in place of the aid consortium there is the 'consultative group'. This is a somewhat weaker form of multilateral framework, lacking the pledging element or element of commitment of the aid consortium but otherwise proceeding in a very similar way. Recently the major donors, with their growing unwillingness to commit themselves, have accordingly developed a preference for consultative groups rather than consortia.

Closer to the multilateral end of the continuum there is aid extended, not by global institutions (e.g. the World Bank or UN Development Programme), but by such institutions as the regional development banks (e.g. the Inter-American Development Bank, the Asian Development Bank, the African Development Bank and the Arab Development Bank) or subregional development banks (e.g. the East African Development Bank). Other institutions of a non-global nature extending multilateral aid include the European Development Fund in Brussels, which is the organ of the EEC. This kind of aid is usually included as multilateral even though its sources are less than world-wide.

The term 'bilateral' is applied more to the source of the aid than to the recipient; e.g. UK or US aid directed to the East African Community in Arusha, rather than to Kenya, Tanzania or Uganda separately, is still classified as bilateral, even though there is a multilateral recipient.

The percentage of total aid flowing through the multilateral channel is gradually increasing. For a number of reasons, by no means all involving glowing enthusiasm for international coopera-tion, donors as well as recipients are coming to prefer the multilateral channel. Smaller countries particularly prefer the multilateral chan-nel because it enables them to avoid the heavy administrative overhead expenses of building up their own aid organizations, which would be a very heavy charge on a small aid programme.

One difference between multilateral aid and bilateral aid arises in the criteria for allocating aid among different recipients. In the case of bilateral aid, allocation is obviously heavily influenced by political considerations, historical links and commitments, diplomatic links, etc. Thus the bulk of UK aid goes to the Commonwealth and few remaining colonies, the bulk of French aid to Francophone African countries, the bulk of US aid to Latin American or strategically important countries along the periphery of the USSR and China, and the bulk of USSR aid to allies such as Syria, Iraq, Cuba and India. By contrast, the global multilateral aid sources (e.g. the World Bank and UNDP) tend to spread their aid more or less evenly – widely but thinly – over all their member countries. There are strong pressures to do so. In the case of the UN Development Programme, the wide and even distribution has been inevitable and is now in fact enshrined in 'indicative planning figures' for each country. In the case of the World Bank, such distribution is concealed by the apparent insistence on 'sound projects'.

In both the bilateral and multilateral programmes, the large countries tend to be discriminated against in the sense that their per capita aid tends to be lower than that of the smaller countries. In the early days of the International Development Association (IDA, the soft-financing agency of the World Bank in Washington) an attempt was made to rectify this by concentrating resources on such large countries as India and Pakistan that were obviously discriminated against, but this move ran into great political difficulties and had to be abandoned. Countries that have no special reason to concentrate aid for political reasons (e.g. Sweden and Canada) have an additional reason here for preferring the multilateral channel.

Hard versus Soft Aid

The question of allocating aid among different countries, which has just been emphasized in relation to multilateral versus bilateral aid, leads to another important distinction. Should aid be allocated according to some criterion of need or according to some criterion of capacity to use the aid effectively?[16] In some ways, of course, the answer must be 'both'. Some criterion of need must be involved, since we limit aid to the poor countries presumably because the rich countries – in the West and Middle East – do not need aid. Similarly, we do not want to see aid wasted; we want to see it effectively used for the purpose for which it is given, even if these purposes are purely humanitarian. For example, if we give aid to help the victims of earthquakes or civil war, we do not want to see the aid money go into the pockets of civil servants or speculators.

The answer 'both' has still another meaning. The best type of aid is aid that benefits the needy and at the same time makes them more capable and more effective in improving their own situation by their own efforts; in this way the criterion of need and effective use are ideally combined. Perhaps the best way of doing this is to channel aid into employment creation, to utilize the unemployed and underemployed manpower of the recipient country for productive investment (e.g. irrigation or rural roads) that creates a permanent basis for continuing development and additional employment. Unfortunately, the present rules of the aid game are very ill designed to have this ideal effect; employment involves largely local expenditures, whereas aid is mainly geared to providing the import components of large-scale capital-intensive projects.

But when all this is said there does remain a real dilemma: whether to place aid where it is most needed, or whether to place it where it will lead to the most immediate increases in output. Even if, to the economists, this dilemma is more apparent than real (since the increase in output constitutes real development only if it benefits the

186

lowest income groups of the LDCs), to the aid officials, whether multilateral or bilateral, the dilemma is real enough.[17]

And now for the third meaning of the answer 'both'. Both objectives, i.e. need and effective use, are legitimate aid criteria, but they require different forms of aid. Normally aid allocated on the criterion of need should be soft aid, without payment obligations. This is clear in the case of financing rural public works for the purpose of employment creation and in financing local expenditures generally. In the case of aid given on the criterion of effective use, hard terms can be justified in so far as the repayment can take place out of the increases in production, which will still leave the recipient better off if the terms of repayment are not exorbitant. There is, however, a proviso in the latter case, which is that repayment of aid involves a double sacrifice: (1) the real resources must be found and kept away from home investment, and (2) the foreign exchange needed for repayment must be found and kept away from imports or must be found by additional exports. Thus, aid on hard terms is only justified if the recipient is enabled by the aid both to produce the additional real resources needed and also to produce the additional foreign exchange resources needed, by expanding exports or replacing imports. There is thus a place for both hard and soft aid. It cannot be said that the present division of aid between these two forms corresponds very closely to a rational distinction of the kind just made, though things seem to be gradually moving in this direction.

It was pointed out above (pp. 177–80) that aid should be defined as *quid sine quo*. This means that in the case of hard aid only the grant element should be counted as aid. But, of course, it does not mean that there is no place for hard aid in the aid picture. It is only when hard aid is mistakenly fully counted as aid and displaces soft aid that it becomes hypocritical to rely on it. Provided the true aid, or the grant element in aid, reaches agreed and acceptable targets and volumes, there is no reason not to have a rational policy whereby part of this grant element is embodied in soft aid and part of it in hard aid on repayable terms. In the past, however, hard aid was given without much consideration for the repayment burden and repayment capacity of the recipient. Partly as a result of this, the debt burden of developing countries has increased at an alarming rate and constitutes one of the major unsolved problems in relations between the rich and poor countries.

187

Project Aid and Programme Aid

Aid either may be tied to the execution of a specific development project (e.g. building a dam, setting up a cement factory or building a hospital) or may be given without such specific project tying (e.g. in the form of budgetary support, a credit line of free foreign exchange or supply of surplus food at the disposal of the government). The tying of aid to projects is only one possible form of tying; aid can also be tied to goods from the donor country, or to foreign exchange requirements (imports) as distinct from local currency expenditures. Normally, 'tied aid' or 'untied aid' refers to the tying of aid money to the purchase of goods from the donor country, and it is in this sense that the term will be used in the next section. There is no necessary relationship between the tying of aid to projects and the tying of aid to goods from the donor country. The World Bank, for example, seems firmly wedded to the principle of project aid to what many critics believe an excessive degree; on the other hand, the Bank, as an international organization, does not and obviously cannot tie its aid to buying goods from any particular donor country. By contrast, the United Kingdom may well give, say, India a loan not tied to any specific project but in the nature of a general line of credit for spare parts or raw materials, or it may give the loan even without restriction and yet tie the expenditure of this credit line to British goods only. It is therefore somewhat confusing to speak of tied and untied aid generally without specifying the nature of the tying referred to.

Is it justified to tie aid to specific projects? There are many arguments *for* answering this question positively or negatively. The main arguments for project aid include:

1. The donor country or agency has a better judgement of what is required than the recipient government would have if the expenditure of the money were left to its own judgement.
2. By tying aid to projects the donor makes certain that the recipient is forced to develop a proper project, properly prepared, studied, programmed and executed, while in the absence of such a tie the aid, for lack of carefully prepared projects, might not be spent for developmental purposes or would be wasted on hastily prepared projects.

3. By tying the aid to the project and doling the aid out as the project materializes and proceeds, the donor maintains some kind of leverage and control over the money, which would be absent in the case of more general support.
4. Project aid makes it natural and easy for the donor to combine financial aid with the proper technical assistance in regard to a particular project, e.g. skilled consultants for feasibility studies, pilot schemes, training of staff for running the project and writing of proper specifications for the supplies needed.
5. There is the demonstration effect of good project preparation; if the recipient country is forced to develop effective projects in order to attract aid it will learn by doing the proper organization for project appraisal, and project preparation is more likely to develop.

This is not an exhaustive list[18] and there are a number of arguments *against* tying aid to projects:

1. If the donor uses aid as a leverage to force his own idea of priorities upon the developing country, this violates national sovereignty.
2. It may also be ineffective because a country will not be wholehearted in supporting projects that do not reflect its own priorities.
3. It is somewhat arrogant of aid donors to believe that they know the priorities of development better than the government of the recipient country that is directly faced with the problems.
4. There is an element of illusion in project aid. If the recipient LDC is given money for project A, which is in any case part of its own priorities, its own money will be released to carry out another project much lower down the priority list for which the money otherwise would not be available. Thus, while aid donors and recipients sit together to discuss the details of project A – the top priority project into which aid is supposed to go – in actual economic fact the aid serves to finance a quite different project, project X, which is not discussed or analysed and may not even be known to the aid donor or identified by either side. Meanwhile, both the taxpayers of the donor country and the citizens of the LDC are cheated into believing that the aid goes

into the priority dam or road, with ambassadors and prime ministers solemnly snipping ribbons, making speeches and inspecting labels: 'This factory/dam/road/etc. comes to you through the aid of the friendly people of the United States/the USSR/the United Kingdom/China/Sweden/etc.

This last point is known as the principle of 'fungibility' or 'switching'. By now, both aid donors and aid recipients generally are well aware of this principle. As a result, aid donors do not normally extend project aid without satisfying themselves that the total programme of the recipient country (including project X, the marginal project) is such that they can aid it with good conscience. The aid recipients, on their part, are often quite happy to accept project tying precisely because they know full well that in actual fact it may release money for quite different projects and enable them to enlarge their total development programme. For political reasons, or for some of the other reasons mentioned above, both sides may be quite happy to maintain the fiction involved in project aid.

The situation in fact may be further complicated. For example, if the aid finances only a small part of the aided project (e.g. the cost of imported machinery) whereas the recipient LDC is required from its own resources to find the major part of the cost, switching or fungibility operates in reverse. Instead of setting resources free to carry out project X, resources have to be withdrawn from project X to cover the recipient's share in the cost of project A; in the aided LDC the development pattern is in fact being distorted in the direction of the priorities of the donor country. This may be a good or bad thing, depending on where the superior wisdom resides. If an LDC really believes firmly in its own priorities, it should not accept aid for a project outside its priority scheme if that aid ties down its own resources; i.e. it should not accept aid unless that aid covers the local and recurrent expenses of the project as well as the direct cost of imports.

An economist's judgement at the present time would be that there is too much project aid and not enough programme aid. It is noteworthy that the great success story of international aid, the US Marshall Plan, was not tied to specific projects. If it is objected that the European beneficiaries of the Marshall Plan could be more trusted than the present LDCs to put their money into good projects, this is a judgement that it would be very arrogant to take for granted today. It ought to be assumed that by now the governments of many LDCs have learned enough about the development business to justify something more like the Marshall Plan treatment.

The whole concept of development as consisting of specific 'projects' of new investment was the product of a very limited type of thinking, in which development was identified with growth of production, and growth of production in turn was identified with new net investment combined with a certain capital/output ratio.[19] Experience has shown this view to be wrong, yet the prevailing aid practice of project aid has failed to adjust itself to evolving experience and insight. However, life has developed its own adjustments. For instance, the aid consortia already mentioned provide not only bilateral aid in a multilateral framework but also 'project aid in a programme framework'. Even though the aid is given on a project basis, the aid consortium discusses the total programme of the countries to which project aid is extended. One cannot help feeling that there is a great deal of institutional inertia involved in the adherence to project aid, even more so in the case of the World Bank than for the bilateral aid programmes. The aid relationship would be healthier if more aid took the form of money placed at the disposal of the LDCs in general support of reasonable and agreed development plans. The developing countries' attempt to link aid with the creation of international liquidity may be seen, among other things, as an attempt to move away from project aid.

Other evolving compromises between project aid and programme aid are (1) the broadening of the concept of a project to include groups of related projects, in the end amounting to something close to a sectoral programme, and (2) the channelling of aid through intermediaries in the LDCs (e.g. national development banks) so that the aid can be redistributed over a multitude of smaller projects. This last arrangement helps to deal with what is perhaps the worst aspect of project aid, which is that it puts a premium on the single large project and, within that category, on projects that require a maximum of imported capital equipment. Both of these results of project aid are directly contrary to the real needs of developing countries, which require employment creation, labour-intensive technologies, a maximum of local procurement, and maximum dispersion and decentralization of economic activities. In partial recognition of this, rules concerning local procurement in aided projects have been generally relaxed over the last few years. Many aid donors will now finance local procurement provided that local costs and quality are not grossly out of line with world market prices (for untied aid) or with prices prevailing in the donor country (for tied aid).

Tied Aid

On our previous definition, tied aid is aid where the recipient, as a condition of the aid, is obliged to use the aid money to buy goods from the donor country only.

The main practical problems concerning this definition centre on the word 'only'. We have just seen that, increasingly, aid provides for the possibility of local procurement, often even with a preference price range for the local products; in other words, the aid is available either for the local products or for buying from the donor country. In still other cases, enlightened donors may make exceptions for other developing countries that they also want to aid. For example, the United States may give aid to Thailand for an irrigation project but permit the Thai government to order the water pumps from India where these pumps are made more cheaply or more suitably than in the United States. The reason for this exception from tying is that the United States also wants to help India. The minor question of definition arising is whether the aid to Thailand should still come under the category of tied aid, in view of the exception made for India (and possibly other developing countries). The major question is whether this should be counted entirely as aid to Thailand or whether part of it should be counted as aid to India, which it really represents. As is the case with aid definitions throughout, numerous practical difficulties and borderline cases exist.

Tied aid is less valuable to the recipient than untied aid. With untied aid, as with free foreign exchange, the recipient can buy the most suitable product in the cheapest market, taking into account other relevant circumstances (e.g. suitability of the product, availability of installation, repair and maintenance services). In the limiting case where the products of the donor country in many cases are the cheapest and most suitable for the aided project or for the development needs of the recipient country, the tying of aid is both unnecessary and ineffective; on the other hand, it does not represent a burden on the recipient. Normally, however, there is a burden. How heavy this burden is will depend, among other factors, on the degree of project tying, on the range of goods that the donor country can offer and their prices relative to other sources of supply, and on the advantage that the firms of the donor country are willing and able to take of the fact that the tying of aid has placed them in a monopoly position as far as tendering for the aided projects is concerned.

Empirical data are scanty, but in view of the wide spread of project tying and other realistic circumstances the evidence seems to suggest that tied aid may be worth about 20 per cent[20] or so less to the recipient than untied aid.

To the economist, this loss of 20 per cent is sad and unnecessary. If the donor countries are put together, their total gain from tying aid to their own products must be precisely zero. If one donor country gains from tying, in the sense that its own firms obtain a larger share of the total imports of aided LDCs than would otherwise be the case, by definition other donor countries must lose. The only exception is if the LDCs use their untied aid to order goods either locally or from other LDCs that are not aid donors – but this exception is in any case desirable and already allowed for, to some extent at least, even in tied aid programmes. Broadly, it may be assumed that the advantages to individual aid donors from tying their aid are more or less cancelled out through the actions of other aid donors' tying *their* aid. Each aid donor hopes to gain by tying, but this turns out to be an illusion because *all* aid donors tie their aid. Meanwhile, though no aid donor gains, all aid recipients lose because the value of aid is to them depreciated by perhaps as much as 20 per cent. Looked at in this way, the wonder is why the donors could not have reached general agreement to untie all their aid.

In real life, however, the situation is somewhat more complicated. In the first place, some aid donors may in fact gain from tying their aid. This is the case either if the donor country's normal share in the imports of the LDCs is less than its share in total aid, or if the donor country gives more aid relatively than other donors, or if the aided projects relate to commodities in which the donor country is less than averagely competitive with other donors. Once such donors actually benefit by tying their aid, it becomes rational for other donors – who really would benefit from a general untying of aid – to tie *their* aid in turn as a defensive measure.

Secondly, it is possible, and in fact likely, that aid would be less acceptable to the producers, taxpayers, parliaments and other interest groups in donor countries if it were not visibly tied to their products. Tying creates a domestic lobby in favour of aid, including trade unions and workers who are interested in reducing unemployment in specific industries or specific parts of the country. While this argument in favour of tied aid may be partly a matter of lack of economic education and sophistication, it is none the less real. This means that, though the value of each dollar of tied aid may be 20 per cent less than that of each dollar of untied aid, the total *volume* of tied aid may be so much larger than it would be with entirely untied aid that in the end the aid recipients are better off with tied aid than with untied aid. In other words, some – possibly the bulk – of tied aid is additional aid, not an inferior substitute for untied aid.

All this helps to explain why in practice it is not so easy to reach an agreement on untying aid. Even so, there is tremendous scope for agreement among the donor countries to go a long way further towards the untying of aid, to nobody's loss and to the gain of the LDCs. Fortunately the donor countries realize this, and considerable efforts and some progress are being made within the framework of the DAC of the OECD.

It has already been mentioned that multilateral aid is usually untied aid. Even this is not entirely accurate. For instance, in the case of multilateral technical assistance under the UN Development Programme, a number of contributors make their contribution in tied currency that can only be used for buying equipment, hiring experts or using training facilities of the donor country. Similarly, in replenishing the resources of the IDA, the United States, being in balance-of-payments trouble, has often made attempts to tie its contribution to the degree to which the IDA drew upon US resources of supply. It is a pity that even the multilateral programmes cannot be wholly untied.

The aid consortia and other forms of aid coordination can do a great deal to reduce the burden of aid tying on the recipients. For instance, by allocating to each donor those types of projects in which the donor is best equipped, in terms of price and suitability, to provide the relevant equipment and other inputs, the effective burden of tying is reduced. Even this method, however, cannot prevent the firms of each donor country from quoting higher prices for their products when tendering for aided projects, knowing that firms in other countries are not allowed to compete.

Notes

1 Report of the Independent Commission on International Development Issued under the Chairmanship of Willy Brandt, *North–South: A Program for Survival* (London and Sydney: Pan, 1980).
2 The rest of this section is based on H. W. Singer and S. Schiavo-Campo, *Perspectives of Economic Development* (New York: Houghton Mifflin, 1970).
3 This consideration partially underlies the rationale for supplementary financing; it is *prima facie* appealing to link the provision of aid to medium-term export earnings and movements and to use external assistance to help smooth the trade earnings cycle.
4 For thoughtful discussions of the subject see particularly the studies of Harry G. Johnson, *Economic Policies toward Less Developed Countries* (Washington, DC: Brookings Institution, 1967), pp. 55–60 and of John Pincus *Trade, Aid and Development* (New York: McGraw-Hill, 1967), pp. 41–8. Johnson treats the question on a somewhat more theoretical level, while Pincus looks at several practical aspects and makes the important distinction between the developed countries' motives and those of the developing countries.
5 Johnson (n. 4), pp. 58–60.
6 See Pincus (n. 4), pp. 41–8. The following partly parallels Pincus's discussion.
7 Pincus (n. 4), p. 184.
8 One very interesting and potentially promising step in this direction is the 1967 international agreement for GATT–UNCTAD cooperation in export promotion, which includes the setting-up of direct technical assistance activities in this field.
9 R. I. McKinnon, 'Foreign exchange constraints in economic development and effective aid allocation', *Economic Journal*, 74, 1964, pp. 388–409.
10 For a further discussion of this see Chapter 2.
11 In fact, where a very powerful multinational corporation backed by all the power of modern technology and market influence deals with the government and business units of small and poor LDCs, the presumption may well be the other way round, i.e. that the balance of advantage could lie with the source of the funds rather than the recipient.
12 This is a period during which the recipient does not have to make any amortization payments and/or interest payments on the loan. The idea

is that the project supported by the loan may take, say, seven years to bear fruit, and once this has happened the repayment is no longer a burden for the recipient.

13 The annual volumes published by the DAC of the OECD entitled *Development Assistance: Efforts and Policies of the Members of the Development Assistance Committee* are the primary source of information of development in the field of aid, and the data are remarkably up to date for official publications of this kind.

14 The Commodity Credit Corporation.

15 For further details see H. W. Singer, 'Local currency proceeds from food aid', *International Development, Growth and Change* (New York: McGraw-Hill, 1964), Ch. 8.

16 See also pp. 174–7 above.

17 The dilemma is by no means peculiar to external aid. It also faces any government in its internal development policy. For example, should an agricultural extension service or the introduction of new hybrid seeds (the 'Green Revolution') be geared towards the larger farmers who are more educated and more capable of increasing production quickly or towards the small farmers who need the rise in their living standards more than the larger farmers? In the absence of positive action to the contrary, the normal experience is that the larger farmers have more effective access to the opportunities provided thorugh agricultural extension, hybrid seeds and otherwise, and hence an increase in output and improvements in welfare, as immediate objectives, will require rather different policies and approaches.

18 For a further discussion see 'Project aid and programme aid' in Singer and Schiavo-Campo (n. 2), pp. 248–56.

19 The clearest expression of this is the Harrod–Domar model of growth, which dominated development planning for a considerable time.

20 Reference has already been made (pp. 180–3) to the problem of measuring the volume of aid involved.

8 Aid: Trends

The Volume of Aid and its Distribution

In view of the vagueness of the 1 per cent target, no useful purpose would be served by debating whether or not it was met in the 1960s and the 1970s and whether or not it is likely to be met during the 1980s. It is much more meaningful to see if the prevalent trends and patterns of aid disbursement and allocation facilitate the achievement of the twin objectives implied by the 1 per cent target: increased development assistance to the LDCs, on the one hand, and a fair burden of sharing the costs of aid among the donor countries, on the other.

Total net flow of resources increased from an average of $16 billion in the period 1969–71 to an average of $52 billion in the period 1974–9. After reaching a peak of over $88 billion in 1981, total net resource flows stood at $83,650 million in 1984, dropping further to around $80,000 million in 1985 (see Table 8.1). According to recent OECD figures,[1] modest increases were expected for 1986 although this could be caused partly by the fall in the value of the dollar. However, although net flows are expected to rise by about 7 per cent, in real terms the figure would still be 15 per cent below 1983 levels. Official development assistance (ODA) grew from $8.7 billion to $24.1 billion during 1970–8 and, apart from minor fluctuations, rose steadily to $29.6 billion in 1985. The latter figure reflected a real increase of 1.8 per cent over 1984 ODA levels. Other financial flows (which consist of official export credits, direct and equity investment, and portfolio investment in multinational agencies) were more than ten times as high in 1978 as they were ten years earlier, and private flows more than doubled over this period. This trend continued, reaching a peak in 1981, after which, under the shadow of a looming debt crisis, 'other financial flows' showed a

Table 8.1   The total net flow of resources reported by DAC countries to developing countries and multilateral agencies

Country	1980 $m.	1980 As % of GNP	1981 $m.	1981 As % of GNP	1982 $m.	1982 As % of GNP	1983 $m.	1983 As % of GNP	1984 $m.	1984 As % of GNP
Australia	872.3	0.63	826.8	0.53	1,223	0.79	952	0.62	1,636	0.96
Austria	245.4	0.32	405.3	0.62	255	0.38	130	0.19	56	0.09
Belgium	2,881.8	2.43	2,830.0	2.93	664	0.79	957	1.17	3,766	4.88
Canada	2,754.6	1.12	4,100.3	1.50	1,529	0.54	2,399	0.76	2,841	0.87
Denmark	786.1	1.22	949.3	1.71	824	1.53	1,076	1.98	625	1.19
Finland	196.5	0.40	209.5	0.44	204	0.43	127	0.27	284	0.57
France	11,521.8	1.77	11,468.8	2.01	13,580	2.51	9,334	1.81	8,897	1.82
West Germany	10,584.0	1.28	8,086.8	1.18	6,970	1.06	7,007	1.07	6,507	1.06
Italy	3,998.7	1.01	3,713.9	1.07	4,969	1.44	2,208	0.63	2,308	0.67
Japan	6,765.9	0.65	12,231.3	1.09	8,768	0.83	8,663	0.75	16,049	1.30
Netherlands	2,312.8	1.46	2,211.3	1.59	2,510	1.84	2,178	1.66	2,048	1.65
New Zealand	106.3	0.48	92.0	0.39	116	0.49	123	0.56	81	0.37
Norway	853.2	1.49	671.4	1.18	826	1.47	740	1.34	1,541	2.90
Sweden	1,836.2	1.51	1,462.8	1.32	1,765	1.82	1,308	1.48	1,262	1.36
Switzerland	2,698.4	2.60	2,292.0	2.35	3,207	3.22	3,253	3.22	3,369	3.50
United Kingdom	12,795.0	2.43	10,113.5	2.01	6,097	1.27	5,728	1.25	3,793	0.88
United States	13,852.0	0.53	26,374.9	0.90	30,159	0.99	22,948	0.69	28,585	0.78
Total DAC countries	75,061.3	1.04	88,039.8	1.21	83,669.0	1.15	69,131	0.91	83,650	1.06

Source: OECD, DAC Review, (Paris), 1981, Table A.10; 1982 Table A.8; 1983, Table I.2; 1984, Table II.A.8; 1983, Table I.2; 1984, Table II I.2; 1985, Table 17.

negative growth rate, although they still account for almost two-thirds of total net resource flows.

Bilateral grants and loans still constitute the major proportion of ODA funds. However, 'bilateral grants and grant-like flows' have declined as a ratio of total ODA and also as a ratio of total net flows. In 1960 they constituted 78 per cent of total ODA and about 45 per cent of total net flows; by 1975 the figures had declined to 72 per cent and 30 per cent, respectively; by 1984 the ratio had fallen further, to 54 per cent and 19 per cent, respectively. The contributions to multilateral institutions increased dramatically by 1977 to represent about 30 per cent of the ODA of the DAC member countries, a level that has been maintained since.

Development assistance was given in the form of food aid, technical assistance and financial grants usually used by the LDCs for the purchase of capital equipment, though financial loans accounted for most of the capital assistance. The growth rate of expenditure on technical assistance exceeded the growth of food aid, loans, etc.,[2] a trend that continued into the 1980s.

Over the 1960s and 1970s the United States was by far the biggest donor in quantitative terms. However, its contributions declined consistently over the period: in the early 1960s its share amounted to almost half the total disbursement, but in the late 1970s the proportion shrank to about one-third, around which it has remained since. The other main donors have been France, the United Kingdom, Japan and West Germany – the first two countries having extensive commitments to nations that were once a part of their empires. It is significant to note that, whereas aid from the ex-colonial powers showed a declining tendency, Japanese and West German assistance has tended to increase rapidly over the later period. In recent years, aid from Canada and the Netherlands has tended to increase significantly.

In the 1980s, a major portion of net financial resource flows from the Scandinavian countries, Canada, the Netherlands and West Germany (though not to the same extent) has been in the form of aid made up of ODA and 'other official flows'. For the United Kingdom, France, West Germany and the USA, the situation is radically different: 'private flows at market terms' make up the major portion of net financial resource flows, in some years being almost double that of ODA and 'other official flows'. For example, in 1984, out of a total of $28.5 billion, the USA provided approximately $9.7 billion in ODA and 'other official flows' while the category 'private flows at market terms' accounted for $17.4 billion.

Table 8.2 shows the aid contribution of the major donor countries expressed as a proportion of their GNP at market prices during 1964–75, 1980–1 and 1985. Only five DAC members exceeded the UN-determined 'critical minimum' figure of 0.75 per cent by 1985, of which only Norway and the Netherlands achieved the 1.00 per cent level. It must be pointed out that the figure for France includes flows to its dominions, without which France's ODA to independent countries accounted for only 0.54 per cent of GNP in 1985.[3] The US ratio was well below the group average, while UK aid as a proportion of GNP had fallen slightly from early 1980s levels.

In general, the value of the ratio of ODA/GNP seems to be going down. For example, in 1960, the combined DAC ratio was 0.51 per cent while the US ratio in the same year was 0.53 per cent, the same as the UK ratio in 1964. The French ratio was an astonishing 1.38 per

Table 8.2 *ODA in relation to GNP*

	1964–75	*1980–1*	*1985*
Australia	0.54	0.45	0.49
Austria	0.13	0.34	0.38
Belgium	0.52	0.55	0.53
Canada	0.44	0.43	0.49
Denmark	0.44	0.74	0.80
Finland	0.15	0.25	0.39
France	0.65	0.68	0.79
West Germany	0.35	0.45	0.47
Italy	0.13	0.18	0.31
Japan	0.24	0.30	0.29
Netherlands	0.42	1.05	0.91
New Zealand	0.29	0.31	0.25
Norway	0.43	0.83	1.00
Sweden	0.54	0.81	0.86
Switzerland	0.15	0.24	0.31
UK	0.39	0.39	0.34
USA	0.30	0.23	0.24
Total DAC countries	0.35	0.36	0.35

Sources: DAC, Development Co-operation (Paris: OECD), 1974, 1979 and 1982 Appendix tables; OECD, *Observer,* No. 141, July 1986.

cent in 1960 but only 0.58 per cent ten years later. Twenty-five years later, in 1985, the DAC ratio was down to 0.35, the US to 0.24, the UK to 0.34 while the French ratio had recovered from the 1970 low to 0.79.

Next we may turn to examine the terms and conditions on the basis of which assistance has been offered to the developing countries since the mid-1970s. Once again the OECD figures are the best.[4] Unfortunately, as the OECD document points out, the terms can only be assessed on the basis of aid commitments rather than actual aid disbursements. According to OECD estimates in the late 1970s, Sweden was the 'kindest' donor in terms of the maturity index and also in terms of the grace period index, as well as charging the lowest (average) rate of interest on development assistance. France was a particularly bad donor by these criteria. In 1984 the DAC average maturity period was 30.4 years, the average rate of interest 2.9 per cent, and the average grace period 8.2 years. The grant element as a ratio of total ODA commitment was 82.5 per cent for the United States, 98.5 per cent for the United Kingdom, 76.7 per cent for France, 46.1 per cent for Japan and 63.7 per cent for West Germany in 1984. Apart from the UK, which seems to have increased the grant element marginally over the past few years, the others, especially West Germany and Japan, appear to have reduced this proportion. For 1984, Australia, New Zealand and Sweden maintained a 100 per cent grant element with regard to ODA commitments.

An examination of the countries to which the major aid donors allocate loans leads to the conclusion that the overwhelmingly important determinants of aid allocation by the larger donor countries are political considerations and colonial ties. There seems to be a significant correlation between the allocation of military assistance and of development aid in the case of the United States – hence its substantial contributions to South Korea, Turkey, Indonesia (after 1965) and Pakistan, and to Central America in the 1980s. France and the United Kingdom have mainly been assisting nations that once were part of their colonial systems – hence French commitments to Algeria, Senegal, Morocco and the Cameroons, and UK concern with the South Asian and East African countries. Similarly, Japan's obvious preference for South and South-east Asian regions may indicate the importance of geo-political considerations. However, it would be rather superficial to assume away the problem of aid allocation by stating that it is determined entirely by political factors. The terms on which assistance has been extended to the poor countries have also been influenced to some extent by the economic conditions prevailing in those countries. This becomes obvious when it is realized that there is in fact a two-way relationship between political preferences and economic structure.[5] The nature of this relationship cannot, however, be specified with any degree of certainty given the existing state of social knowledge.

If the pattern of aid allocation among the LDCs is compared to some indicators of economic performance, the only thing that can be safely said is that there is a definite association between GNP per capita and the term structure of aid (measured by the proportion of funds included in the grant element out of total ODA). The ratio of grant elements to ODA is low in the case of countries with GNP per capita greater than $450 and relatively high for countries with GNP per capita of about $200. No clear association can be discerned between the level of indebtedness and the value of the ratio of grant element to ODA. Similarly, other measures of economic perform-ance also do not adequately 'explain', in a regression equation sense, the pattern of aid distribution, on the one hand, or the term structure of aid, on the other.

In conclusion, we may again ask the questions we raised earlier. Has there been a substantial increase in the flow of resources from the rich countries to the poor? And has the sharing of the aid burden between the donor countries become more equitable?

The first question may be dealt with briefly. It is clear that there has been an increase in the volume of foreign assistance: the net flow/GNP ratio rose from 0.76 per cent in 1963 to over 1 per cent in 1978. However, the average ODA/GNP ratio for the DAC countries declined over the period. In view of these trends the objective of increasing the annual flow of resources by the magni-tudes envisaged by the Brandt Commission is certainly an ambitious one. The current economic crisis has further worsened aid expansion prospects. The major aid donor countries are under considerable economic stress: inflation, unstable oil prices, slower growth and rising unemployment have all contributed to the development of a cautious international economic approach. At present, we are in the middle of a protracted bargaining session that seeks thoroughly to overhaul the international trade and monetary systems. Aid prospects are related closely to the success of these negotiations. An adoption of recessionist beggar-my-neighbour policies will preclude an expansion of aid.

The oil-rich countries of the Third World have to some extent sought to offset the decline in assistance; they have sponsored aid programmes that are generous compared to the programmes of the major donors. However, the pattern of aid allocation by the new-rich countries leaves a lot to be desired. Aid allocation seems to be primarily influenced by their political and strategic considerations; indeed, foreign aid is explicitly employed as an instrument of economic warfare. It is thus the political stance of individual countries and not their economic condition that makes them eligible for favourable treatment by the new-rich. An expansion of the aid programme of the new-rich countries will have an optimum impact on the Third World only if such an expansion is accompanied by a revision of aid allocation policies.

Let us now turn to the second question identified above: what has been the change in the pattern of burden-sharing by the donor countries during this period? We have tested a number of hypotheses to determine the burden-sharing effect. The acceptance of the 1 per cent target has a number of implications. In statistical terms, by failing to relate the share of GNP expected to flow from individual donor countries to LDCs progressively to the varying levels of per capita GNP of the various donor countries, the UN target set up the share of GNP represented by financial flows to LDCs as a constant (i.e. 1 per cent). Thus, if the target was effective over a certain period we would expect (a) that at the end of the period the correlation between per capita GNP and the share of GNP to LDCs would be zero, and (b) that over the course of the period this correlation coefficient would move in the direction of zero.

A simple test shows that neither of these expectations was in effect satisfied during the 1960s. The correlation in 1960 between per capita GNP and the total flows as a percentage of GNP was $r = -.21$, while in 1968 it was $r = -.43$. It thus appears that the movement during the decade was in fact away from the hypothesis of zero correlation; the mild correlation at the beginning of the decade became, if anything, more pronounced (even though by itself it is statistically not clearly significant). Moreover, the sign of the increased correlation is negative. This means that there was a tendency for the relatively poorer OECD countries to transfer a relatively higher share of the GNP to the LDCs. The spirit, if not the letter, of the UN 1 per cent target presupposes some progressive rather than regressive relationship, in the sense that the richer OECD countries should find it easier to reach or maintain the 1 per cent target than the poorer OECD countries. Considering, therefore, that the total target was not fulfilled in 1968, we would have expected the richer OECD countries to improve on their performance, and vice versa for the poorer OECD countries. This is in fact what has happened. The correlation coefficient between GNP per capita and the aid/GNP ratio for the year 1978 was +.12. For 1984, the correlation coefficient was +.24. The richer OECD countries now contribute more to development assistance than they did in the 1960s and 1970s.

This simple test may be repeated separately for the two components of the total flow of financial resources to the LDCs, that is, ODA on the one hand and private investment on the other. The results confirm those previously reached. The ODA/GNP ratio moved from a correlation of $r = -.20$ with per capita income of donor countries in 1960 to a more pronounced negative correlation of $r = -.39$ in 1968. Similarly, the correlation of private flows with per capita income of donor countries moved from $r = -.02$ in 1960 to $r = -.19$ in 1968. Hence the statement previously made concerning the apparent ineffectiveness of the 1 per cent target can also be made separately for the components of the total flow. It should be remembered, of course, that during the 1960s there were no separate explicit subtargets, corresponding to the 1 per cent target, for official aid and private investment.

The 0.7 per cent target for official aid was established in the 1970s but performance to date does not give much encouragement that it will be effective. Although it is true that in the 1980s official aid was more closely related to the level of per capita GNP, private investment seems to bear out this relationship to a greater extent. For 1978 the correlation between the ODA/GNP ratio and GNP per capita was not significantly different from zero; but for private flows it was +.136. For 1984, the correlation between the ODA/GNP ratio and GNP per capita was +.11; for private flows it was +.26.

While in the last few years net private flows have fallen dramatically, in the late 1970s and early 1980s commercial bank finance dominated resource flows to LDCs. According to the OECD *Observer* of September 1986, the official sector accounted for just 35 per cent of financial flows in 1980. While the debt crisis has resulted in a sharp decline in private sector financial flows, and a reversal of the 1980s position, tests show that, although the richer DAC countries now make a more positive contribution to official aid, this progressive relationship with regard to private flows was even clearer.

Another test may be made to correlate the growth rate of per capita GNP of the donor countries with the change in percentage of GNP transferred to the developing countries. From the point of view of relating donor capacity to the burden of resources transfer, this relationship would be expected to be positive; that is, the more rapidly growing countries would tend to increase their share of GNP transferred to the LCDs more (or rather diminish it less) than the less rapidly growing countries. This hypothesis is, in fact, much better satisfied than the first hypothesis. The correlation between growth of per capita GNP and percentage of GNP transferred to the poor countries is very close to zero for the seventeen DAC countries in the 1960s: r = +.10 for total flows, +.04 for official aid and +.04 for private investment. For the 1970s the values of the coefficients are broadly similar; the sign (for what it is worth) *is* positive, but the correlation is practically zero. In the 1980s, however, the picture changed somewhat and test results show the expected relationship: by 1984, r = +.34 for total flows, +.07 for official aid, and +.33 for private investment.

The results of our two simple tests require some conciliation. On the one hand, the negative correlation between per capita income and share of GNP given in transfer and aid was intensified during the 1960s; on the other hand, there was a trace of a progressive (and certainly not negative) association between the incremental growth rate of per capita GNP and the burden of transfer and aid. The reconciliation of this apparent contradiction may be sought in the well-known fact that during the 1960s the relatively poor OECD countries (specifically, of course, Japan and Italy) tended to have faster growth rates of GNP than the relatively richer countries (typically the United States and the United Kingdom). It will be readily seen that this provides an explanation of why, during the First Development Decade of the 1960s, the faster-growing countries tended to increase their aid faster, while at the same time in the overall picture the relatively poorer countries carried a heavier share of the total burden at the end of the decade than at the beginning. The growth rate of GNP per capita was positively correlated with the growth rate of the total flow of resources (as distinct from the percentage share of GNP of the total flow) to the mild degree of $r = +.26$. In the 1970s the value of this coefficient was $+.35$. Moreover, since the richer DAC countries improved their growth performance, this implies an improvement in the pattern of aid burden-sharing. If this test is continued to the more recent years up to the 1983/4, the relationship of the increase in total resource flow to growth rate remains positive ($r = +.26$ for 1970/1 to 1983/4), indicating a shift in the distribution of the transfer burden in a progressive direction towards the more rapidly growing donor countries.

So, as far as the distribution of the aid and transfer burden among donors according to both level and growth rate of GNP is concerned, there has been a gradual shift in the direction of progressivity, and the more recent indices are all positive.

One third and final test may be made. If the concept of burden-sharing among donors, as symbolized by the existence and activities of the DAC and as implicit in the 1 per cent target, were in fact operationally effective over a certain period, the differences among donor countries in the burden of transfer (as measured by percentage of GNP) would be expected to diminish over the period. This last hypothesis is clearly borne out by the figures for the 1960s and 1970s, but not for the 1980s. The differences in the aid burden carried by the OECD donor countries – as measured by the dispersion of the percentages of transfer of resources to LDCs around the average – were in fact clearly reduced during the 1960s. The standard deviation for total flows was 0.55 per cent of GNP in 1960, but fell to 0.30 per cent in 1969. In 1978 the standard deviation had fallen to 0.128 per cent. This figure then rose to 0.27 per cent in 1984. For official aid, the standard deviation fell from 0.48 per cent in 1969 to 0.33 per cent in 1978, and dropped still further to 0.15 per cent in 1984. For private investment, the corresponding movement was from 0.33 per cent in 1969 to 0.25 per cent in 1978, rising sharply to 0.59 per cent in 1984.

Thus it may be concluded that the idea of burden-sharing and measurement of comparative performance based on GNP shares was most effective during the First and Second Development Decades in the sense of *equalizing* the performance of donor countries; that is, the donors carrying a big burden reduced their transfer and aid relatively to those donors carrying a smaller burden. In the 1980s, however, this was only true with regard to ODA, the higher standard deviation for total flows being influenced by the increased dispersion of private investment flows around the average. Thus, the 1 per cent target was effective only during the 1960s – not in reaching the target, not in any way in adjusting the distribution of aid to real capacity, but only in making the distribution of aid more 'equitable' (in the sense of more equal) among the different donor countries.

The Burden of Aid: The Recipients' Dilemma

In our discussion of the implications of the 1 per cent target we talked a great deal of the equitable distribution of the burden of aid among the donor countries. Despite the obvious importance of this problem, the concern that has been shown by development economists, multinational agencies, public bodies and governments has been viewed with considerable cynicism by the poor countries – as if a transfer of about 0.05 per cent[6] of the GNP of a country like the United States can create insurmountable balance-of-payments and other problems for the donor and jeopardize the future of the international economy, whereas the ever-widening gap between the rich and poor countries is an inevitable structural characteristic of the twentieth-century world economy that we shall have to live with! Such an attitude is also evidenced by the bland complacency with which the corresponding problems of the burden of aid to the poor countries are being treated by the 'development establishments' of the developed world. Indeed, until well into the 1960s the developed world never acknowledged that aid could constitute a burden to the recipient countries.

The economic impact of the aid burden to the developing countries can manifest itself in two forms. First, there is the problem of 'debt-servicing'. Since most of the so-called aid to the LDCs is in the form of interest-bearing loans, the poor countries have perpetually to find the means to pay off the annual interest charges. Second, the 'aid' that is received by the LDCs is also usually tied to the donor countries in one form or another. Both of these 'aid costs' are becoming increasingly important and will have to be taken into account by those who consider a comprehensive reorganization and reform of the whole international aid system imperative. We have looked at tied aid in Chapter 7 and will consider debt in greater detail in Chapter 9. However, it is worth pointing out that if debt-servicing payments were to be subtracted from the annual flow of financial resources from the rich to the poor countries over the last few years, the net real financial flows would be seen to be decreasing gradually. This tendency is the joint effect of an increase in the repayment and amortization funds by the LDCs, unmatched by a corresponding increase in the inflow of financial resources in the form of either 'aid' or investment. Moreover, the rise in debt repayments has also not been matched by the growth in the export earnings of the LDCs. This is not very surprising. There was a time, not so long ago, when development was thought of as an instantaneous process: all that was needed was the money, and, given the money, productivity would rise in no time, enabling the borrower to repay without too much trouble. This has not happened; for development effort to be initiated at all it is necessary to make substantial investments in the socio–economic infrastructure (e.g. schools, hospitals and roads), and projects of this nature have long gestation periods. On the other hand, the loans contracted by the underdeveloped countries in the post-war period were of short duration and were made available on relatively hard terms. The debt repayment capacity of the LDCs has therefore lagged behind their debt obligations. This poses a very important threat to the prospects of development in the poor countries. As Eugene Black, then President of the World Bank, remarked as early as 1961, 'the machinery of economic development could be overloaded with foreign debt until it sputtered to a halt amid half-built projects and mountains of discarded plans'.[7]

An UNCTAD study[8] in 1971 drew the attention of the world to the acuteness of this problem. This study tried to estimate the gross flow of aid into the LDCs that would be required merely to keep the net flows constant. Its projections are concerned only with reported debt. The total outflow of financial resources is, of course, much larger, for to debt repayments have to be added short-term capital outflows and the repatriated profits of foreign private companies.

The UNCTAD paper showed that, if the 1971 terms of lending were maintained, in order for the *net* inflow to remain at the 1965 level (at 1965 prices) the *gross* inflow of financial resources would have to rise to $17,500 million, as debt-servicing charges would themselves rise to $10,400 million by 1975. These debt charges would constitute about 23 per cent of the export earnings of the LDCs; in 1971 they constituted about 19 per cent. If *all* future lending from official sources were to be contracted on the terms given by the IDA (i.e. interest-free, with a nominal service charge, fifty years' maturity and ten years' grace period), the gross inflow of financial resources to the LDCs would still have to rise by about $14,000 million merely to keep the net inflow to the poor countries at the 1965 level.

However, the debt problem that emerged in the early 1980s was of a far greater magnitude than that envisaged at the beginning of the 1970s. Between 1979 and 1983, developing countries were exposed to a series of external shocks. Oil prices rose sharply and so did real interest rates, which reached historically high levels in 1980–1. These were compounded by a prolonged recession in the industrial economies between 1981 and 1983. Balance-of-payments deficits of all developing countries reached unmanageable levels, and their dependence on external finance became critical – the total external liabilities of all developing countries reached almost $900 billion in 1984. According to World Bank estimates, the debt-service ratio to export earnings stood at 22 per cent in 1984; debt-service payments amounted to $100 billion in that year. In 1970, they amounted to $9.3 billion. Interest payments of all developing countries alone totalled $58 billion in 1984, far exceeding their combined current account deficits of $36 billion. According to World Bank reports, ODA has fallen since 1970 when it provided 50 per cent of all the developing countries' inflows; for the low-income countries, its share was 78 per cent. By 1983 these figures had fallen to 46 per cent and 45 per cent respectively. What did increase dramatically was the volume of commercial bank and private lending for which repayment conditions in terms of time and interest rates were relatively severe.

What is needed today is an initiative on the part of the developed countries not only to ease the burden of debt being carried by the LDCs but also to increase ODA and the grant element in such resource flows. In recent years the West has shown an increased willingness to expand some forms of assistance to the Third World. Food aid in particular has won wide support within the donor countries. The next section discusses the prospects for the growth of food aid in the medium run.

Food Aid

Concern about food shortages gained importance in the 1960s and 1970s but was heightened in the 1980s as widespread famine conditions affected most parts of sub-Saharan Africa. Since the creation of the World Food Programme in 1961, numerous institutions have been set up to deal with chronic and temporary food shortages. However, the volume of food aid in cereals has declined since 1971, when it amounted to 17.5 million tons. The current Food Aid Convention signed in 1980 took steps to guarantee a minimum supply of 7.6 million tons per year from twenty-two donor countries. In 1982–3, food aid in cereals amounted to 9.1 million tons. In 1984–5 more than 100 developing countries received about 12 million tons of cereals from twenty-five donor countries. Vegetable oil, skimmed milk powder, other dairy products, and meat and fish products made up another 1 million tons approximately. Less than 5 per cent of food aid came under the category of emergency food aid.

The USA, which gave 94 per cent of all food aid in 1965, still continues to be the largest donor, although its share has now dropped to around 50 per cent. This reflects both a decline in volume as well as increased activity by other donors. The European Community accounts for about 30 per cent of food assistance, while Australia, Canada and Japan account for around 14 per cent, collectively.

In recent years, food aid valued at world prices amounted to about $2.6 billion annually, or 10 per cent of ODA. The distribution, quantity and nature of food aid is affected by factors other than those directly related to need. For example, Egypt receives 20 per cent of all cereal food aid, which reflects its strategic importance to the

USA. The whole of sub-Saharan Africa on the other hand receives roughly 27 per cent of all food assistance. The level of food aid is also affected by world prices: when high, they result in a lower volume of food aid, as was evident in 1973–4. Factors within the recipient countries also adversely affect the effectiveness of food aid. For instance, the lack of storage and distributional facilities results in waste on the one hand, and prevents food from getting to the most needy on the other.

In order that food aid achieves the objectives it is designed to meet, a number of factors have to be considered and a number of conditions met. First, the volume of food aid must be increased to at least the 1971–2 levels. Secondly, aid should be determined by dietary deficiency and need and not by political and price considerations. Thirdly, information and early-warning systems are needed so that famine conditions can be pre-empted and contingency operations initiated before crisis point is reached. Fourthly, improved infrastructure to facilitate efficient food storage and distribution is essential and should be emphasized as a priority aspect of food aid. In the long-term, strategies aimed at increasing domestic production of essential food should be formulated and implemented, so that fluctuations in national food production, the chief source of food insecurity, can be overcome. The many projects being undertaken by a number of international agencies constitute an attempt to tackle this problem. However, it is clear that much more resources and commitment need to be geared toward this end.

Future of Aid: Aid Reform

It is impossible to forecast the future of aid over, say, the next twenty years or so with any degree of confidence. Too many political, economic and other factors are involved. Who, thirty years ago, could have predicted the rise and subsequent stagnation of foreign aid, and the various phases and transformations through which aid has gone?

What we can do instead is to discuss some of the ideas which seem hopeful and important and appear to have a reasonable chance of being implemented, and also to follow up some trends that are

211

already visible. The total volume of aid proper would have to double in order to reach the UNCTAD target of 0.7 per cent of GNP, and then continue to expand in line with the expanding GNPs of the rich countries. It is difficult to believe that this will happen in the near future. The potentially largest aid donor, the United States, which on the GNP criterion ought to account for about half of total aid, is in a retrenchment mood that seems more than ephemeral and appears to extend to both the major political parties, though for different reasons. One can still expect, hopefully, countries like Japan and the EEC to expand their aid programmes rapidly, and perhaps also the USSR and other eastern countries if a political détente between East and West is firmly established. But this does not seem to amount to anything like the combination of doubling the present level and putting the whole flow on a rising trend of 5 per cent per annum in real terms.

Compared with real aid, private investment in the LDCs as well as hard loans, export credits, etc. have held up remarkably well in recent years in circumstances that have appeared rather unfavourable. The ratio between aid and other financial flows to the LDCs has been far from the 7:3 ratio implied in the UNCTAD target (i.e. 0.7 per cent of GNP aid, 1 per cent of GNP total flow); it has been more the other way around. At any rate, the main growth dynamics seem to be in private investment, export credits and hard loans. There is nothing wrong with this, provided that the investments really help the LDCs and that the debt repayments do not become too burdensome. This last proviso suggests a possibly hopeful future development: why not let foreign investments, export credits, hard lending, etc. grow and redirect aid so as to reduce the debt burden on the LDCs? Various technical possibilities of doing this exist, ranging from generous debt rescheduling towards financial aid to LDCs related to their outflows in respect of profits and dividends of foreign investment.

The trend towards multilateral aid has already been mentioned. Such a multilateralization can be helpful if it contributes to the untying of aid. It is to be hoped that more progress will be made towards aid untying, and that aid increasingly will take the form of free foreign exchange placed at the disposal of the LDCs, which are trusted by the donors to make effective use of this aid on the basis of mutually agreed policies and development plans. This would remove much of the friction from the aid relationship, particularly when combined with progressive multilateralization.

A special step towards both multilateralization and aid untying can be taken by forging the much discussed link between the Special Drawing Rights (SDRs) of the IMF and aid to developing countries. The issue of the SDRs itself was a big step forward in the aid business, since it removed the balance-of-payments burden that donor countries pleaded both for reducing aid and for tying it. It was also directly helpful to LDCs because they themselves were allocated a certain share of the SDRs (though a minor share corresponding to their IMF quotas), contrary to the original intention. What is now under discussion is the possibility of allocating the major share of the rich countries (about 75 per cent of the SDRs) not directly to them but rather to aid agencies, perhaps the IDA and the regional development banks. This means that the rich countries would not *get* the SDRs as a matter of right, but would have to *earn* them by supplying aid goods to the LDCs. From the point of view of the rich countries, the aid would no longer be a burden because it would increase rather than diminish their foreign exchange reserves; in fact, it would be a *failure* to aid that would result in a depletion of foreign exchange reserves, because other countries would earn the SDRs. Such a link has a great deal to recommend it. It could become one of the social inventions that make the world go round, like money itself. The technicalities can be solved if the will to act exists. The link cannot be taken for granted, but the difficulties have been well explored and shown to be by no means insuperable.

The most serious objection is that the SDRs are primarily meant to increase international liquidity and prevent balance-of-payments crises, which is itself a major interest of the LDCs. The liquidity purpose suggests a distribution of SDRs among both the rich countries and LDCs that could – and normally would – be different from that suggested for aid purposes. The ideal solution would be to have separate SDRs for aid purposes, additional to the SDRs issued for liquidity – but this is too much to expect. In a second-best world, the link remains a desirable objective that would go far towards smoothing the way to more effective aid. The developing countries have continued to press for the adoption of the aid–SDR links.

Other new aid ideas under active discussion include special aid to be given to counteract unpredictable losses in the export earnings of the LDCs due to drops in the prices of commodities, sudden crop failures, political emergencies, etc. The principle of such aid has already been conceded and operational for some time,[9] but its broad application still has not produced substantive results. It has been the subject of extensive study, even more so than the link between SDRs and aid. Again the technicalities of implementing such 'compensatory aid' are not well established and await a political decision to go ahead wholeheartedly.

Another proposal that has withstood the test of prolonged discussion and study is the 'Horowitz Plan'. Essentially, this consists of using aid to reduce the interest rates that the LDCs would otherwise have to pay on money raised commercially in the capital markets of the world for the purpose of financing development. It is not difficult to show that aid money used in this way could have a considerable leverage or multiplier effect, compared with more traditional forms of aid. The Horowitz proposal belongs in the same general family of ideas as the one mentioned a little earlier, i.e. to use aid to relieve the LDCs of some of their debt burden arising from hard forms of development financing.

It would also be a great advance – and at no real cost to the donor countries – if aid commitments could be made on a longer than yearly basis, e.g. for five years, tying in with the LDCs' development plans, or preferably on a rolling basis for five years ahead. Such extension might require changes in legislative procedures in some donor countries, but this would be justified by the importance of this matter to the LDCs and for the sake of the more effective use of any aid actually given.

Yet another aid development that could perhaps have more leverage effect than any other, and that still largely awaits implementation, is the financing of research and related pilot development work on technical problems of special importance to developing countries. The tremendous technological capacity of the rich countries has as yet hardly been tapped as a contributor to the development of the poor countries. The present technical assistance programmes are only a faint taste of what could be done. Here also the problem has been much studied. For example, in 1971 the UN Advisory Committee for the Application of Science and Technology to Development drew up a World Plan of Action in which some forty to forty-five priority problems were identified, and concrete plans for the creation of a World Plan of Action fund or account were put forward.[10] The target suggested by the UN group and accepted by the Pearson Commission[11] was for the rich countries to devote 5 per cent of their public expenditures on research and development to the specific problems of developing countries. This would not be very expensive in terms of the sum of money involved, but it should result in major breakthroughs in development. It would also help to do away with the idea that aid should be defined as something that happens geographically within the developing countries. What happens within the rich countries can be just as important, or more important, for the future of the LDCs. Again, there are some hopeful signs that, through the DAC of the OECD, the richer countries may begin to move in this direction. It would be desirable if a greatly strengthened UN Development Programme would backstop such an international effort by providing seed money, and it is unfortunate that until recently the Programme has been tied down entirely to the method of 'country programming'. This prevents it from giving the kind of leadership with global problems that an international organization ought to give.

More recently, a group of least developed and most seriously affected countries have been singled out by the United Nations and UNCTAD for special aid. This is a good development, provided that aid to the least developed countries is additional and does not result in discrimination against other poor countries. In general, though the Pearson Commission was wildly optimistic, and more diplomatic than honest, when it thought that aid could become unnecessary by 1990, there is an element of truth in saying that successful aid should become less and less burdensome to the donors. More and more of the LDCs will leave the category of recipients and enter the intermediate group, and more and more countries from the intermediate group will move up to become potential aid donors; in this sense the donor/recipient ratio should become increasingly favourable. The concentration of aid on the least developed countries could be the beginning of this process.

Finally, let us return to the thought that the future of aid may be determined essentially more by what the rich countries do within their own borders than by what they do within the LDCs. The hope is that, in future, aid will not be negated by restrictive trade policies or by obstacles to migration or, on the other hand, by a brain drain of the needed skills from the LDCs or by social policies that create antagonisms between interest groups in the richer countries and the development of the majority of mankind. Thus, it must be hoped that the aid donors will increasingly let their total action and total policy be of one piece in giving more support to the LDCs: by giving adjustment assistance and retraining to workers displaced by imports from LDCs, by pursuing full employment policies at home, by developing SDRs and other rational methods of balance-of-payments adjustment, by giving some priority in their research and development to the technological problems of the LDCs, etc. It is aid-supporting *total* action that is needed rather than an increase in the volume of aid itself. But such a hope for the future depends on the deepening of the recognition that we are fellow-travellers on a precarious journey in the 'Spaceship Earth'. Perhaps our growing worries about the environment will produce such recognition. Without it, the environment could just as easily deal a death blow to aid as it would otherwise serve to give it a solid foundation. The sub-title of the Brandt Report, 'A Program for Survival', is an indication of the growing recognition of our mutual interdependence.

Notes

1 OECD *Observer*, No. 142, September 1986, p. 15.
2 Statistics are taken from Development Assistance Committee, 'Twenty-five years of development co-operation', 1985 Report (Paris: OECD, 1985).
3 OECD *Observer*, No. 141, July 1986, p. 21.
4 Figures taken from DAC, *Development Co-operation, 1974* (Paris: OECD, 1974), Appendix tables.
5 Such a relationship is acknowledged by free enterprise and Marxist economists alike.
6 This is a very generous estimate of the grant element within the financial resources transfer to most LDCs.
7 'Address of the President of the World Bank to the Annual Meeting of the Fund Aid Bank, 19 September 1961', *International Financial News Survey*, 29 September 1961.
8 UNCTAD, 'The outlook for debt service', TD/7/Supp. 5, October 1971, mimeo.
9 This scheme is operated through the IMF: the 5th quarter, i.e. an extra drawing facility of 25 per cent over and above a member country's full IMF quota. Also refer to Chapter 6 on other stabilization schemes.

10 *World Plan of Action for the Application of Science and Technology to Development* (New York: UN, 1971). Examples of priority problems include: drought-resistant crops, use of brackish water, control of bilharzia, labour-intensive construction methods, etc. Also see *Science and Technology for Development: Proposals for the Second Development Decade* (New York: UN, 1970).

11 L. B. Pearson, *Partners in Development*, Report of the Commission on International Development (New York, Washington and London: Praeger, 1969).

9   *The Debt Crisis*

A Debt Profile of the Third World

The debt problems of the developing countries have been a matter of grave concern throughout the western world in recent years. The accumulated debt of LDCs currently stands at well over $1,000 billion and the debt-service burden has increased so substantially that there is now a net *outflow* of capital from the poor countries in many parts of the Third World. Table 9.1 presents a debt profile of the Third World over the period 1978–83. The countries included in the table accounted for over 80 per cent of the total debt of the South and for almost the total credit extended by the private banks – the Eurocurrency institutions in particular – to the LDCs. High-income LDCs (including Brazil, Mexico, Argentina, South Korea, Venezuela, Chile and Malaysia) accounted for the largest proportion of total Third World debt and for almost four-fifths of debt incurred from private sources. Almost half of total debt was incurred during 1979–83 and the share of the private sector in total debt stood at 54.8 per cent in 1983. The share of private to total debt rose for all groups of LDCs but, whereas private debt accounted for almost 80 per cent of the debt of the high-income LDCs, the corresponding share of the poor LDCs was only 13 per cent. The debt/GNP ratio increased most significantly for the high-income LDCs, but their debt-service/export ratio actually declined by almost 2 percentage points over the five-year period. As against this, middle-income LDCs experienced a near doubling of their debt-service ratio during 1978–83. Table 9.1 also shows that interest rate variations have been the major cause of the rising debt-service burden: the implicit interest rate rose by one-third during the period and interest repayments accounted for over half of all debt-service transactions. New net capital outflows accelerated alarmingly over 1978–83, turning

218

clearly negative for the high-income LDCs and falling sharply for both the poor and middle-income developing countries.

Two major conclusions can be drawn from the preceding analysis. First, it is the high-income LDCs, particularly those in Latin America, who have mainly absorbed the growing debt volumes. Large developing countries in Asia such as India and China have kept international borrowing to manageable proportions.

Table 9.1 *The debt profile of the Third World (based on sample of 65 countries), 1978–83 (%)*

	65 LDCs	Low-income LDCs	Middle-income LDCs	High-income LDCs
Share of sample in debt of all LDCs:				
in total debt	83.0	17.6	21.1	44.2
in private debt	97.3	4.8	19.1	73.4
Percentage of 1983 stock of debt accumulated during 1978–83				
of total debt	47.2	36.4	54.2	48.1
of private debt	57.5	49.5	60.4	57.3
Share of private debt in total:				
1978	44.9	10.4	36.9	65.1
1983	54.8	13.1	42.7	79.1
Debt/GNP:				
1978	23.8	24.0	21.1	25.0
1983	34.8	25.9	34.3	40.7
Debt-service/exports:				
1978	24.3	16.9	15.8	33.1
1983	28.1	19.4	27.3	31.5
Implicit interest rate:				
1978/9	7.0	3.3	6.5	9.2
1981/3	9.5	3.6	8.0	12.8
Total debt-service to total disbursement:				
1978	58.3	47.6	47.3	65.9
1983	87.6	67.3	72.1	103.7

Source: UNCTAD, *Trade and Development Report 1985* (New York: UN, 1985), p. 77.

Although bank loans to the export-oriented East Asian countries such as South Korea and Taiwan have increased rapidly in recent years, export growth has generally kept pace with increases in debt. On the other hand, the debt-service ratios of many middle-income and poor LDCs – including Burma, Ethiopia, Kenya, Madagascar, Malawi, Pakistan, Sierra Leone, Somalia, Tanzania, Uganda, Cameroon, Colombia, Ivory Coast, Mauritius, Morocco, Nicaragua, Nigeria, Peru, Tunisia, and Zambia – have increased alarmingly. Five poor LDCs, seven middle-income countries and almost all high-income countries in the sample had negative net transfers of capital in 1983.[1]

The rising number of countries with negative capital transfers reflects the second major conclusion that can be drawn from Table 9.1. This is that debt repayment burdens have increased despite a general decline in new lending due to a hardening of terms. The implicit interest rate went up for all groups of developing countries during 1975–83 and the share of interest repayments in debt source obligations increased substantially – once again for all groups of LDCs. This would suggest that proposals to reduce the debt burden must address the problem of international monetary reform and must be particularly concerned with the regulation of the international banks, whose lending policies during the 1970s was a major factor in increasing the debt obligations of the LDCs.

The Genesis of the Debt Crisis

During the 1970s a marked change occurred in the pattern of international lending to the developing countries. There was a rapid increase in borrowing from the private sector. As Table 9.2 shows, the share of bank loans in total long-term financing increased from 4 per cent to 22 per cent over the period 1970–83. In 1979 (that is, before the beginning of the world recession), bank loans accounted for 32.7 per cent of total long-term financing, whereas the share of ODA had been only 22.4 per cent.[2] The rise in the share of bank loans was particularly marked for the relatively higher-income newly industrializing countries in Latin America and East Asia. On the other hand, the poorer LDCs remained mainly dependent on official flows. Even in 1979 bank loans accounted for only 2.4 per cent of their total long-term external financing and in 1983 loan and interest repayments from the poor LDCs exceeded new bank loans by $10 million. On the other hand, bilateral and multilateral ODA accounted for about 80 per cent of total flows to this group of LDCs in 1983.[3]

During the 1970s, multilateral financing did not keep pace with the growth of private portfolio lending to the developing countries. Although efforts had been made during the 1960s and 1970s to expand the resources and the development financing role of the IMF,[4] LDCs refused to borrow from the IMF because of the stringent conditions that were attached to such loans. The Eurocurrency institutions had ample liquid funds during most of the 1970s, so developing country governments found it possible to obtain sizeable sums at relatively low cost and within highly flexible repayment schedules. The banks often had little alternative to lending to the LDCs because OECD governments were reluctant to expand investment and were concerned primarily with containing domestic inflationary tendencies. The explosion of commercial lending to the developing countries that occurred during 1973–9 owed as much to the eager enthusiasm of cavalier bankers willing to

Table 9.2 *Sources of long-term financing to the Third World, 1970–83*

	1970		1983	
	Volume US$M.	%[a]	Volume US$M.	%[a]
Total long-term finance	9,317	—	52,107	—
Bilateral[b]	8,137	87.3	40,152	77.0
ODA	3,202	34.4	13,855	26.6
Other official	542	5.8	5,037	9.7
Private direct investment	2,243	24.1	8,093	15.5
Export credits	1,650	17.7	2,501	4.8
Bank loans	380	4.1	11,453	22.0
Multilateral	1,076	11.6	11,097	21.2
Socialist countries	104	1.1	858	1.6

Notes:
[a] the total does not add up to 100 because of omissions.
[b] from OECD and OPEC countries.

Source: UNCTAD, *Handbook of International Trade and Development Statistics 1985* (New York: UN, 1985), p. 330.

take risks that later proved to be injudicious, as it did to Third World policy-makers who borrowed incautiously. During the 1970s, the commercial banks developed a series of financing techniques that made it possible to spread risks widely. The practice of syndication associated with most large-scale Eurocurrency banking distributed the risks among members of the syndicates and enabled smaller banks to enjoy the expertise of the major financial institutions. Funding risks were also reduced by the development of the large inter-bank markets and the increasing use of variable rate credit to eliminate interest rate risk. Syndicated Eurocurrency loans were readily available to the newly industrializing LDCs, which generally enjoyed high credit ratings. Such loans were much more flexible than export credit arrangements and subject to less stringent conditions than loans obtained from the IMF. Moreover, countries such as Brazil and Mexico were able to raise very large sums of money – often amounting to hundreds of millions of dollars in single loan packages – through the Eurocurrency syndicates.

The rapid expansion of bank credit during the 1970s reflected the widespread belief of both developed and developing country governments that the economic crisis that began with the break-down of the Bretton Woods system in 1971[5] (and was accentuated by the four-fold increase in oil prices in 1973) was of a temporary nature and that the severe recession in the West would quickly come to an end. LDC governments therefore strained to maintain high investment levels despite drastic reductions in export earnings. The IMF encouraged the LDC governments to maintain high expenditure levels and established a series of special financing facilities to mitigate the balance-of-payments effects of the slackening of export growth and the rise in oil prices. Both the International Monetary Fund and the Bank for International Settlements (BIS) turned a blind eye to the explosion of Third World borrowing in the Eurocurrency markets and made no attempt to contain or direct these financial flows.[6]

By 1976 there was a general realization that the export earnings shortfall of the LDCs was likely to be of a prolonged character and investment levels were reduced. However, the current account deficit of non-oil-exporting LDCs remained significantly higher than in the period 1971–3 and long-term borrowing from the international banks also continued to expand. In theory these expanded borrowings should have contributed to growth in the debtor country's repayment capacity. An IMF study showed that growth in international indebtedness was positively associated with growth in the savings/GNP ratio throughout the 1970s for a sample of the twenty larger LDC borrowers.[7] This would suggest that international borrowings were not absorbed in rising levels of consumption. Moreover, the study also showed a close correspondence between the growth of investment and gross national product. On the other hand, many sub-Saharan countries during the 1970s had average investment/GNP ratios in excess of 20 per cent but the rate of growth of GNP was negative in many of these years.[8] This raises many questions about the efficiency of investment and the effective utilization of the funds that financed them. In recent years, many African countries have become increasingly burdened by 'white elephant' projects that continue to absorb large volumes of foreign exchange without generating any marketable products.[9]

Some Latin American countries remained concerned with enhancing investment and external competitiveness. Chile under General Pinnochet is the outstanding example of a developing country that eagerly embraced a monetarist macroeconomic programme.[10] Such countries increased wage flexibility, lifted restrictions on capital movements and accelerated the pace of privatization of the economy. These policies were usually accompanied by a rise in the consumption of luxuries, speculation, unemployment and capital flight. It is estimated that over the period 1974–82 capital flight amounted to as much as 40 per cent of the total accumulated external debt of the Latin American countries.[11] On the other hand, export earnings did not expand significantly.

An unfavourable international trade environment constituted an important constraint on the debt-servicing capacity of both Latin American and African LDCs. In 1983, BIS argued that the difficulties experienced by many LDCs in servicing their debt were due more to the deterioration in the international macroeconomic environment than to failures in domestic management and resource allocation.[12] During the 1970s, however, very few LDCs were faced with serious debt-servicing crises, and IMF reschedulings of debt repayment arrangements were confined to a handful of cases. From 1979 there was increasing realization that debt repayment difficulties were not likely to remain confined to exceptional cases.

The average debt-servicing ratio for LDCs doubled from 10 per cent in 1974 to 20 per cent in 1979. This was accompanied by a significant rise in the price of oil and the adoption of a deflationary monetarist policy by many OECD countries – most notably the USA, West Germany and Britain – leading to a restrictive protection-enhancing trade strategy. The current account deficits of the LDC debtors were thus subject to increased strain. Moreover, the change in US monetary policy in the early 1980s led to sharply increased and highly volatile interest rates. Debt-servicing obligations therefore increased very significantly, and this drastically changed international environment induced world creditor institutions radically to revise their views about the nature of the debt situation and the policies considered appropriate to deal with it. For example, in the 1970s the IMF had remained concerned with maintaining investment levels in the LDCs (as noted earlier); in the 1980s, it became the leading advocate of 'payments adjustments' involving drastic cutbacks in import levels and reductions in domestic consumption and investment.

The rapidly deteriorating trade environment initially led to a rapid increase in international borrowing by the LDCs. There was a large rise in gross commitments of Eurocurrency credits to developing countries during 1980–1 and the attitude of the international banks remained liberal.[13] Furthermore, there was a much greater use of IMF credit than during the 1970s. These borrowings significantly increased the stock of Third World debt – by almost 50 per cent according to the figures in Table 9.1 – and the cost of servicing it. Since the middle of 1982 an alarmingly large number of LDCs – including Mexico, then the world's largest debtor nation – have been facing a squeeze on their external liquidity. Long-term debt is increasingly being refinanced by short-term borrowing. Debt rescheduling has become common and a number of developing countries – including Bolivia, Mexico, Nigeria and Peru – have had to declare unilateral moratoriums on debt-servicing transactions. Moreover, since 1985 there has been a net *outflow* of capital from Latin America and many countries in Africa.

The response of the international financial community to the growing debt problems of the Third World has taken the form of the provision of emergency relief negotiated on a case-by-case basis.[14] The IMF now plays a pivotal role in the rescheduling of debt and the organization of the so-called 'involuntary' loans necessary to restore debt-servicing capacity. The relationship between IMF and commercial bank lending has become increasingly close. In recent years the IMF has made it clear that the availability of its resources is conditional on parallel commitments of funds by the international banks. The banks have also made further lending conditional on a debtor country accepting IMF advice.

Since 1985 the ability of the IMF to enforce policy changes has declined, and the net outflow of funds from the IMF has fallen significantly. It has often been unable to collect its debts and many LDCs – including Argentina, Brazil, Mexico, Nigeria and Tanzania – have for long periods refused to accept its proposals for macroeconomic policy changes. In 1985, the United States recognized the need for a change in the system of international financial management and presented a series of proposals for increasing the role of the World Bank and downgrading that of the IMF.[15] Without fundamental reforms in the international financial system, a general revival of lending from the international banks is unlikely and even if such a revival were to take place there exist no mechanisms for channelling the new bank loans to areas where they are most needed or can be most effectively utilized.[16]

The fall in international bank lending during 1982–87 was accompanied by a stagnation in the flow of official development assistance funds. ODA has declined in nominal value terms in every year since 1980 (although its share in total funding has sometimes gone up owing to the greater decline in other sources).[17] This has had a devastating impact on the sub-Saharan LDCs in particular and on most low-income LDCs in general. For most of these countries, official funds still constitute well over four-fifths of external financing. A fall in these funds has drastically reduced the opportunities for growth and structural change in the low-income LDCs. Moreover, as the sub-Saharan countries are typically very import dependent, they have had to attempt to substitute commercial borrowing for official funds, wherever possible, thus considerably increasing the overall cost of external development financing. Thus, both the middle- and high-income LDCs that relied primarily on bank borrowing during 1973–82 and the poor LDCs have had to adopt large-scale adjustment measures to deal with the problems of falling external resources and a rising debt burden.

Patterns of Adjustment and the Impact of the Debt Crisis

The growing balance-of-payments deficits of most LDCs – including many oil-exporting countries – during 1979–86 were principally due to stagnant export volumes, falling terms of trade and rising interest rates on accumulated debt (see Statistical Appendix, Tables S.4 and S.7). New borrowings during this period were generally insufficient to fill the gap between foreign exchange earnings and expenditure.[18] Increased interest payments absorbed a large proportion of the additional borrowing in most cases. Thus much of the debt accumulation since 1979 has been used to compensate for declining export earnings and rising debt-servicing obligations, and has therefore had little direct impact on productivity growth within the borrowing countries. This is reflected in the rising debt GNP ratios, which as Table 9.1 shows increased by about almost 50 per cent over the period 1978–83. The debt-servicing ratio also rose significantly during this period. In the case of the high-income countries with large accumulated debt this was principally due to increases in interest rates. In the case of most low-income LDCs, on the other hand, the rise in the service payment to exports ratio was mainly due to falling commodity prices and stagnant export earnings. For the vast majority of LDCs, whereas the growth of accumulated debt has declined significantly since 1982, the debt-service obligation – measured both in absolute terms and as a ratio of exports – has continued to increase despite the many reschedulings and conversions of official loans into grants that have been arranged by the IMF and some of the OECD governments. These trends have led to a situation whereby since 1985 most Latin American countries and many low-income sub-Saharan countries have been exporting more capital to the rich countries in the form of interest and principal repayments than they have obtained as grants or loans. This has meant a substantial loss of development finance and has had very serious adverse effects on the economies of the Third World.

This is reflected in a sharp fall in imports (measured in both volume and value terms) to the LDCs over the period 1981–5. The value of imports over this period to the LDCs fell by 5 per cent.[19] Despite substantial increases in export earnings during 1986, imports by the LDCs continued to decline, owing to rising debt-servicing obligations. The fall in imports in the non-oil LDCs during 1982–4 was sufficient to offset the trade deficit that had emerged during 1979–81. Import reductions were most drastic in the case of the low-income LDCs – mostly situated in sub-Saharan Africa – which could not obtain commercial loans and whose terms of trade and export earnings declined substantially during the early 1980s. The relatively high-income countries of Latin America experienced a very sharp decline in bank lending during 1982 and 1983 and were forced drastically to cut imports in those years. Most of these cuts were concentrated in the capital imports sector. Imports of intermediate goods and industrial raw materials, on the other hand, were maintained at pre-recession levels. The Latin American countries thus adopted a strategy that sought to maintain production at high rates of capacity utilization but cut back sharply on investment and capital formation programmes. The low-income LDCs reduced capital goods imports much less in percentage terms because, even before 1979, such imports were at very low levels in their countries. On the other hand, imports of intermediate goods and raw materials fell substantially. As most sub-Saharan LDCs have very high levels of import dependence, the fall in intermediate imports led to a very substantial fall in production and to the emergence of very high rates of capacity underutilization. This process is sometimes described as 'import strangulation'. The low-income sub-Saharan countries faced a very difficult situation during the 1980s. Commercial loans were not available, in most cases ODA levels were stagnant and a large proportion of grant income had to be committed to increased food imports ncessitated by the persistence of drought, and export earnings remained low owing to the relatively slow expansion of European countries, which were the main markets for sub-Saharan commodity exports.

Since the early 1980s, the IMF has put increasing pressure on the LDCs – particularly those with serious balance-of-payments difficulties – to increase exports. It has advocated a strategy emphasizing the need to raise the producer prices of cash crops and to permit a large-scale devaluation in the exchange rate of the deficit countries. Such macroeconomic policies are theoretically expected to lead to a switching of investment resources from domestic demand-oriented production to production for exports. Such a switching of expenditure requires a depression of domestic demand – to be achieved in the

IMF programme by a reduction in the domestic budget deficit. In most cases, an increase in exports by the LDCs thus involves very substantial sacrifices in consumption by the poorer sections of the community. This is because more often than not they are the main beneficiaries of government expenditure programmes and consumers of goods that are export substitutes (such as food crops instead of cash crops, homespun cloth instead of high-quality wearing apparel, etc.)

In general, developing countries have found it very difficult to switch resources from domestic demand to export-oriented production because of the necessary cost in terms of domestic consumption loss and the relatively low mobility of resources within the economy. Moreover, there are important constraints on the demand side as well. Thus, throughout 1981–5 the IMF put pressure on Tanzania to deflate, raise producer prices and devalue the Shilling in order to stimulate exports. Although Tanzania adopted many of these measures, export earnings remained stagnant. This is partly explained by the fact that Tanzania's main export is coffee and the International Coffee Agreement (of which Tanzania is a member) has not permitted an increase in Tanzania's export quota in this product.[20] Rising protectionist pressure in the West has seriously constrained the growth of both primary commodities and manufactured exports from the developing world. In general, however, it is mainly the manufactures-exporting, high-income LDCs that have succeeded in substantially increasing export earnings during 1982–6.

The fall in imports and the rising burden of debt-servicing has imposed a heavy cost on the developing world. GNP per capita growth was negative for a very large number of LDCs – including most low-income countries – during 1979–83. Most sub-Saharan countries experienced negative GDP growth during these years. Negative GDP growth was significantly positively associated with rising debt-servicing.[21] Moreover, a large proportion of LDCs also experienced negative investment growth during 1980–3. Table 9.3 summarizes the relationship between falling import and export levels and associated declines in GDP and investment. During 1979–81, 61 per cent of countries with negative import growth had negative growth in GDP and for investment. The ratio rose to 83 per cent in 1982–83. This ratio had similar levels for all groups of LDCs. Only 35 per cent of countries with positive export growth experienced negative GDP and/or investment growth in 1979–81. During 1982–3 this ratio rose to almost 60 per cent. The ratio rose most markedly for the low- and high-income countries (with no substantial change for the middle-income LDCs). This would suggest that in many cases increased export earnings were not being channelled to financing new investment; they were being used up in the debt-servicing necessitated by rising interest rates.

Thus, most LDCs incurred a heavy domestic cost in their attempt to adjust to deteriorating conditions in international export and financial markets. Latin American countries in particular paid a heavy price for the liberal economic policies they had pursued during the 1970s. They borrowed heavily during this period, freed capital movements and attempted to switch expenditure to export-oriented activities. Rising interest rates and growing protectionist barriers have ensured the failure of this type of economic strategy. Developing countries – such as China and India – that have pursued import-substituting policies and carefully limited their international borrowing have been much less seriously affected by the crisis. The cost of adjustment to the changed international environment has been much lower in their case.

Table 9.3 *Relationship of changes in imports, exports, GDP and investment, 1979–83*

		1979–81				1982–3		
	Total	Low-income LDCs	Middle-income LDCs	High-income LDCs	Total	Low-income LDCs	Middle-income LDCs	High-income LDCs
Number of countries[a] in which import volume fell	34	14	16	4	30	8	14	8
of which GDP and/or investment fell	21	8	11	2	25	6	12	7
Number of countries[a] in which export volume rose	28	13	9	6	29	8	10	11
of which GDP and/or investment fell	10	6	3	1	17	6	3	8

Note:
[a] These countries are taken from an UNCTAD sample of 65 LDCs for which data on investment and GDP growth are available.

Source: UNCTAD, *Trade and Development Report* (New York: UN, 1985), p. 92.

For the majority of LDCs the cost of structural adjustment in the short run has been substantial also in terms of price instability. Currency depreciation exerts pressure on prices, rendering it even more difficult to reconcile the balance-of-payments adjustment with price stability, and attempts to maintain 'realistic' exchange rates in the face of widespread misalignments among the floating exchange rate currencies often add to the problems. Rising interest rates – to contain capital flight – also add to the pressure on prices. Combined with currency depreciation and falling domestic demand this creates problems for the corporate sector and inevitably governments have to mount expensive rescue operations. Thus, removal of subsidies on food stuffs in order to reduce fiscal deficits can simply result in a change in the mechanism through which inflationary pressure is generated rather than a fall in the inflationary rate. Moreover, cuts in public expenditures on utilities and other forms of investment generally entail significant reductions in both employment and production. Indeed, the main casualty of adjustment to the international crisis has been public expenditure in the developing countries, and reduction in public expenditure has usually had a significant negative impact on the pattern of income distribution within the Third World.

The falling levels of public expenditure and of investment in the developing countries in response to the debt-servicing crisis have created a serious dilemma not only for the LDCs but for the international financial system as a whole. As noted earlier, many developing countries are currently experiencing a net outflow of capital, so that external funds are not likely to substitute for falling domestic investment. The attempt to switch expenditure from domestic-oriented to export-oriented activities has not so far proved successful and export growth has been nominal in most years. However, export earnings must rise to service debt. This seems very difficult given the sluggish nature of the recovery in the West and the rising tide of protectionism. If a generalized debt crisis is to be avoided there must be action on the one hand to reduce protectionist barriers and on the other to improve the export competitiveness of the LDCs in international markets. This would require new investment to stimulate efficient production, and new investment on a significant scale can occur only if the deflationary policies advocated by the IMF and forced upon the LDCs are abandoned and foreign exchange resources are provided to stimulate the imports essential for investment in the export-oriented industries.

The rate at which investment must grow in an LDC to avoid a debt crisis will be determined by (1) the initial stock of debt, (2) its rate of growth, and (3) the growth of the structure of interest rates. The higher these factors, the greater the 'critical minimum' level of investment necessary to generate export revenue sufficient to offset the annual capital outflow. It is important to stress, however, that an increase in investment is in itself not sufficient to avoid a generalized debt crisis. If such investment is provided by high-cost commercial borrowings, the debt burden will continue to rise and the critical minimum level of investment to stave off a debt crisis will very soon become too high. It is therefore essential that new financial flows to the LDCs are provided significantly more cheaply than in the past and the overall debt burden is – at least gradually – reduced. This must imply a substantial reduction in real interest rates.[22] However, an improvement in the terms on which international finance is provided to the LDCs can be effective only if it is achieved as part of a general overhaul of the international financial system. Such reform is, however, a very complex matter and the prospects are discussed in Chapter 11. The next section analyses some more modest proposals that have been put forward in recent years for dealing with the debt crisis of the developing world.

Debt Management Reform Proposals

Debt crisis management has in recent years been concerned primarily with the stability of the international banking system and the survival of individual banks. It has not generally addressed the question of mitigating the long-term adverse effects of the growth of the debt burden on the development prospects of the LDCs. The result is that, whereas bank failures have been few and far between, the debt burden has continued to grow. Thus, in spite of many restructuring packages, the net outflow of capital from Latin America averaged $25 billion a year over 1982–5 (equivalent to 25 per cent of the annual export earnings of the region).[23] Furthermore, debt management during 1982–6 was concerned with short-term containment and not with the type of systematic changes that would make debt crises less likely and less damaging in the future. There was little serious consideration of the need to develop a more appropriate system of international financial mediation to deal with the debt crisis of the Third World.

The need for fundamental reforms in the international debt management system has meanwhile become considerably greater as new bank lending has been drastically reduced since 1984 and the risk of debt-service arrears moratoriums and even default has grown rapidly. Debtor governments have since the early 1980s been pressing for fundamental reform in the international debt management system. The fact that there is now an annual outflow of a large sum of capital from the LDCs has meant that the bargaining power of these countries in international financial markets has increased and they are in a strong position to influence the terms and conditions of debt management. This is partly recognized in the so-called 'Baker' initiative of 1985 (discussed in Chapter 11), which asserts that greater priority ought to be given to stimulating growth in the LDCs through a transfer of development assistance. Many countries and groups are thus seriously considering proposals for reform in the debt management system.

Many such proposals have been put forward in recent years.[24] There have been suggestions for a liberalization of the IMF's Compensatory Financing Facility (CFF), enabling the provision of loans under this scheme to compensate for fluctuations in nominal interest rates and widening the export coverage of this scheme (see Chapter 6). It is argued that the net cost of introducing an 'interest window' within the CFF would be relatively low if compensating payments through this window were linked to members' quotas at the IMF, but its beneficial countercyclical effect would be small as well. There is therefore a case for 'de-linking' compensatory payments (for both interest and export variations) from quotas. The opening of an interest compensatory window might also lead to a reduction of funds available for the compensation of export short-falls unless the total resources of the IMF were substantially enhanced. If the total liquidity of the Fund were to remain unchanged, the opening of an interest window would in all likelihood lead to a transfer of resources from low-income LDCs (which are presently the main beneficiaries from the export compensatory facilities) to the middle- and high-income LDCs, which have large outstanding commercial debt and are likely to be the main recipients of interest compensatory payments. Cline has proposed therefore that the interest window of the CFF be financed through the emergency funding conditionality already available to the IMF. This would imply a significant expansion of the General Agreement to Borrow (GAB)[25] Financing facilities within GAB have been increased on a number of occasions, and the main OECD countries (who are the members of GAB) can authorize provision of credit through GAB for interest compensation. An important problem here is that, whereas CFF-related credit is relatively cheap, the use of the GAB facility has generally required high conditionality, upper credit tranche arrangements. This would significantly raise the cost of debt-servicing to the LDCs.

Several proposals to reduce this cost have been concerned with 'interest capping' – that is, restraining interest rate rises.[26] It has been suggested that interest rates should be 'capped' to stabilize interest repayments over time. A ceiling should be set on both new and rescheduled loans, and if market rates rise above this ceiling the difference should be added to the principal due to be paid at maturity. Such a proposal has attractions for the LDCs if the capping of interest rates is accompanied by policies that substantially reduce the long-term real interest rates – otherwise it amounts to no more than a postponement of the crisis. There is a need to reduce the debt burden, which can be addressed only by developing mechanisms for shifting the burden of increased interest payments (over and above generally agreed 'normal' levels) from LDCs to other agencies such as the central banks of the rich countries, which could compensate commercial banks for the loss of interest payments necessitated by some form of 'concessionary' interest capping. Such compensation, it is argued, is required to maintain the net flow of bank credit to the Third World.[27] Such 'concessionary' capping might be linked to schemes that suggest that debt-service repayments should be related to the production or export capacity of the debtor nations.

The proposals discussed above do not require major institutional change and taken individually they can have only a minor impact on the debt management process. However, as Griffith Jones has pointed out, 'the adoption of several of them would imply a significant change in the way that international flows to developing countries occur. The undertaking of several relatively minor changes may imply the first steps towards more fundamental reform'.[28]

More ambitious proposals than the ones outlined above have also been put forward. They seek to increase the flow of private credit to the LDCs, enhance the stability of the international banking system and substantially reduce the volume of outstanding debt (the so-called 'debt overhang'). In recent years, attention has been focused on proposals that suggest mechanisms for insuring loans to the LDCs. Thus Wallich[29] argues that total loan portfolios (rather than individual loans) should be insured, and the fund established for this purpose should have sufficient resources to inspire confidence in the banking community. In other words, resources should be adequate to ensure that even very large losses could occasionally be covered. Resources could be provided by the multilateral institutions such as the World Bank and the IMF (although this would once again raise problems about the reduction of other forms of concessional assistance to provide investment-guaranteeing funds) or through borrowings in the capital markets.

Another proposal to increase private lending to the LDCs has been put by Harold Lever.[30] He proposes an extension of the powers of the national export credit agencies to insure the export of capital to cover current account deficits as well as the export of goods. Lever proposes the establishment of an international organization that would fix total and national limits for insured bank lending to LDCs – these limits being determined with reference to guidelines provided by the IMF. Thus new lending for financing exports and current account deficits would be provided by commercial banks but would – within the limits established by the new central international organization – be insured by national export credit guarantee agencies. Export credit agencies would have to agree to accept credit limits determined by the new central body. In practice this is likely to be a very difficult task, as the policies of national export credit agencies have more often than not been at variance, particularly since 1982.

Coordination in national policies is an essential prerequisite for improving the structure of international lending. A fundamental cause of the existing international financial chaos is the uncoordinated and haphazard growth of international lending by the private banks. As discussed in Chapter 11, the Eurocurrency institutions have developed in a manner that has intensified the trend towards international financial anarchy and an important existing need is the subordination of the policies of the international banks to a properly constituted central international monetary authority – along the lines of the international clearing union (ICU) proposed by Keynes as early as 1942.[31] Implicit in the Lever proposals – and in proposals put forward by some other authors as well – is the need to establish a new international agency that could act as an insurer of funds invested in the Third World as well as a lender of last resort to overextended banks. Such an institution would inevitably also possess the authority to regulate the lending activities of the international commercial banks.

The establishment of a new ICU could go a long way towards closing the gaps not covered by national lender of last resort and supervisory authorities and towards reducing the risk (and thus stimulating the growth) of international lending. As a first step in this direction Griffith Jones and Lipton have proposed that western central banks should make explicit their commitments in international lender of last resort arrangements.[32] This should be accompanied by supervision to monitor both the volume and terms of international lending. The development of such an institution, particularly if coupled with substantial concessionary interest capping and a generous extension of the CFF, could go a long way towards easing the debt burden of the developing countries.

Proposals have also been put forward to reduce the 'debt overhang' by emergency action. Thus 'non-performing' debt can be written off the books of the lender banks and they can be 'compensated' by its conversion into equity stock or other less risky financial assets. Debt burdens can also be reduced by a straightforward writing off of bad debts – as was done in the late 1970s and early 1980s when many loans to the poorest countries were converted into grants. The 'discounting' of private sector debt to LDCs could be financed by donor central banks, which could then insist that some fraction of the fund involved in this transaction be channelled back to the LDC in the form of a new loan.[33] Most proposals for reducing the debt 'overhang' relate debt rescheduling to some measure of the trade and/or growth performance of the debtor LDC.

Debt repayment capacity is strictly limited in most developing countries. Forecasts by the IMF, the World Bank, UNCTAD and other international bodies show that many LDCs with severe debt-servicing problems will in 1990 have real per capita income levels at or below their 1980 levels.[34] There is thus a strong *prima facie* case for writing off a large proportion of the 'non-performing' outstanding debt of the Third World. Steps must, however, be taken to ensure that this does not negatively affect the flow of new loans to LDCs. Careful regulation and management of international financial mediation procedures can contribute towards a gradual lowering of the debt overhang and the conversion of the portfolio of the commercial banks. Substantially increased public funds would, however, be needed for achieving these targets. There is also a need to abandon the case-by-case approach that has in the recent past determined all rescheduling arrangements and to establish new general guidelines for the restructuring of debt. These general guidelines should cover issues such as multi-year reschedulings, grace and repayment periods, greater uniformity of interest rates, and criteria to determine overall resource transfer in the medium run. Some movement towards the development of such a general policy framework has been made in the debt negotiation process involving countries such as Mexico, Sudan and Pakistan.

Movement towards reform of the debt management process has, however, been slow in recent years. This has induced many LDCs – including Argentina, Brazil, Mexico, Nigeria, Peru and Tanzania – to take unilateral action and to defy the IMF for long periods. The traditional IMF package for dealing with debt-servicing difficulties – involving domestic deflation, currency depreciation, liberalization and privatization – has lost credibility. The IMF now finds it difficult even to collect its own debts and its international authority to regulate lending to the Third World has been reduced; in this regard it has now to act in concert with the World Bank. Debtor countries are thus in a relatively strong bargaining position in international financial markets. They can unilaterally – or collectively within the context of a debtors' union – decide to relate debt-service payment to some objective measure of debt-servicing capacity. Such a policy could lead to a suspension of net capital outflow from the LDCs – provided that LDC governments can effectively check capital flight. It must be supplemented by attempts at increasing national productivity and the competitiveness of the country's (or region's) exports in world markets. The development of such an approach has been impossible because of the different interests and perceptions of the major Third World debtors – for example, Mexico, a large oil producer, stands to lose from falling oil prices, while Brazil stands to gain substantially. This makes the coordination of international financial policies very difficult. Nevertheless, without substantive economic cooperation, Third World debtors will not be able to utilize their increased bargaining power within international financial markets. This power could be – and ought to be – used constructively, i.e. in a manner that stimulates growth throughout the world economy. It is in the interest of the rich countries to ease the debt burden of the poor. This will involve a substantial increase in the flow of resources to the Third World. Rich country policy-makers currently put great stress on direct foreign investment as a means for stimulating economic development – this potential is discussed in the next chapter. More fundamentally, an increased flow of international finance must be supplemented by an improvement in the terms on which the transfer of resources takes place. This requires a comprehensive overhaul of the international financial system. This question is addressed in Chapter 11.

Notes

1 UNCTAD, *Handbook of International Trade and Development Statistics*, Supplement 1985, (New York: UN, 1985) pp. 388–9 and UNCTAD, *Trade and Development Report 1985* (New York: UN, 1985) pp. 198–203. The countries with negative net capital transfers in 1983 were: Ghana, Kenya, Malawi, Pakistan and Sierra Leone (poor LDCs); Congo, Guyana, Ivory Coast, Mauritius, Morocco, Peru and Tunisia (middle-income LDCs); and Algeria, Argentina, Brazil, Chile, Gabon, South Korea, Panama and Venezuela (high-income LDCs). Botswana and Gabon were the only two LDCs with negative capital transfers in 1978.
2 These figures are from UNCTAD *Handbook* (n. 1) 1985, p. 330.
3 UNCTAD *Handbook* (n. 1) 1985, p. 332.
4 This is discussed in Chapter 11 and Chapter 6.
5 On this, see Chapter 11.
6 On the role of the IMF during the early 1970s, see IMF, *Annual Reports* (Washington DC: IMF), 1971, 1972, 1973, 1974, and 1975. US Senate Committee on Foreign Relations, Subcommittee on foreign economic policy, *International Debt, the Banks and US Foreign Policy* (Washington DC: USGPO, 1976), and T. Brett, *International Money and Capitalist Crisis* (London: Heinemann, 1983) pp. 175–88.

7   IMF, *World Economic Outlook 1983* (Washington DC: IMF, 1983), pp. 140–4.
8   S. Griffith Jones and R. H. Green, *African External Debt and Development* (Brighton: Institute of Development Studies, 1984), pp. 36–41.
9   UNIDO, *Industrial Indebtedness in Africa*, IS.217 (Vienna: UNIDO, 1985).
10 Under the guidance of no less an economist than Professor Milton Friedman.
11 UNCTAD, *Trade and Development Report 1985* (n. 1), p. 68.
12 Bank for International Settlements, *Fifty Third Annual Report 1985* (Zurich: BIS, 1985), p. 68.
13 According to the Governer of the Central Bank of Brazil, they were able to borrow 'automatically' at the rate of $1.5 billion a month in the Eurocurrency market during the first half of 1982 (*Eurocurrency*, October 1983, p. 20).
14 The relationship between the international banks, the IMF and LDC governments in the debt renegotiation process is described in J. A. Ansari, *The Political Economy of International Economic Organisation* (Brighton: Wheatsheaf, 1986), pp. 73–80. See also pp. 231–4 above.
15 These proposals are referred to as 'the Baker initiative' after the then US Secretary for Trade, James Baker. For a fuller discussion of these proposals see J. A. Ansari and H. W. Singer, 'International financial reform and the developing countries: Is Keynesianism irrelevant?' (forthcoming). On the changed role of the IMF and the World Bank within the international financial system see T. Hayter, 'The World Bank and the IMF', *Third World Quarterly*, April 1986.
16 Chapter 11 addresses the question of international financial reform.
17 This is discussed in Chapters 7 and 8.
18 For evidence on this, see, for example, B. Balassa, 'Adjustment policies in developing countries: A reassessment', *World Development*, 12(9), 1984, pp. 960–9.
19 UNCTAD, *Trade and Development Report 1985* (n. 1), p. 83.
20 UNIDO, *Industrial Development Review: United Republic of Tanzania*, I.S 628 (Vienna: UNIDO, April 1986), pp. 1–3, 32–6.
21 UNCTAD, *Trade and Development Report 1985*, (n. 1), p. 90.
22 On the relationship between debt servicing, investment and export growth, see R. E. Feinberg and V. Kellalilog, *Adjustment Crisis in the Third World* (New Brunswick, NJ: Overseas Development Council, 1984) and W. Cline, *International Debt and the Stability of the World Economy* (Washington DC: Institute of International Economics, 1983).
23 United Nations Commission for Latin America and the Caribbean, 'Preliminary overviews of the Latin American economy, in 1986 (Santiago, 1985), mimeo, p. 17.
24 These proposals are discussed in detail in S. Griffith Jones, 'Ways forward from the debt crisis', *Oxford Review of Economic Policy*, 2(1), 1985, pp. 39–61.

25 W. Cline, *International Debt: Systemic Risk and Policy Response* (Washington DC: MIT Press, 1984).

26 See e.g. H. Wallich, *Insurance of Bank Lending to Developing Countries* (New York: Group of Thirty, 1984).

27 F. Bergestein, F. W. Cline and J. Williamson, *Bank Lending to Developing Countries, the policy alternatives* (Washington DC: MIT Press, 1985).

28 Griffith Jones (n. 24), p. 47.

29 Wallich (n. 26), pp. 17–23.

30 H. Lever, 'The international debt crisis: a concerted way out', *The Economist*, 9 July 1983. The proposal is discussed at some length in Griffith Jones (n. 24), pp. 49–51.

31 For a description of Keynes' original proposal about the ICU (as contained in the 1942 White Paper), see G. Moggridge (ed.), *Collected Works of John Maynard Keynes* (London: Macmillan, 1980), vol. 25, pp. 310–23.

32 Griffith Jones (n. 24), pp. 52–3.

33 Such a proposal has been developed by P. Leslie, 'Techniques, of rescheduling', *The Banker*, April 1983.

34 S. Page, *Economic Prospects for the Third World* (London: Overseas Development Institute, 1973), p. 12.

10   The Multinational Corporation in the Developing Countries

One of the more important changes that have taken place in the thinking of development economists since the 1960s has been the shift in the analysis of the effects of foreign investment on LDCs. Not so long ago the mainstream of economic thinking directed attention on the foreign investor as a provider of capital. Nowadays we are much more concerned with the role that the foreign investor plays in the process of the transfer of technology from the rich metropolis to the poor periphery. In other words, the modern economist is principally worried about the *quality* of foreign investment, i.e. about the effect of a given unit of foreign investment on factor productivity. If (as has been argued throughout this book) the dependence of the poor countries on the rich is fundamentally technological in nature, an elimination of this dependence will require an international diffusion of technological knowledge. It is surely right, therefore, to concentrate on the role of the foreign firm as an agent of technology transfer to the LDCs.

Colonial Private Investment

Why is that foreign private investment has never in the past been an important instrument of the transfer of technology to the LDCs, whereas in the now developed countries it has played a very important role in the process of technology transfer? In order to understand this difference in impact let us look at the pattern of international investment in the heyday of colonialism.

In 1914, the stock of long-term international investment was equal to $44,000 million, of which $24,500 million was invested in Europe and the United States and $19,500 million in Latin America and Asian countries (Africa's share was very small). The major creditors were the United Kingdom, France and Germany; the major debtors were the United States (up to about 1900, when it became a creditor), Canada, Australia, New Zealand, South Africa, Argentina and India.[1]

Up until 1914, portfolio investment in the form of bonds and debt investments was a much more important component of international financial flows than was direct foreign investment: in 1914, about 70 per cent of total UK and French long-term investment consisted of government and railway bonds.[2] The governments of the debtor countries borrowed heavily on the foreign capital market for the purpose of infrastructure investment and in order to protect the convertibility of their domestic currencies. Despite the fact that the major international borrowers were the governments of the capital-importing countries, the lenders were invariably private individuals.

There were important variations in the pattern described above as far as the LDCs were concerned. It is generally acknowledged that the fundamental difference in the role of foreign investment in Europe and North America, on the one hand, and the African, Asian and Latin American countries, on the other, lay in the nature of the relationship between foreign and domestic investors. Foreign investors in Europe and North America were controlled by a national government that was prepared to tolerate foreign investment only to the extent that it served the economic interests of the borrowing country. The governments of the non-White colonies, on the other hand, saw their primary responsibility as one of preserving the interests of the colonial power, which was, in ninety-nine cases out of a hundred, the only foreign investor. The government of the borrowing country was the agent of the investing country and was entrusted with the task of contributing to the maintenance of the stability of the imperial system. This was the overriding objective, and commercial and economic interests were all subject to it. Investment was channelled to sectors that were linked to the economy of the investor country. Foreign investment, whether direct or portfolio or controlled by a number of intermediate devices (e.g. the managing agency system in India), was invariably directed to economic activities connected with the export trade of the borrowing economies. The socio-economic infrastructure, the complex of commercial institutions and the structure of production were all geared to increasing the export potential of the colony.

The consequences of such a pattern of development were two-fold. First, and most important, the economy found itself sharply divided into an 'advanced' sector and a 'backward' sector. The advanced sector was logically a periphery of the economic system of the investor country. The backward sector was linked to the advanced sector in a one-way relationship: it provided the advanced sector with the labour force and/or raw materials it required but did not share in the gains that accrued to the advanced sector as a result of international trade.

Second, the advanced sector was advanced only in relation to the rural hinterland in the colony. It used a technology that changed little with the times and was primitive by western standards. The investor in the advanced sector, whether foreign or domestic, was concerned with maximizing export earnings, and this, given the commercial and economic policies of the mother country, could only be done by keeping down costs and maximizing output. Local investors and entrepreneurs were in no position to improvise, through imitation or innovation, an indigenous technology that would allow for an increase in labour productivity. Such innovation has usually taken place behind high tariff walls when foreign investment has been used by the protectionist country to supplement the national development effort. Lacking governments that could develop such policies, it was inevitable that the colonies remained incapable of using foreign investment as a vehicle of technology transfer.

Both these characteristics – economic dualism and an inability to assimilate and adopt sophisticated and advanced technologies – have been, as it were, built into the structure of most underdeveloped economies. Economic theory, especially since the seminal work of Gunnar Myrdal,[3] has held that private investment within the colonial framework and the pattern of international trade that goes with it have been the prime factors that have led to the growth of this structural deformity in most LDCs. It is natural therefore that the poor countries have been rather wary of private investment in the recent past and have in general tried to control inflowing private capital, so as to use it in a way that is complementary to their achievement of long-run development targets.

Modern Foreign Private Investment

After the Second World War, most of the colonies attained political independence. Consequently the climate for foreign investment changed dramatically. Foreign private investment had now to deal with an environment in which the major preoccupation of the government was with the achievement of rapid and sustained development. The centre–periphery relationship fostered by the previous colonial administration, and to which foreign private investors had – willingly or unwillingly – geared their activities, was now viewed with abhorrence. The management of the foreign enterprise in a newly independent LDC was faced with the challenge of re-orienting its business so as to make it appear acceptable to the new government. The development of the multinational corporation (MNC) has enabled foreign private enterprise to develop an adaptability that is nothing short of amazing. Barring a very few exceptions, underdeveloped countries have eagerly sought direct foreign investment and collaboration with multinational corporations. Even the USSR, China and most Eastern European countries have tried to secure foreign participation in industrial development on a long-term basis. The spate of nationalization that threatened to destroy the 'empire' of the large multinationals seems to have halted. The developing countries and the multinational companies, after an initial period of mutual distrust, suspicion and intolerance – intensified briefly in the aftermath of the Arab-Israeli War of October 1973 – are slowly grasping the fact that they cannot wish each other out of existence! Both the multinationals and the LDCs are relatively permanent units of economic activity. They cannot afford either to ignore each other or to launch a full-scale war. They must work towards compromises in which each party sees that its basic interests are being promoted.

There is some evidence that compromises of this sort are gradually emerging. The most important evidence lies in the increasing volume of foreign private investment in the LDCs. Total foreign investment to the poor countries from the DAC members has increased from an annual average of $3.1 billion in 1960 to about $21 billion in 1983, of which direct investment now constitutes about one-third.[4] Between 1971 and 1981, foreign investment in LDCs rose at an annual average of 2–3 per cent in real terms. On the other hand, bilateral official concessional flows from the OECD countries remained stagnant. The share of private flows in total financial transfers from the developed to the developing countries increased from 43.1 per cent in 1970 to 54.0 per cent in 1981. By 1983 the share had fallen to 41.9 per cent (Statistical Appendix, Table S.5), indicating that the recession had led to a significant contraction of foreign private investment. Moreover, whereas until 1973 direct foreign investment had grown considerably more rapidly than portfolio investment in the poor countries, the trends were reversed during 1973–81, with commercial bank lending growth substantially exceeding the growth of direct foreign investment (see Table S.4). In 1973, direct investment accounted for about 51 per cent of total private flows to LDCs, whereas the share of bilateral portfolio investment (including commercial bank lending) was only 8.6 per cent. In 1983, the share of direct foreign investment had declined to 38.1 per cent and that of portfolio investment had increased to 53.9 per cent. However, the contraction of bank lending during the recession has been much more pronounced than the corresponding decline in direct foreign investment: the annual flow of portfolio investment declined from $22.6 billion in 1981 to $11.4 billion in 1983, while direct foreign investment to the LDCs fell from $12.2 billion to $8.1 billion over the same period (Table S.4). A rapid increase in direct investment flows to the LDCs is not particularly likely, whereas an improvement in the international policy-making environment can be expected to have a substantial positive impact on the flow of commercial bank lending even in the short run. (This theme is developed in Chapter 9.)

Direct foreign investment has remained heavily concentrated in a small number of developing countries. As Table 10.1 shows, twenty-seven middle-income countries have accounted for over 90 per cent of the total, and within this a very small number of countries – Brazil and Mexico, joined more recently by Singapore and Malaysia – dominate the figures. Of the 1973 total, just over 50 per cent went to these four countries; by 1981, their share was about 60 per cent. Even among these, it was the largest source of finance only for Singapore and Malaysia. Foreign investment is, however, probably more important than this might indicate in manufacturing in most of the countries listed in Table 10.1. A high proportion, frequently as much as 50 per cent, comes from reinvested earnings. This and the evidence on the direction of flows suggest a serious limitation on foreign investment as a source of finance – its concentration in a very limited number of countries and the slowness with which any changes, in level or in distribution, are likely to take place.

For the last twenty-five years, the United States has been the major source of investment flows to developing countries, on average responsible for over half the total. Japan has increased its share, taking second place, while France and West Germany have also increased their outflows. British investment has not risen, so that its share has fallen sharply. It is important to put these trends in the context of these countries' total foreign investment. Developing countries account for about half of Japan's investment abroad, while the US and British share is under a quarter, with France and West Germany even lower.

Latin America and Asia are important for both the United States and Japan. Recently, Japan has shifted more towards Asia, where its flows are approaching the US level. The distribution among host countries within Asia and Latin America is similar for the United States and Japan.

Excluding some special cases of banking countries, most US

Table 10.1 *Net foreign direct investment to LDCs, 1973–83*

	1973–8	*1979–83*
Total	$20.82 billion	$53.30 billion
27 LDCs	73.9 per cent	91.9 per cent
Asia (as % of total)	36 per cent	38 per cent
Singapore (as % of total)	(14 per cent)	(16 per cent)
Malaysia (as % of total)	(10 per cent)	(11 per cent)
Latin America (as % of total)	57 per cent	50 per cent
Brazil (as % of total)	(36 per cent)	(21 per cent)
Mexico (as % of total)	(16 per cent)	(16 per cent)
Africa (as % of total)	7 per cent	13 per cent

Sources: IMF, *International Financial Statistics* (Washington, DC: IMF, January 1985); IMF, *Foreign Private Investment in Developing Countries* (Washington DC: IMF 1985).

investment in developing countries is in manufacturing or mining, with chemicals and machinery the most important. For Japan, mining also has a large share, particularly in Asia, in line with the traditional view of Japanese investment as a means of ensuring supplies of raw materials for Japan; within manufactures, metals, chemicals and textiles have been important. For France, commercial and, more recently, financial services and energy have been important.[5]

Direct foreign investment is then not the most important source of external finances for the vast majority of LDCs. However, as noted earlier, the main provider of direct foreign investment – the MNC – is generally regarded as a key actor in the international technology markets. Developing country governments seek to develop a working relationship with the MNC that will induce it to transfer appropriate technology on mutually advantageous terms to the Third World. In the next section we shall examine the nature of the relationship between the MNC and Third World governments with a view to assessing the scope for enhancing the contribution the multinationals can make towards the economic development of the poor countries.

Multinational Corporations and the LDCs

The multinational corporation is a comparatively recent phenomenon in the world of business and industry. Conventional economic theory has not been very useful in helping to form a correct appreciation of the behaviour of a typical multinational firm. However, developments in the theory of the growth of the firm have provided an analytical framework within which the operations of the multinational can be meaningfully studied.

The large multinational corporation has been likened to a large self-governing bureaucracy, mainly independent of the control of both its shareholders and financiers. Autonomy, however, does not imply omnipotence, as the firm is subject to pressure from many groups (e.g. the government of the home country, the government of the countries where it is investing, the press and international agencies). The large multinational cherishes its independence in the business world, and sets great store by the ability of a firm to increase its growth rate on the one hand and its rate of self-financing on the other. Therefore, in the subsequent analysis it will be assumed that (1) the overall objective of the typical multinational is to maximize long-run profits, and (2) the multinational also tends to maximize the rate of retention out of the earnings of the company over time.

The multinational corporation has to pursue these objectives on a worldwide basis, and this naturally leads to a number of special problems. First, multinationals have a 'dominant' nationality,[6] i.e. that of the parent company, regardless of the nationality of affiliates, licensees or junior partners. The dominant nationality is important because most of the shareholders of the parent company are likely to share its nationality and because the foreign investment of a multinational is treated as the investment of the country in which the parent is incorporated. There will usually be a flow of funds from the firm as a whole to the citizens of the country of the parent company (as they are the main shareholders). This involves, among other things, a movement of funds away from the economies in which the subsidiaries of the multinational are operating. The dominant nationality of the multinational also determines to a large extent its use of personnel, equipment and technology. Firms tend to buy factor services and technical equipment from their own country, 'not necessarily because they are concerned with nationality as such but . . . because they are accustomed to certain ways of doing things'.[7]

Second, the retained profits of the multinational corporation represent its savings, some of which may have arisen because the corporation has had monopoly power to influence prices in the markets of foreign countries. The reduction in consumption that has made this saving possible has been spread over a number of economies. The investment of retained income has been similarly spread. There is, of course, no correspondence in the geographic distribution of the savings and investments of the multinational.

All multinational corporations are integrated across national frontiers, either horizontally, vertically or both. A high degree of integration inevitably introduces an important element of arbitrariness in allocating overhead costs to different operations and in setting the prices of the goods that pass from one subsidiary to another. Usually these price adjustments reflect the desire of the corporation to take advantage of tax differentials between different areas in which it is operating. Generally speaking, multinationals are in a better position to avoid taxation in a given country than are national firms. With a high degree of vertical integration, a multinational has great scope for adjusting *transfer prices*. This is bound to affect the distribution of income within countries. The governments of the countries in which the multinational has made investments in one form or another are naturally concerned with the danger of the deterioration of the balance-of-payments position of their country as a consequence of the pricing policy of the corporation. Thus the government's trade, tariff, tax and economic policies are, in a sense, a constraint on the multinational, which is therefore inevitably involved in a process of protracted negotiations with the host governments. These negotiations determine the extent to which the corporation is allowed to pursue policies that would lead to a maximization of profits and/or retained income.

The multinational corporation's behaviour can best be analysed in the context of an oligopolistic or duopolistic model. In a typical LDC economy, the multinational is in competition with the public sector and a few large national firms. Its course of action is circumscribed by the agreements with the local government that determine its area of operation. The following propositions, put forward by Rothschild as early as 1947, concerning the behaviour of oligopolistic producers, describe the pricing policy of the typical multinational:[8]

- Price rigidity is an essential aspect of normal oligopolistic price strategy.
- Oligopoly leads to a multitude of conditions surrounding the quoted price.
- Under oligopoly the price tends to be the outcome of a variety of conflicting tendencies within the firm.
- Price wars, while tending to occur infrequently, are a dominant feature of the oligopolistic situation. Preparation for them leads to the adoption of measures that are peculiar to oligopoly.

In other words, the rigidity of the price structure indicates that the multinational may forgo short-run advantages if these endanger the overall security of its interests or investments in a given country.

What is the likely impact of investment undertaken by an

economic organization of this type on the economic performance of a typical Third World country? Dunning has shown that the extent to which an MNC is likely to be interested in investment abroad is determined by three main factors:

1 the extent to which it possesses ownership-specific advantages, in the form of production technology, marketing, purchasing or organization skills relative to its competitors in a given market;
2 the extent to which it finds it profitable to use these advantages itself – i.e. 'internalize' them rather than lease or sell them to firms in foreign countries;
3 the extent to which it is profitable to combine mobile ownership advantages with the relatively immobile resources located in foreign countries.

Neo-classical theory suggests that the greater the ownership advantages of an MNC that can be exploited by production abroad, the greater is its likely positive impact on the economic structures of both the home and the host country. The international distribution of investment and production that such a strategy generates, however, may not be regarded as optimal or desirable by a host LDC. Dunning himself recognizes that

the common ownership of production by MNCs may lead to the concentration of high value added activities in some countries and less value added activities in others. From the point of view of the firm (concerned with short run profit maximisation) this may be the most sensible strategy. But it may freeze a host country into an existing and unacceptable international division of labour.[9]

Divergence between the perspectives and strategies of the MNCs and their host (and sometimes also home) governments is particularly pronounced in the area of what is now generally referred to as 'rationalized production'. This is production undertaken not on the basis of differences in international comparative advantages but on the basis of the exploitation of economies external to a given subsidiary (located, say, in a developing country) but internal to the MNC. In such a situation the corporate strategies of MNCs are more important determinants of the international distribution of invest-

249

ment than differences in national resource endowment. The growth of rationalized production has accelerated in recent years,[10] largely in association with the corresponding growth of *intra-firm trade* – that is, trade between the subsidiaries of the same multinational family. In the early 1970s it was estimated that intra-firm exports accounted for over a quarter of all US exports.[11] This share has undoubtedly grown substantially in recent years and with it has grown the scope for both transfer pricing and rationalized production.[12]

LDCs have attempted to develop a policy environment to boost the impact of MNC investment within their economies. A liberal economic policy stance by the government enhances the contribution of MNCs to the development process – although it also increases their ability to transfer resources abroad if they so desire. The international environment is an equally important determinant of MNC behaviour; in recent years, movements of funds have often reflected variations and expected variations in foreign exchange markets. Similarly, the structure of international *intermediate* product markets is also likely to be an important determinant of MNC investment decisions. Thus, whereas the MNC clearly has the potential to raise the technical efficiency of developing countries, by employing a more efficient technology and by developing subcontracting and other forms of linkages with local firms, it is not always the case that it will be induced to realize this potential. The spillover and linkage effect of MNC investment in developing countries has generally been low and it has directly and indirectly generated relatively few jobs in the Third World. Manufacturing MNCs employ only about 2 per cent of the industrial labour force of the Third World and total employment provided by all MNCs in the poor countries did not exceed 4 million in the late 1970s.[13] If the domestic market is small, MNC investment might lead to a squeezing out of local firms and a consequent increase in the concentration of economic power.[14] Furthermore, MNCs prefer to centralize their R&D activities in their home countries: currently about 90 per cent of the R&D expenditure of American MNCs is undertaken in the home country. The corresponding figure for the UK is 85 per cent and for West Germany 90 per cent.[15] Even when some R&D is undertaken in a host economy subsidiary – and this is very rarely the case as far as LDCs are concerned – by an MNC its parent company will retain control over its type and usage and there is no guarantee that it will be profitable to use such technological capacity in a way consistent with the long-term development goals of the host country.

The nature of the multinational corporation is the main determinant of the pattern of its investment in the developing countries. It contributes to the development process in order to maximize its gains by operating in an environment that gives it a chance to make a profit. A development process that is being sustained by organizations interested primarily in profit maximization is organically different from a development process in which the public sector sets the pace. The former is likely to generate tendencies that accentuate income inequalities within the developing country. In particular, the employment problems of an LDC are likely to be increased as a consequence of large-scale investment by a typical multinational. The direct effect of the multinational's investment is largely confined to the employment of a small, elite, semi-skilled and highly skilled labour force, the members of which earn incomes that are substantially higher than the incomes of the domestic labour class. The indirect effect of investment undertaken by the multinational depends upon the willingness and ability of domestic enterprises to adapt to the production and marketing techniques devised by the corporation and of the government of the LDC to tax the profits earned by it.

Nevertheless much hope has been placed on the multinational corporation as an agent of development. It is the only world organization that has to date demonstrated its ability to integrate vertically entire industries and to integrate horizontally economic activities over a very widely spread area. The multinational has been undergoing an unending metamorphosis in order to be able to exploit its own growth potential. The typical multinational is forever seeking new markets and devising new products. It possesses an extremely flexible internal organizational structure – new production and marketing processes can be adopted and old ones discarded with a minimum of friction. Moreover, the financial strength and manoeuvring capability of the organization allow its managers to develop a corporate strategy with a very long view and very wide horizon. It is inevitable, therefore, that the multinational will seek to integrate the world economy in order to take the fullest possible advantage of the potential of such an organization.

What form will this integration take? And will it be a good or a bad thing from the point of view of the developing countries? Here there is a sharp division between 'the Right' and 'the Left' among academic economists. The Right has come up with a theory of the 'withering away of the state', based ironically enough on work by Professor Galbraith (who himself can hardly be called a 'Right' economist). Galbraith's thesis of the domination of the US economy by what he calls 'the technostructure' has been used by economists of the Right to argue that the multinational is the first truly international economic organization that has evolved in human history.[16] The multinational will raise capital in those parts of the world where funds can be obtained cheaply, invest these funds where labour costs are low and thus tend to equalize factor incomes all over the world. The Left insists that such a transfer process will never occur, mainly because the integration that can take place under the multinational is unlikely to reduce international inequalities.[17]

If the multinational corporation is to be an important agent of development and if the type of integration that it aims at promoting is to contribute towards an elimination of international inequalities, surely its main impact must be on factor productivity in LDCs. The Right argues that an increase in factor productivity will be brought about by a gradual process of technology transfers from the developed to the developing countries. The Left disagrees with this position. This question is of the utmost importance, because the economic division of the world between the developed and underdeveloped countries is – as this book has argued throughout – determined primarily by the technological advancement of the former and technological backwardness of the latter. The unequal relationship between 'North' and 'South' is characterized by the technological dependence of the latter on the former. If, and only if, the multinational demonstrates an ability to reduce this dependence, can it be argued that it is capable of promoting international development. What is the potential of the multinational corporation as an agency for the transfer of technology to the LDCs?

The Multinational Corporation and Technology Transfer[18]

Professor Vernon has argued that, for many years to come,

developing economies will not be in a position to develop modern science-based industries. He has developed the now well-known technological gap theory of trade,[19] which runs in terms of a product cycle. It is in only the second stage, i.e. perhaps many years after the commercialization of a given innovation, that the developing economies can hope to start producing the commodity concerned. The increased emphasis on the production of capital-intensive and research-intensive goods in the developed countries may not be totally disadvantageous from the point of view of the developing economies. Ideally, the importing of technically superior goods should increase the technological potential and absorptive capacity of the developing economy.

The multinational corporation has been a source of technology transfer to the underdeveloped countries. Broadly speaking, the problems it has faced are related to certain institutional characteristics of underdeveloped economies. These are problems of adjusting the needs and demands of science-based industries to traditional industries, problems of the replacement of conventional techniques and patterns of production by new methods, problems of technological bottlenecks and problems of adequate social and economic responsiveness to rapid structural change.

Technology transfer takes place in many forms, the most usual being either direct investment or some form of cooperation between the multinational corporation and domestic enterprises. The following paragraphs discuss problems that arise when the transfer takes the forms of direct investment, joint ventures, licensing, and management contracts and sales.

Direct investment

The multinational corporation invests in underdeveloped countries with a view to taking advantage of expansion in demand as the economy of the country in question develops or to protecting its stake in the market, which might be threatened by tariff barriers. Very little investment by MNCs has been undertaken in LDCs with a view to exploiting export opportunities. MNC investment in the developing countries is more likely to come from firms already involved in the market of the country concerned than from new investors. This is to be expected because the insider has greater knowledge about the potentialities of a project within the economy and because the cost to him of investing may be less than to an outsider, owing to the existence of a network of distribution and sales organizations under his control.

Having decided to invest in a developing economy, a multinational corporation has to tackle the important problem of how best to manage the local subsidiary unit that has been set up. In the developing economies, successful growth and production demand efficient top-quality management. The managers of the overseas subsidiary of the multinational face several special problems: the operating environment differs from that of the home country; the subsidiary is open to criticism from public opinion in the host country; often nationals with different, and possibly inferior, levels of technical training have to be employed; managers have to be locally recruited; and 'special' relations with the government of the host country have to be worked out. As a result of all these factors there is a tendency to leave at home potentially useful technical concepts and managerial techniques and practices. This is particularly so in the areas of labour management, production control and procurement, which are generally under local supervision.

Thus, direct investment by the multinational corporations tends to be restricted to a relatively small group of industries, which either can easily be controlled from the metropolis or do not require rapid changes in production and marketing methods. The growth of both of these types of industries cannot be expected to contribute directly, to a significant extent, towards the diffusion of technical and scientific knowledge within the LDC.

Joint ventures

Multinational corporations seek local collaboration for a wide range of reasons. The most important is the need for local intermediaries in order to cope with officialdom, to obtain licences and to get sympathetic interpretation of regulations. Mediation with local financiers is another incentive to collaboration, particularly for firms primarily interested in the sale of know-how and licences and for firms that wish to keep their own financial commitments to a minimum. Local partners also usually handle sales, labour relations and publicity. In developing economies, when partnerships take place there seems to be a rigid functional specialization: the multinational deals mainly with technical operations, management, foreign supplies and finance; the local partner plays the role of mediator and deals directly with the local market. Joint ventures between MNCs and public sector enterprises have become increasingly popular in Latin America and East Asia.

In general, developing economies have tended to prefer the purchase of licences and know-how to the establishment of joint ventures, and the establishment of joint ventures to the setting up of independent subsidiaries by the multinational corporation. On the other hand, there seems to be very definite preference on the part of multinational corporations for wholy owned affiliates. It is widely believed that United States parent companies move towards a partnership only when they are pushed to do so. European companies share these tendencies.

There are many reasons why a multinational corporation should seek control of a foreign enterprise. Fundamental is the inherent logic of the process of efficient management, which demands effective centralization and coordination of decision-making. Furthermore, in developing areas especially, situations are likely to emerge in which the global strategy of a multinational may necessitate the adoption of policies or actions that may be detrimental to the interests of the domestic enterprise or public authority of the country concerned.

On the whole, joint ventures tend to work better in developed countries because the contracting partners are of equal bargaining strength and possess similar technical and managerial potential. When multinational corporations set up joint ventures in developing countries, the scope for misunderstanding, mistrust and suspicion is greater, as the junior partner is usually not in a position to assess the deal that the multinational offers. Moreover, the junior partner is unable to contribute towards the evolution and development of a technology that would allow the corporation to make a better use of the resources of the LDCs. Hence joint ventures between multinational corporations and local enterprises also tend to be confined to industries that use the technology developed largely in the rich countries. Joint ventures have not proved to be better channels of technology transfer to the LDCs than the subsidiaries of the multinationals.

255

Licensing

Licensing an independent company to use the patents and trademarks of the multinational corporation is becoming an increasingly important source of technology transfer – more important than the licensing of affiliates. The reasons for licensing a subsidiary are usually financial or legal. If exchange restrictions favour the remission of royalties paid for know-how or patents rather than the remission of dividends, or if there is a tax advantage, the multinational may choose to license or sell patents to its subsidiary.

The possibility of a profitable return on royalties is a major inducement for licensing. Non-royalty income in the form of dividends may also be sought. Trade restrictions and restrictions on currency remittance may also provide an important reason for licensing. Import controls have been another major stimulus to licensing. Licences may become relatively useless, however, if import policy does not permit the import of the equipment necessary to make the licence worthwhile.

The expansion of business at home and the drive world-wide to keep up with new developments are in themselves an important incentive for licensing, because the results of research in the developed countries thus become available for transfer abroad. Between countries of the developed world, licensing has tended to increase significantly: about 85 per cent of all licenses are given to firms in the developed countries. The relative sophistication of production techniques has a bearing on the decision of the multinational corporation whether to invest or to give licences for goods with short product cycles (e.g. pharmaceuticals). In underdeveloped areas, licensing is generally easy for the multinational, since the technological gap between it and the licensee is great and (usually) offers no threat to the corporation's technological leadership. However, for industries where research and development costs represent a high proportion of expenditure, the multinational usually prefers to make direct investment. Furthermore, in considering whether to enter into a licensing arrangement, the technical absorptive capacity of the recipient firm is also a major factor.

The areas of conflict between the parent and recipient firms with respect to technology transfer involve pricing, ownership and long-run technological development. These factors are usually affected by competition among parent firms, the relative bargaining power of the contracting partners and the policy of the host governments. It is commonly the developing countries' view that the price of technology is too high. They prefer licensing to foreign control. On the other hand, multinational corporations usually prefer direct investment to licensing in LDCs, the desire to maintain the quality of the product being cited as one reason for this preference.

The main reason for the meagre use of licences by multinational corporations lies first of all in the inappropriateness for the LDCs of the technology used in the developed countries. Second, the weak financial position of firms in the poor countries has reduced their bargaining power vis-à-vis the multinationals. This factor, along with their limited technological absorptive capacity and low marketing and production capabilities, makes them reluctant to invest in new technology, whether in the form of machinery or human commital. The multinationals, on the other hand, consider many firms in the LDCs to be incapable of assimilating technical know-how and hence prefer direct investment to licensing.

Management contracts

The shortage of skilled personnel is an important characteristic of developing countries. Most of the top-level managerial staff employed by, for example, US multinational corporations have to be imported from the United States. Where joint ventures are set up, the multinational has to supply most of the technical and managerial staff, since it is usually responsible for the technical side of the business. Know-how is purchased from the multinational if it holds a minority interest in a joint venture.

Technical assistance agreements are also made between multinational corporations and their subsidiaries in foreign countries or independent foreign firms. Payment is usually on a royalty basis, but sometimes fixed sums are stipulated. In some cases, know-how is built in to a foreign plant constructed by the multinational but payment is extended over a longer period and may not take the form of royalties on net sales.

Technical assistance contracts usually accompany patent or

trademark agreements. To use the patent, special knowledge may be required, and if the seller refuses to disclose all the necessary knowledge along with the patent the technical assistance agreement becomes vital. Special techniques, for example, may be necessary to maintain the quality of a product or to produce it efficiently. Technical assistance may take the form of a guarantee on the part of the multinational to inform foreign firms of all developments in this product line. Technical assistance programmes include product specifications and layouts, formulas, 'trade secrets', selling techniques and the training of technical personnel. In developing economies, such agreements – both technical and managerial – are indispensable if foreign participation is desired. Usually they are part of the overall policy of a multinational corporation when it is investing in or collaborating with firms in developing economies.

The most important constraint on the multinational corporation as an agent of technology transfer to the developing countries has been the nature and character of modern technology itself. Expenditure on scientific and technological research is made with a view to the requirements of the developed countries. Much of the new science and technology has little or nothing to contribute towards the solution of the problems of the LDCs. Some of it is positively harmful, not merely in a global sense (typified by the increasing pollution consequent on industrial and urban growth) but also in a specific sense. For example, the development of a number of synthetics has been, at least in the short run, of very real disadvantage to the primary-producing LDCs.

Technological development that is of relevance to the LDCs can take place within a number of organizations: international bodies, government agencies (in both LDCs and developed countries), consultant firms and multinational corporations. It is conceivable that the multinationals could contribute significantly towards the development of the relatively more sophisticated technologies (e.g. communications technology, agricultural technology and technology used by the pharmaceutical industry) in accordance with the requirements of the LDCs. This would require a change in production methods and marketing techniques – the multinationals produce with methods that take the fullest advantage of economies of scale, and such economies of scale are, of course, unattainable in the large majority of small LDCs. The multinationals would have to explore the possibility of producing for small markets. More importantly, they would have to grapple with the problem of devising a capital-saving technology that nevertheless is efficient; a labour-intensive technology that inhibited the growth of factor productivity would be self-defeating in purpose. There is some evidence that modern 'best practice' production technology, usually thought of as capital-intensive, actually economizes on all factors of production. Moreover, as labour skill increases in the LDCs, a sophisticated and relatively capital-intensive technology will be required. This points to the fact that the transfer of technology to the LDCs involves the creation of an international institutional structure that will arrange for the provision of a bundle of embodied and disembodied technology suitable for the resource potential of the developing country concerned and one that will alter with the changes in the quality and quantity of the factors of production in the LDC.

Technology transfer and offshore assembly

MNC investment in LDCs often has the effect of integrating them within the 'high-technology' industries; the manufacture of computer punch cards in South America is an example of this form of participation. A multinational may ship the many components of a manufactured product to a low-wage country for assembly and processing and re-export the half-finished product to the metropolitan countries. A large number of LDCs have established 'enclaves' that the multinationals use for activity of this sort.

Even if the short-run effects of such investment are beneficial in terms of income generation within the LDC, it seems unlikely that the process of technology transfer from the developed to the developing countries will be adequately modified as a consequence of investment in such assimilating and processing plants by the multinational corporations. The technology employed in such ventures is invariably of an unskilled labour-intensive type that tries to capitalize on the relatively lower labour costs prevalent in the LDC. The backward and forward linkage effects of such production processes are likely to be low within the LDC: these linkage effects are produced within the production structure of the multinational itself. Similarly, the nature of the technology used by the multinational in manufacturing for export also precludes the possibility that the 'learning' effect of such investment will be substantial. The multinational is simply not interested in a diffusion of skill within the LDC when it sets up a processing plant in a low-wage country, for it requires such skill further along the production line. Furthermore, the development of manufacturing for export by multinationals tends to increase the technological and financial dependence of the LDCs on the rich countries. The export-processing 'enclave' is completely unintegrated with the rest of the economy of the LDC: it is totally integrated into the marketing and production structure of the multinational. The LDC that possesses this enclave is in an extremely weak bargaining position vis-à-vis the corporation, for the MNC is its only buyer. Since activities of this sort are extraordinarily 'foot-loose', the multinational is forever threatening the poor country with shifting production. The LDC is at the mercy of the multinational, and decisions about plant location, product diversification, market allocation and choice of technique cannot be made without the consent of the foreign firm. It is unthinkable that a large-scale diffusion of appropriate technical knowledge to the LDCs can take place when their governments are for all practical purposes powerless before the multinationals.

The multinational corporation and the government of a developing country find themselves at cross purposes rather frequently. However, the multinational is perhaps the only organization that will in the near future be capable of generating massive flows of embodied and disembodied 'hardware' and 'software' technology to the LDCs. In a world where aid and technical assistance programmes are shrinking daily, the multinational will in all likelihood increase in importance as the agent of technology transfer to the developing countries. None the less, the quantity and quality of the technology supplied by the multinational leaves a great deal to be desired. The form of international economic integration that the multinationals seem to be aiming for will not, at least in the short run, lead to a closing of the gap between the rich and poor countries. It is of extreme importance that the state should not be allowed to 'wither away' in the LDCs but should actively seek to influence the decisions of the multinationals investing in its country. Only then can it be hoped that the MNCs will be induced to consider seriously the adaption of existing technologies and the creation of new technologies so as to meet the specific requirements of the LDCs. South Korea represents an important success story for the development of a mutually beneficial relationship between the MNC and a developing country. The next section tells this story.

Government Policy and Multinationals in South Korea: A Case Study[20]

South Korea has been among the most successful developing countries in the recent past. During the period 1962–82, Korea was transformed from a mainly agricultural to a largely industrialized and modernized economy, registering an annual average real GNP growth rate of 8 per cent. Exports grew at the rate of 35 per cent per annum throughout the 1960s and 1970s. In 1982, manufactured exports accounted for 94 per cent of total export earnings. It is widely recognized that it is the very rapid growth of exports that has been the main determinant of the pace of economic progress.

Korean development was achieved by the execution of a strongly state-interventionist economic strategy, and not by merely reducing market distortions and 'getting the prices right', as the neo-classical economists suggest.[21] In 1962, the government adopted an export-oriented industrialization strategy and has pursued this strategy vigorously ever since. The government also placed emphasis on attracting foreign investment, as a source both of finance and of technological inflow. Throughout the period the government closely monitored the activity of MNCs and attempted to channel investment in accordance with its own sectoral priorities. It did not allow the multinationals to become dominant in any major sector, and MNC investment remains small in comparison with investment undertaken by Korean public and private enterprises, particularly within the manufacturing sector.

MNC investment began in 1962 and was originally located in the area of import substitution of key raw materials. The main import-substituting industries – chemicals and petroleum products – accounted for three-quarters of all foreign investment in South Korea during the 1960s. During the first half of the 1970s some diversification of MNC investment into other domestic demand-oriented industries, such as basic metals, non-synthetic petrochemicals, food processing, paper products and automobiles, also occurred. From the early 1970s, MNCs also became increasingly involved in the export industries – electronics, garments, plastic products and machine parts – as Korea's political stability and suitability as a low-cost, labour-abundant site for sourcing-type investments became widely known. In the late 1970s and 1980s, foreign investment was increasingly concentrated in the heavy industries – chemicals, machinery and electronics.

Over the period 1961–80 the government tightly controlled the approval procedures through which direct foreign investment entered South Korea. Foreign firms were permitted to operate mainly in sectors that were accorded priority in the government's development strategy. Generous tax and other incentives were offered to export-oriented subsidiaries and there were very few restrictions on their operations. On the other hand, the government sought to intervene directly in the planning and operation of large import-substituting subsidiaries, often insisting on their participation in joint ventures with public industrial enterprises. Foreign firms were generally excluded from most domestic demand-oriented consumer goods and service industries. The government has tended actively to discourage the establishment of wholly owned subsidiaries, except in the area of export-oriented or high-technology intensive projects. Domestic enterprises have been induced to acquire and improve technology in the domestic demand-oriented industries producing TVs, washing machines, elevators and even automobiles.

Foreign investment in South Korea has been highly responsive to government policy. MNC growth remained concentrated in the export-oriented industries – in accordance with the government's strategy – throughout the 1970s. Since 1973 the government has emphasized the development of domestic demand-oriented heavy industries such as electronics, machinery, automobiles and other consumer durables. Foreign investment has moved into these branches, despite the fact that government policy has significantly reduced the opportunities for the profitable exploitation of the ownership-specific advantages that the MNCs enjoy in these product areas. Government policy has been a much more important determinant of the intra-industry distribution of foreign investment in South Korea than changes in the country's relative comparative advantage (RCA).[22] Koo found that the correlation coefficient between the inter-sectorial distribution of direct foreign investment and the RCA index was insignificant over the period 1968–80.[23]

The contribution of the MNC subsidiaries to Korean development has been rather limited both in terms of the development of linkages and as sources of technological transfer. As a result, Korean enterprises have developed an independent base of technological and market power over a surprisingly short period of time.[24] The main contribution of MNC affiliates has been the enhancement of allocative efficiency within the domestic economy and the provision of international market access, particularly in the early stages of Korean industrialization. Since 1981 the government has relaxed many of the regulations governing the entry and operation of MNCs in Korea; it is felt that domestic enterprises have now achieved a level of development whereby they can compete effectively with foreign firms.

Many LDC governments have sought to develop coherent policies to influence MNC operations in their countries. However, multinationals have developed an organizational structure that allows them to confront and challenge the decisions of the strongest and most powerful governments in the West. The governments of most Asian and African 'soft states' can hope to have only very limited influences on their policies. The head office of the company is located in Europe or the United States, and it is there that the most important decisions are made. The LDC will find that it has only restricted legal power over the multinational. Moreover, the multinational will be able to circumvent the monetary and fiscal measures undertaken by the government of the LDC – by adjusting the prices of its inputs and outputs at different stages of production, by converting profits into management salaries, by drawing on the head office and other subsidiaries for funds, and by a hundred other methods. All this, of course, creates serious problems of domestic resource allocation as well as balance-of-payments disequilibria. The once frequent use of the technique of wholesale and outright nationalization of foreign enterprises by LDCs reflects mainly increasing frustration at their inability to control the multinationals. If private international investment is to be an agent of development in the future, the problem of increasing the bargaining power of the LDCs vis-à-vis the multinationals will have to be seriously tackled.

Nevertheless, the South Korean example shows that a viable relationship can be developed with the multinationals. The multinationals, it has been seen, are willing to accept a substantial amount of regulation if the economic environment within which they operate is healthy and there are good prospects for enhanced profits and growth.

There are now strong pressures on the developing countries to accept and 'encourage' foreign investment. The World Bank has established a Multilateral Investment Guarantee Agency (MIGA) to supplement national schemes for the promotion of investment. It is expected that the rate of growth of direct foreign investment in the LDCs will accelerate during the next decade.[25] This growth must be accompanied by the development of coherent regulatory policies at both the national and the international level. This should involve a revival of the discussion for the formulation of an international code of conduct for the transnational corporation, which has been stalled within the UN since 1979. Such a code of conduct could provide an essential policy framework for enhancing the development impact of direct foreign investment in the Third World.

Appendix: Third World Multinationals

Since the mid-1960s a small number of LDCs have significantly increased their investment abroad. Over the period 1960–80 the stock of direct investment abroad by Third World transnational corporations (TNCs) increased from $700 million to $14 billion. Developing countries increased their share of global direct foreign investment from 1.04 per cent to 2.73 per cent over this period.[26]

Despite their relative insignificance in global terms, TNCs have in recent years rapidly increased both their size and their range of operation. TNCs cannot of course possess competitive advantages in frontier technologies and advanced marketing. Their comparative advantage must lie in special knowledge of Third World regions, adoption of widely diffused technologies to suit local resource potential and markets, and special managerial skills. This would imply that TNCs could be a particularly suitable source for the transmission of technology from the newly industrializing countries – such as China, India, South Korea and Brazil – to the other poor countries. The technology they deploy could potentially be more suitable in terms of factor price structures and quality conditions obtaining in the poor countries. This might involve the adoption of imported technology or the development of indigenous production processes. Similarly, the products manufactured by the TNCs might be more suitable for Third World markets, reflecting lower incomes, different tastes and a preference for joint consumption. Moreover, TNCs have considerable scope for developing informal marketing networks – through the development of links with buyers – which could overcome the barriers erected by international advertising and mass promotion.

It has been argued that TNCs produce at low costs with small production runs. They thrive in areas where price competition is marked, the scope for product differentiation is limited and there is little need for complete production and market packages. Often they prefer participation in joint ventures to the establishment of a wholly owned subsidiary.[27] The net effect of TNC investment is thus described as a 'de-scaling' – a reduction in the capital intensity of technological process in the Third World that are now obsolete in the West.[28] Sanjaya Lall has argued that 'de-scaling' is only one of a number of technological options available to the TNCs.[29] In many instances no evidence of de-scaling exists and the capital intensity of TNC investment is not significantly different from that of the investment of the traditional MNCs.[30]

TNCs may broadly be divided into two distinct types. Hong Kong based TNCs are specialized in light consumer goods. Their investment is directed to import-substituting industries. They provide management and marketing expertise but export little technology to their host countries. TNCs based in India and China, on the other hand, are large-scale providers of embodied and disembodied technology to host LDCs. These TNCs invest in a whole range of industries from light consumer to heavy capital goods. They are also basically oriented to import substitution and somewhat reluctant to develop export opportunities. Both China and India have developed a high technical capacity, due invariably to government policies that favoured import substitution. This is reflected in the foreign investment of their TNCs. Hong Kong based

TNCs also possess significant technical capacity, but prefer to transfer only relatively low technical processes to host countries. There is some evidence to show that a large MNC presence in a home developing country inhibits the export of embodied technology by its TNCs to other LDCs.[31]

Empirical evidence compiled for TNCs based in Brazil, Argentina and India shows that these firms engage in a wide range of technical development activities in both their home countries and their host LDCs. This included efforts to assimilate and adopt imported technology and to innovate new technical processes from first stages. Export-oriented TNCs – and these are relatively few in number – emphasize improvements in product design. The technological strength of the Indian TNCs lay in their mastery over the basic design and production engineering of various technologies – the technology transferred abroad represented the best at home. As pointed out, there is relatively little evidence of conscious technological de-scaling, except perhaps in the case of the Hong Kong based TNCs.[32]

There is some difference, therefore, in the technological impact of investment undertaken by TNCs on the one hand and the traditional MNCs on the other. TNCs, by transferring a more suitable technology to the developing countries, have created a niche for themselves in these economies. It is important to stress, however, that this does not represent a difference in corporate motivation. As Lall concludes:

> Third World MNCs [are] no better or worse at manipulating the existing structure of host countries than other firms. They are not better 'corporate citizens' than developed countries' MNCs – any observed difference in behaviour . . . [is] simply the consequence of possessing a different . . . set of monopolistic advantages.[33]

Notes

1 The figures are from N. Bloomfield, *The Pattern of Fluctuation in International Investment before 1914*, Princeton Studies in International Finance, No. 21 (Princeton, NJ: 1968), Princeton University Press.
2 *Ibid*. p. 4.

3   G. Myrdal, *Economic Theory and Underdeveloped Areas* (London: Allen & Unwin, 1957).

4   Figures are from DAC, *Development Assistance. 1971* (Paris: OECD, December 1971), p. 89, and UNCTAD, *Handbook of International Trade and Development Statistics 1985* (New York: UN, 1985), pp. 334–8.

5   Figures on which these estimates are based are taken from IMF, *Foreign Private Investment in Developing Countries* (Washington DC: IMF 1985).

6   The term 'the international firm' is a misnomer and may introduce a lot of unnecessary confusion, as it implies that the multinational corporation is in some sense a supernational institution.

7   E. Penrose, *The Large International Firm in Developing Countries* (London: Cambridge University Press, 1968), p. 73.

8   P. Rothschild, 'Prices theory and oligopoly', *Readings in Price Theory* (New York: American Economic Association, 1947).

9   J. H. Dunning, *Multinational Enterprises, Economic Structures and International Competitiveness* (Chichester: Wiley, 1985), pp. 8–9.

10 J. H. Dunning and G. Norman, 'Intra industry production as a form of international economic involvement' in A. Erdilek, *Multinationals as Mutual Invaders* (London: Groom Helm, 1985).

11 S. Lall, 'The pattern of intra firm exports by US multinationals', *Oxford Bulletin of Economics and Statistics*, 40(3), 1979, pp. 209–22.

12 Dunning notes that 'the fastest growth in MNC activity is occurring in sectors in which rationalised investment is taking place . . . There is also evidence of a growing amount of intra industry trade' (Dunning, n. 9, p. 408).

13 For a survey of the literature on the employment impact of MNC investment and the linkages issue, see J. Ansari, R. Ballance and H. Singer, *The International Economy and Industrial Development* (Brighton: Harvester, 1982), Ch. 7. For estimates of MNC employment, see T. Brett, *The World Economy since the War* (London: Macmillan, 1985), Ch. 4.

14 This was the case for example in Singapore during the 1970s. See D. Lecraw, 'Singapore', in J. H. Dunning (ed.), *Multinational Enterprise, Economic Structure and International Competitiveness* (Chichester: Wiley, 1985), pp. 379–406.

15 Dunning (n. 9), p. 419.

16 For Professor Galbraith's description of the role of the technostructure, see J. K. Galbraith, *The New Industrial State* (Harmondsworth: Penguin, 1967). For a view of the Right, see C. Kindleberger, *American Business Abroad* (New Haven, Conn. and London: Yale University Press, 1967), and H. G. Johnson, 'The multinational corporation as an agency of economic development', in B. Ward, *The Widening Gap* (Baltimore, Md: Johns Hopkins University Press, 1972), pp. 242–52.

17 The Left position ranges very widely. See, for example: P. Streeten, 'Costs and benefits of multinational enterprises in LDCs' and R. Murray, 'The internationalisation of capital and the nation state', in J. H. Dunning (ed.), *The Multinational Enterprise* (London: Allen &

Unwin, 1971), pp. 240–59 and; S. L. Hymer, 'The multinational corporation and the law of uneven development', in J. Bhagwati (ed.), *Economics and World Order* (New York: Little Brown & Co., 1970).

18 This section has incorporated some part of H. W. Singer and J. A. Ansari, 'The multinational corporation as agent of technology transfer', OECD CT/4861, 1971, mimeo.

19 R. Vernon, 'International investment and international trade in the product cycle', *Quarterly Journal of Economics*, May 1960.

20 This section is mainly based on B-Y Koo, 'Korea', in J. H. Dunning (ed.), *Multinational Enterprise, Economic Structure and International Competitiveness* (Chichester: Wiley, 1985), pp. 281–308.

21 There exists a vast literature attempting to explain the Korean 'miracle'. See L. G. C. Bradford, 'East Asian models', in J. Lewis and W. Kallah, *Development Strategies Reconsidered* (Washington DC: Overseas Development Council, 1986), pp. 115–28.

22 See Chapter 6, pp 151–2, for a definition of this concept.

23 Koo (n. 20), p. 295.

24 I. Westphal, Y. W. Rhee and G. Pursell, 'Korean industrial competence. Where it came from', World Bank Staff Working Paper No. 469 (Washington DC: 1981), mimeo.

25 IMF, *Foreign Direct Investment in the Developing Countries* (Washington DC: IMF, 1985), pp. 73–7.

26 J. M. Stopford and J. H. Dunning, *Multinationals. Company Performance and Global Trends* (London: Macmillan, 1985), p. 5.

27 These characteristics are enumerated by L. T. Wills, *Third World Multinationals* (Cambridge, Mass: MIT Press, 1984).

28 Ibid, Ch. 6.

29 S. Lall, *The New Multinationals* (Chichester: Wiley, 1983), pp. 11–15, pp. 259–66.

30 D. T. Lecraro, 'Direct investment by firms from LDCs', *Oxford Economic Papers*, 1977, pp. 442–57.

31 The experience of both Brazil and Hong Kong based TMCs may be cited in this context. See Lall (n. 29), pp. 88–136, 220–49.

32 This empirical evidence is summarized in Lall (n. 29), pp. 259–62.

33 Lall (n. 29), p. 267.

11 The International Financial System and the Developing Countries

The Developing Countries in the Bretton Woods Era

The two decades of the Bretton Woods system (1946–71) were characterized by unparalleled steady growth, high levels of employment, very little inflation and gradual movement towards a more equal level of income distribution in the rich OECD countries. Furthermore, this period saw a closing of the income gap between these countries: the poorer economies of the West grew more rapidly than the better-off ones. The developing countries of the South taken as a group also experienced higher levels of growth than in any previous period, although there were divergencies within this group: the better-off Third World countries tended to grow at a faster rate than the poorer ones.

The international monetary and financial system that had been erected in 1944 centred upon the role of the United States within the world economy: the US dollar was the only currency that was directly convertible into gold; all other major currencies were to be linked to the dollar. The International Monetary Fund was given the responsibility of ensuring exchange rate stability. Almost as soon as the IMF began operations it realized that a substantial increase in its resources was essential if it was to fulfil its role effectively. Keynes, who was the leader of the British delegation at the Bretton Woods Conference in 1944, had foreseen that the creation of a new international currency under the control of an international central bank would be essential.[1] The developed countries who dominated the decision-making process took seventeen years to come to this conclusion, and during this period had made extensive swap arrangements. This allowed them to deal adequately with the recurrent 'dollar shortages' that the European countries were facing. This, coupled with the US reluctance to establish an international unit of account that could in time rival – and maybe even supplant – the dollar, ensured that the Group of Ten, which was constituted of the leading western countries, and which was the effective controlling body in international financial negotiation, would not be particularly enthusiastic about the creation of an international reserve asset.

In the middle 1960s the US government gradually became convinced of the need to redefine the role of the dollar within the international monetary system. By 1966 it had endorsed the main recommendations of the Ossola Report, submitted by a group of experts established to study the problems of and prospects for the creation of a new international reserve asset. By 1967 the creation of the Special Drawing Rights (SDRs) facility had become a virtual certainty and in March 1968 the Group of Ten formally approved the First Amendment to the Fund's Articles of Agreement empowering it to create the SDRs.

Negotiations for the approval of the First Amendment were carried on entirely among the members of the Group of Ten. 'The developing countries were absent from these negotiations. Consequently they were unable to win any major concessions.'[2] From the late 1950s the developing countries had been arguing that the Fund had not been able to meet their needs. Despite the fact that many developing countries had joined the Fund during the 1950s they found themselves unable to use the services it had to offer. The Fund simply did not have the orientation or the structure to meet the liquidity requirements of the developing countries. Until the establishment of the Oil Facility in 1975 the Fund was able to offer only short-term financial assistance on very stringent terms. Moreover, the Fund's approach to the problem of the adjustment of balance-of-payments disequilibria has been to place the burden of such adjustment on the deficit countries and to persuade them to adopt deflationary policies. The poor countries have been particularly vulnerable to such pressures[3] and have traditionally been reluctant to accept international surveillance that could impede their development policies.

During the debate on the First Amendment the LDCs believed that a way to increase the usefulness of the IMF from their point of view could be found if a link could be established between an expansion in its resources and an expansion in the volume of aid. The SDR aid link scheme has been extensively elaborated and examined.[4] In 1968, the western countries rejected the proposal to establish a link on the grounds that its institution would mean that donor countries would lose effective control over the level and distribution of their aid programmes. The increase in international liquidity would ensure that the balance-of-payments constraint on aid disbursement would to a large extent be alleviated, but the developed countries clearly did not consider this sufficient to undertake a commitment for augmenting foreign aid. In other words, they demonstrated a reluctance to reduce the political element in the determination of aid volumes. Furthermore, the rich objected to the creation of a mechanism that would automatically transfer resources to the LDCs, as this would encourage them to put into effect policies that might endanger international financial stability. The developed countries argued that the Group of Ten had to remain firmly in control of the IMF if financial indiscipline was to be avoided and the Bretton Woods system was to be preserved.[5] The adoption of the First Amendment thus did little to make the Fund a more effective instrument for serving the international financial requirements of the developing countries. The SDRs were distributed in accordance with the quotas of individual members within the IMF – in the initial years, over two-thirds of SDRs were allocated to the rich countries. No account was taken of the special development needs of the poor countries.

The Poor Countries in a Regime of Floating Exchange Rates

Contrary to developed countries' pronouncements, it was not the Third World that destabilized the Bretton Woods system. In September 1971, President Nixon unilaterally delinked the dollar from gold, and attempts at creating a system of fixed exchange rates have floundered ever since. Furthermore, the early 1970s saw a massive increase in the rates of inflation all over the world despite the strict control that the Group of Ten was supposed to be exercising on the conduct of international money markets. During the period 1974–8 inflationary pressure eased in some western countries but remained strong in others, so that there was a marked increase in the dispersion of national rates of monetary expansion and growth of GDP over this period. For seven industrialized countries – Canada, France, West Germany, Italy, Japan, the United Kingdom and the United States – the dispersion of annual national inflation rates averaged 1.5 per cent over the period 1960–70. During 1972–7 this increased to 4.3 per cent. These high rates of inflation and the rapid increase in the dispersion of national inflation rates were major factors behind the acceleration of exchange rate variability.

Following the Nixon proclamation of September 1971, most major western countries decided to float their currencies. Today, more than four-fifths of world trade is carried out across floating exchange rates.

In the early years of the 1970 decade, attempts were made to reduce exchange rate variability. In December 1971, the Group of Ten initiated the Smithsonian Agreement, which represented a new general realignment of currencies. When, in 1972, it became apparent that this arrangement would have to be abandoned, an *ad hoc* committee – the Committee of Twenty – was appointed to negotiate a reform of the system. This committee consisted of representatives of the twenty constituencies of the IMF that elected or appointed its executive directors, and thus LDC delegates became its members. The poor countries may have seen this as a first step towards the democratization of the Fund – something they had been pressing for since the early 1970s. However, the Committee of Twenty failed to negotiate any major reforms during the two years of its existence.

The period 1973–6 saw the emergence of new difficulties for both the rich and the non-oil-exporting developing countries. In retrospect it can be argued fairly conclusively that the rich industrial countries succeeded in dealing with the unprecedented increases in the price of oil fairly effectively. Taken as a group, the OECD industrialized countries had a deficit on the current account of their balance-of-payments to the tune of US$4 billion in the year 1974. They succeeded in converting it into a $25 billion surplus in 1975, and over the period 1975–9 their annual current account surplus averaged about $16 billion. As against this, non–oil–exporting LDCs had an average annual deficit of almost $32 billion over this period.[6] The rich countries therefore put a premium not on augmenting international liquidity (this problem was taken care of by the decision to float) but rather on the need to ensure exchange rate stability. The LDCs, on the other hand, required massive increases in international financial resources. The concern of the rich and poor countries with international monetary reform thus reflected different needs, and an Interim Committee of the Board of Governors was established to attempt to coalesce and unify the approach of these two groups.

This committee worked out the details of the Second Amendment of the Articles of Agreement of the IMF in Jamaica in 1976. This Amendment came into force two years later. It required members to collaborate with each other and with the Fund in order to ensure exchange rate stability. Individual members were expected to follow domestic and foreign trade policies consistent with the objective of maintaining a stable international financial system. Members were free to choose a floating or a pegged exchange rate system, and they were free to peg the value of their currency or some other currency to a 'basket' of other currencies or to SDRs, but not to gold. The IMF was given the responsibility of ensuring that members complied with the general requirements on exchange regulations and of overseeing the operation of the whole system. The fund was also empowered to expand the role of SDRs within the world economy and to establish them as the main international reserve asset. It was authorized to demonetize gold, to sell off its gold holdings, and to use the proceeds to aid the poorest LDCs.

Along with the Second Amendment came the Sixth General Review of Quotas. This increased the IMF's quota resources by about a third, and also provided for a redistribution of quotas. In 1979, a further redistribution was proposed and an additional allocation amounting to SDR 4 billion to be issued over the period 1979, 1980 and 1981 was also envisaged. Quota revisions and issues also took place during the period 1980–4. Quota redistributions have in general increased the quota share of the OPEC countries, reduced the share of the industrialized countries, and left the share of the non–oil–producing countries virtually unchanged. The Second Amendment and subsequent quota reviews thus went some way to ensuring a firmer commitment to exchange rate stability and to augmenting international financial liquidity.[7]

From the point of view of the LDCs, two important developments have taken place as a consequence of the adoption of the Second Amendment. First, as we have noted, the IMF has been given increased powers of surveillance over its members' exchange rate policies. Members are under obligation to provide the IMF with information necessary for it to exercise effective surveillance, and the Fund is empowered to organize consultations, not necessarily limited to exchange rate policies, with its members. Members are required to exchange their national currencies for freely usable currencies – at present the US dollar, the French franc, the Deutschmark, the Japanese yen and the pound sterling – at the behest of the Fund. The developing countries are particularly concerned about the way the new apparatus of surveillance has been used. At the 1978 Annual Meeting of the IMF the Venezuelan delegate expressed the opinion that 'surveillance . . . should be concentrated on the countries with the most weight in international trade'.[8]

The Fund has attempted to develop a policy framework for exercising surveillance. The production of the annual document *World Economic Outlook* and the *Annual Report* provides the Fund with an opportunity to review economic policies and prospects and is supposed to constitute an essential input into the surveillance process. Consultations are also held with members on an annual basis and include a wide-ranging discussion of many aspects of macroeconomic policy. However, although 'under the Fund articles a member has the procedural obligation to provide information and undertake consultation at the request of the Fund, there is no requirement that the Fund and the member reach agreement on the appropriateness of action taken or not taken'.[9] It is thus often the case that there is significant divergence in the views of the IMF and member countries and these divergencies have tended to persist for long periods of time.

During 1978–87, as in earlier periods, the IMF has remained virtually powerless as far as the developed western countries are concerned. Originally Keynes had proposed that mechanisms should be established to regulate the policies of the surplus countries – involving the imposition of a penalty on countries with large balance-of-payments surpluses and permitting debtor countries to restrict imports from these countries.[10] The fact that such mechanisms have not been institutionalized has meant that large industrial countries – both those with substantial surpluses and those (such as the USA) that can easily finance their deficit through large-scale capital inflows – can afford to ignore the IMF. The process of surveillance has had no effect on the severe imbalance of macroeconomic policies in the United States – reflected in rapidly growing balance-of-payments and budgetary deficits. Instead, coordination among DCs has been achieved outside the IMF – within the framework of the annual economic summits bringing together the leaders of the five major industrial nations. The relative powerlessness of the IMF vis-à-vis these countries has increased since the collapse of the Bretton Woods system because it has virtually no role to play in the determination of exchange rates or the international movements of private capital.

As against this, the IMF's authority to influence the macroeconomic policies of the LDCs has increased, particularly during the 1980s. In the period 1973–81, creditworthy LDCs found international private credit to be readily available. Moreover, the IMF itself adopted a relatively liberal attitude – establishing a number of special financing facilities during this period. The period also saw a relatively widespread conversion of loans into grants. This was of considerable benefit to the poorest LDCs.

The situation has changed radically since 1981, however. Private credit has been reduced, ODA levels have stagnated and the IMF has adopted a tough monetarist attitude. The Fund's 'typical' stabilization assistance package includes recommendations advocating:

- A drastic reduction in public expenditure leading to a significant deflation of the domestic economy.
- A switch of investment from domestic demand-oriented commodites to exportables. This usually has a severe adverse effect on income distribution and is very difficult to achieve because of supply-side rigidities.
- A large devaluation of the domestic currency. This fuels inflation and, because of protectionism and low price elasticities of the major primary exports, does not guarantee increased foreign exchange revenue.
- Enhanced privatization and the provision of incentives for the

inflow of foreign investment. Such policies are unlikely to be effective in a depressed economic environment and can lead only to an erosion of the bargaining power of the governments of the developing countries. The net flow of private capital to the LDCs has become negative in many cases and has been reduced to a trickle almost everywhere else.

The international liquidity squeeze on the LDCs has become very severe in recent years. These liquidity problems could be most directly tackled through a renewed issue of SDRs. The Second Amendment of the Articles of Agreement of the IMF provides for a downgrading of gold and the transformation of the SDRs into a major reserve asset. At present, however, SDRs account for less than 5 per cent of total international liquidity. A very high proportion of votes (no less than 85 per cent) is required for a change in the valuation of SDRs. Since the SDRs are composed of the major national currencies, a change in the valuation of SDRs might affect the strength and use of these currencies. The major western countries are thus unlikely to be enthusiastic about a revaluation of SDRs, at least in the near future. The IMF clearly does not have the authority to force members to obey its rules on the use of gold as a monetary asset. The case for renewed SDR issues has, however, received widespread support on the basis of evidence that in the early 1980s SDRs declined significantly as a proportion of non-gold reserves and that the ratio between reserves and imports was well below the level in 1978. SDRs are a particularly appropriate means for augmenting international liquidity in a world facing severe debt problems because they will not create repayment obligations or require expansion of the Public Sector Borrowing Requirement (PSBR) of industrial countries and approval of their national legislatures.[11]

Development Requirements and the New System

Developing countries require an increase in international financial resources, partly to meet their obligations on past borrowings and partly to finance existing investment programmes. We have seen in the previous section that, as a group, developing countries have had a large deficit on the current accounts of their balance of payments since 1974. It reached a peak of $72.3 billion in 1983 but declined to $46.6 billion in 1986 owing to a severe curtailment of imports.[12]

As pointed out in Chapter 9, import restraint has imposed a heavy development cost on the Third World. Most observers believe that, for growth to resume on a sustained basis, the current account deficit of the Third World will have to increase substantially. Thus UNCTAD estimates that in a high-growth scenario – involving annual average growth of about 6 per cent over the period 1985–95 – the current account deficit to GDP ratio of the major LDCs will have to rise from 1.9 per cent in 1985 to 7.7 per cent in 1995. The corresponding ratio for the least developed countries will have to increase from 11.3 per cent to 19.6 per cent over the same period.[13] The development financing needs of the LCDs are likely to increase rapidly if growth is to be resumed in the Third World. But, as noted earlier, the prospects for an expansion in foreign inflows are bleak. Bank transfers to LDCs are expected to remain negative during the 1980s and concessional assistance is unlikely to rise significantly in real terms.[14]

Increasing the availability of foreign exchange resources is therefore an important priority for the Third World.[15] Such an increase cannot be procured on a long-term basis without reforms within the international financial system, because it is the exchange rate regime that emerged after the collapse of the Bretton Woods system, and the existing arrangements for the creation and distribution of international liquid assets, that constrain the orderly growth of international trade and investment. The exchange rate is now frequently used as a protectionist device by governments. Moreover, exchange rate volatility under the present system has been significantly greater than it was during the Bretton Woods period. Since most of the exchange rate alterations have been unanticipated, the international economic environment has become uncertain and unstable and it has become increasingly difficult to develop a coherent foreign trade and investment policy. Exchange rate instability makes it impossible to pursue liberal international economic policies: it encourages the rise of non-tariff barriers (by reducing the 'transparency' of tariff rate protection) and increases the difficulty of estimating a country's dynamic comparative advantage and a company's long-term profitability in international traded goods. This inevitably amounts to a stimulation for strengthening protectionism within the world economy.

Moreover, as the IMF itself recognizes, the floating exchange rate regime has not diminished the need for international liquidity. As far as the developing countries are concerned, the short-run effects of exchange rate changes are often 'perverse'. Increased liquidity is thus required to finance trade deficits that persist despite exchange rate adjustments even if the perversity is corrected in the medium run. During the 1970s, some LDCs with an acceptable credit rating used the Eurocurrency markets to finance these deficits, but that option is no longer available – net transfer of resources from banks to LDCs was estimated to be negative in 1985.[16] Increased international liquidity can be made available on a long-term basis only through international public institutions such as the IMF. It cannot be generated spontaneously through the operation of unregulated international financial markets. That is why even the reputedly neo-classical deputy chairman of the Indian Planning Commission, Manmohan Singh, argues that 'the present debt crisis is a reflection of the underlying inadequacy of existing arrangements of both international trade and transfer of real resources to the developing world'.[17]

The developing countries have put forward a series of proposals for international financial reform.[18] The main concern in almost all these proposals is the securing of a substantial increase in international liquidity. Strong emphasis is placed on expanding the stock of SDRs and on achieving an equitable distribution of this stock. The proposals also stress the need for increasing the resources of the international multinational lending institutions. Various mechanisms are suggested for linking the issuance of SDRs to growth in liquidity needs, trade levels and volume of international concessional finance. Increase in the assets of international public institutions is to be linked to an upgrading of their authority in international financial markets. This is to be achieved, for example, by the establishment of an interest facility at the IMF and by expanding its role (as well as that of the World Bank Group) in the provision and insurance of loans to developing countries. Proposals aimed at reforming the relationship between LDCs and the commercial banks are also concerned primarily with the promotion of international financial stability.

As noted earlier, a small number of 'creditworthy' LDCs made extensive use of credit provided by Eurocurrency institutions during the 1970s. This served to reduce Third World pressure for more general reforms, such as the SDR aid link, that could be of benefit to all, both middle- and low-income countries. At the North–South Dialogue in Paris, some developing countries, concerned that their own creditworthiness might be called into question, raised objections to a global arrangement for the cancellation of debts.[19] This does not mean that middle-income countries that succeeded in acquiring access to the Eurocurrency markets found a long-term solution to the problem of balance-of-payments disequilibrium. The easy availability of external credit in fact created a false sense of security and encouraged a deferment of necessary domestic adjustments.

During the 1970s there existed an excess supply of funds in the Eurocurrency markets,[20] owing mainly to a growing asymmetry between strict regulation of nationals operating in their own currencies and the much more liberal treatment of non-residents operating in foreign currencies within the same banking system. In the early 1970s, the demand for corporate credit within the western countries grew relatively slowly and the commodity price boom ensured that Third World economies became attractive customers. Moreover, a number of innovations were developed to diminish the risk of long-term borrowing. Thus the concept of 'roll-over credit' was created, which ensured that in long-maturity loans the interest rate was adjusted every three to six months in correspondence with changes in the structure of market interest rates. This 'floating' interest rate shifts the burden of one of the most important market risks onto the borrower. Then there have been developments related to consortium banking and to syndicated loans, all of which spread the default risk of foreign loans and make such operations particularly profitable for the larger banks.[21]

These mechanisms ensure that banks can operate flexibly. Conditions in money markets can and do change rapidly. In the early 1970s, costs of loans were low and maturities were high. In 1974–5, however, only 31 per cent of loans to LDCs were for a period in excess of seven years, as against 82 per cent in 1973–4. In 1976, conditions improved once again, particularly for what the market called 'first-class borrowers', and this trend persisted during 1977. In the 1980s, conditions became extremely difficult for LDC borrowers.

279

As soon as the supply of funds falls or the demand from other developed country borrowers rises LDCs find that they are squeezed out of markets. For LDCs with a high spillover ratio a relatively small decline in the availability of funds from the Eurocurrency markets could, other things remaining constant, imply a significant proportionate reduction in net transfer.[22]

There is thus a need to restructure international financial regulatory mechanisms to stabilize world money markets, on the one hand, and to spread the distribution of both official and private credit among LDCs, on the other.

During the 1980s, the adoption of monetarist policies by the leading western countries pushed interest rates up to record levels despite the large supply of funds on the market. The London Inter Bank Offer Rate (LIBOR) has fluctuated widely: it was 5 per cent at the end of 1976, 19.7 per cent in March 1980 and just over 10 per cent in December 1985.[23] By historical standards, real – as against money – interest remained very high during this period.[24] On the other hand, the large supply of funds coupled with increased oligopolistic competition among the international banks kept spreads very low.

While borrowers have paid dearly for their loans, the banks have been living on small margins. Although the large institutions are earning large sums for acting as 'lead' banks and managing consortium operations, the smaller banks are operating on margins that are dangerously thin and subject to increasingly fierce competitive pressures. Banks with thin spreads are also exposed to 'maturity transformation' problems. In the 1970s, many banks adopted a strategy of 'borrowing short and lending long'. Thus they often found themselves with money that had to be repaid at a week's notice covering loans extended for an eight-year period. Such problems can lead to a bankruptcy, as was demonstrated by the collapse of Franklin National, a large US bank, as early as 1974.[25] Since the international banking system is highly integrated – with most short-term loans being raised within the system – a failure of even a minor institution threatens confidence and stability throughout the system. Moreover, as noted in Chapter 9, no 'lender of last resort' exists at the international level and supervision of the international banks is minimal; general international financial crisis is therefore particularly difficult to handle. A series of banking failures in the United States and Europe during 1984 induced governments to take a fresh look at the processes of international financial management.[26]

The indiscipline of the international financial markets is undesirable not merely because it may precipitate a future global economic crisis. It also entails a high presently existing cost. This emerges from the prevalence of what Michael Stewart has called 'a deflationary bias' inherent in modern international financial arrangements. The world financial community – which consists 'of a relatively small number of individuals, perhaps only a few hundred [and] including government . . . officials, key figures in the twenty or so largest international banks, treasurers of multinationals, a few particularly influential stock brokers and financial journalists'[27] – is concerned with risk minimization and thereby necessarily functions in a manner that impedes governments' ability to execute expansionist policies. Higher interest rates and restrictive monetary policies are 'rewarded' by the international financial community: there is an inflow of funds to such a country and its exchange rate rises. Thus, countries that pursue deflationary policies are likely to be successful both in achieving their objectives and also in transmitting deflationary pressures to the economies with which they have significant trade and investment relationships. In contrast, a country pursuing an expansionary policy (such as France in the early 1980s) – particularly if it does so in isolation and is not in the fortunate position of being the world's largest economy – will be punished: its currency will depreciate and pressure on its capital account will increase. The odds will therefore be stacked against it. The international financial market is by the nature of its constitution incapable of encouraging policies that aim at the stimulation of growth through medium-term cyclical adjustments.

Attempts to overcome the deflationary bias of the international financial system have been sporadic and largely ineffective; developed country governments have usually chosen to act unilaterally and on a case-by-case basis. The resources at the disposal of the IMF were increased from SDR 29 billion in 1971 to SDR 90 billion in 1983, and funds mobilized through GAB also increased significantly during this period. However, new SDR issues have been small and a redistribution of SDRs in favour of the LDCs has not taken place.

Since the early 1970s the developing countries have been calling for democratization of the IMF in the hope that this would bring about a reorientation in the fund's approach and make it an instrument for them to shape the international financial system. It is quite clear that such a democratization has not occurred. The dominance of the developed countries on all important issues remains unaltered and the Fund remains committed to an economic strategy that puts the burden of international adjustment on debtor countries. The changes that have occurred in its role within the international monetary order originate from a shift in political and economic power within the Group of Ten. Thus the establishment of the European Monetary System (EMS) and the decision to permit a variety of exchange regimes directly reflect the needs and perceptions of rich countries. Both these decisions, particularly the latter, are likely to affect the LDCs profoundly, yet they were taken with little or no reference to the LDC views.

The LDCs made very little use of the financing facilities provided by the IMF during the 1970s, but as private credit lines dried up during the 1980s borrowings from the Fund increased, despite the increasingly stringent conditions attached to these loans. Currently, repayments to the Fund by its LDC members significantly exceed its provision of new loans and the IMF is experiencing increasing difficulties in collecting its debts. Donor governments are recognizing that there is a need for a drastic revision of the role of the IMF within the international development finance system.

The first clear exposition of this reassessment was incorporated in the so-called 'Baker initiative' launched at the 1985 Annual Meeting of the IMF. James Baker, the then US Secretary of Trade, advocated international policy coordination among the leading western countries, and such coordination created the basis of a planned devaluation of the dollar and reduction of nominal interest rates in international markets. The 'Baker plan' also envisaged a reorientation of international debt management policy. Support to debtor nations should be geared to stimulate growth within these economies, and not merely to achieve 'structural adjustment' as conceived of by the IMF. There was an implied downgrading of the role of the IMF, which was henceforth expected to coordinate its policies with those of the World Bank in the provision of debt relief. The financial resources of the World Bank were to be substantially increased to enable it to play a major role in the debt management process.

The substantive policy content of the 'Baker initiative' is only marginally different from that of the programmes adopted by the IMF during the 1980s. Indeed, the primary short-term purpose of launching the initiative was the desire to rescue the IMF from a difficult position[28] and to ensure a smooth beginning for Mr Barber Conable, the new world Bank President, who is a close personal friend of Mr Baker and a favourite son of the Reagan administration.[29] It became increasingly clear in 1986 and 1987 that the US administration had not abandoned its commitment to international monetarist doctrine in its dealings with developing countries. Despite its advocacy of growth-oriented policies, it expected LDC governments to reduce fiscal deficits, permit a large-scale devaluation of their currency and remove restrictions on capital movements if they desired preferential access to debt relief assistance.[30] Cosmetic reforms in debt management procedures can therefore be expected to have very little effect on the development prospects of the Third World. The international monetary arrangements that have emerged since the collapse of the Bretton Woods system

> seem to have been devised with very little thought of the real needs of the developing countries. They do not meet their principal international financial requirement of additional concessional liquidity. Nor do they provide the . . . built-in mechanisms for ensuring that members adhere to the rules. This has widened the gap between the strong and weak countries, pushed the cost of international adjustment on to the weaker currencies. The poorest developing countries seem to have come off worst. The new system does nothing for them.[31]

We have seen that the Second Amendment allows members to choose exchange rate regimes. The domestic and international circumstances of most LDCs will induce them to peg their currencies. This will mean that they bear substantial costs in adjusting domestic economic policy to accommodate balance-of-payments deficits. Those LDCs that peg their currencies to weak currencies, such as the pound sterling, will be periodically threatened with major devaluations. This will tend to scare off foreign capital, in the form of both loans and direct investment.

Building up foreign reserves and preserving the value of their own currencies has become a risky business and demands considerable expertise and central bank reserves, neither of which is in abundance in the Third World.

Fundamental changes are required in both international financial norms and procedures if the development finance needs of the South are to be adequately met. These changes should envisage:

1 A final abandonment of monetarist doctrine, which assumes (and does not prove) that 'getting prices right' and 'putting one's own house in order' are sufficient measures for the stimulation of world economic growth and for the eventual 'trickling down' of this growth to the developing countries.
2 The development of a supranational institutional framework that does not merely 'coordinate' national economic policies but subordinates and integrates them within the context of global growth and redistribution–oriented economic strategies and possesses adequate resources for this purpose.
3 The establishment of the SDR as the main international reserve asset and the linking of its issuance to movements in world trade, investment and production.
4 An expansion of the flow of concessionary development finance to the Third World and an improvement of the terms on which it is made available.
5 The development of firm regulatory and guidance procedures for subordinating the international Eurocurrency banks to the type of discipline that is currently imposed on financial institutions in domestic capital markets. This is essential to avoid international financial chaos and to reduce the burden of debt, which tends to rise with each 'case-by-case' rescheduling operation currently mounted to 'rescue' LDCs from repayment crisis.[32]

It is perhaps appropriate to recall that Keynes, generally considered to be an architect of the Bretton Woods system, also advocated the creation of a big world development agency during the Bretton Woods Conference. He also argued for the establishment of a world central bank and an international trade organization. He wanted to see an international monetary system in which the burden of adjustment of balance-of-payments disequilibria was placed on surplus – not on deficit – countries. Keynes was in favour of the creation of commodity money. He wanted the international trade organization to stabilize the prices of a representative bundle of primary commodities in terms of the main international monetary standard. He wanted international financial management, which would be able to control the volume and distribution of international liquidity and which would be committed to a programme of economic expansion and development. Today, the authority of the IMF has been reduced and its propensity to discipline weak deficit economies has increased. This is a far cry from Keynes' original perception of the international monetary order. A return to some important features of Keynes' proposals at Bretton Woods might well pave the way for meeting the international financial needs of the Third World.[33]

Notes

1 Both these features were incorporated in his proposal for the establishment of an international clearing union. The proposals were, however, abandoned during the negotiations for the establishment of the IMF. The story of these negotiations is told in G. Moggridge (ed.), *The Collected Works of John Maynard Keynes* (London: Macmillan, 1980), vol. 25, p. 230–5, 459–68.

2 G. C. Abbott, 'Effects of recent changes in the international monetary system on the developing countries', *Separatabdruck aus Aussenwirtschaft*, No. 1, 1979, p. 61.

3 C. Payer, *The Debt Trap: The IMF and the Developing Countries* (Harmondsworth: Penguin, 1972).

4 See, for example, Maxwell Stamp, 'The Fund and the future', *Lloyds Bank Review*, October 1958, pp. 1–22; Tibor Satovosky, 'A new approach to international liquidity', *American Economic Review*, December 1966, pp. 1212–20; UN, *International Monetary Reform and Cooperation for Development* (New York: UN, 1969), Sales No. E10: 11DD2.

5 See Abbot (n. 2), pp. 61–2.

6 M. Goldstein and J. Young, 'Exchange rate policy: Some current issues', *Finance and Development*, March 1979, pp. 7–8.

7 For a review of the main provisions of the Second Amendment and the quota reviews, see Abbott (n. 2), and the *Annual Reports* of the IMF for 1978, 1979, 1983, 1984 and 1985.

8 See M. Blackwell and K. S. Friedman, 'A growing perception of interdependence', *Finance and Development*, December 1978, p. 5.

9 G. Johnson, 'Enhancing effectiveness of surveillance', *Finance and Development*, 22(4), December 1985, p. 4.

10 See *Collected Works of Keynes* (n. 1), vol. 25, pp. 459–68.

11 On this, see J. Williamson, *A New SDR Allocation* (Washington DC: Institute for International Economics, 1984).

12 Figures are from UNCTAD, *Trade and Development Report 1985* (New York: UN, 1985), p. 190.

13 ibid., pp. 137–66, 178–84.

14 J. W. Seivell (ed.), *US Foreign Policy and the Third World Agenda* (Washington DC: Overseas Development Council, 1985).

15 The following paragraphs are based on J. A. Ansari and H. W. Singer, 'International financial reform and the Third World. The continuing relevance of Keynes' proposals', in N. Hatti, H. W. Singer and R. Dandon (eds), *Resources Transfer and the Debt Trap* (New Delhi: Vikas, 1987), pp. 17–33.

16 UNCTAD, (n. 12), p. 109.

17 UNCTAD, 'Statement by Manmohan Singh', in *The Development Dialogue in the 1980s – continuing paralysis or a new consensus* (New York: UN, 1985), p. 83.

18 For a review of some of these proposals, see Commonwealth Secretariat, *The Debt Crisis and the World Economy: Report by a Commonwealth Group of Experts* (London: Commonwealth Secretariat, 1984); W. H. Bolin and J. Del Canto, 'LDC debt: beyond crisis management', *Foreign Affairs*, 61(5), Summer 1983, and International Reports, *The A to Z of Debt Relief Schemes* (New York: Praeger, 1984).

19 G. Fitzgerald, *Unequal Partners* (New York: UN, 1979), p. 30.

20 G. Bird, 'Commercial borrowings by LDCs', *Third World Quarterly*, 11(2), 1980, p. 279.

21 See 'Buddy, Can you borrow a buck', *Eurocurrency*, May 1978.

22 Bird (n. 20), pp. 279–80.

23 These rates are taken from various issues of Morgan Guaranty Trust, *World Financial Markets*.

24 This is explained by the fact that, while money interest rates have fallen since 1982, inflation in the major western countries has fallen at an even faster rate.

25 See J. Spero, *The Failure of Franklin National Bank* (New York: Colombia University Press, 1980).

26 For one analysis of these bank failures, see E. Brett, *The World Economy since the War* (London: Macmillan, 1985), pp. 238–48.

27 M. Stewart, *Controlling the Economic Future* (Brighton: Wheatsheaf, 1983), p. 48.

28 The IMF was finding it increasingly difficult to collect its own debts during 1984 and 1985 and its net outflows to LDCs had become negative in 1985.

29 Mr Conable assumed office in early 1986. For his background, see 'Baker takes tough line', *Financial Times*, 15 April 1986.

30 *Financial Times*, 15 April 1986, and 'Made in America, selling well abroad', *Financial Times*, 7 May 1986. For a 'post-Baker' statement on the IMF's debt relief priorities, see the views of Richard Erb, the American vice President of the Fund appointed in 1985 in R. Erb, 'Adjustment growth and the Fund's role', *Finance and Development*, March 1986, pp. 2–5.
31 Abbott (n. 2), p. 75.
32 For evidence on the increased cost of debt rescheduling, see Brett (n. 26), pp. 238–41.
33 For an elaboration of these proposals see J. A. Ansari and H. W. Singer, 'International financial reform. Is Keynesianism resurgent?' (Brighton: Institute of Development Studies, 1986), mimeo.

PART IV

An Overview

12   *Forty Years of Changing Thought on Development Problems*[1]

The initial approach evolved by development economists in the late 1940s and the early 1950s concentrated on growth of GNP as a handy and supposedly neutral and objective goal and performance test of economic development. This approach was then in the air and thus enabled economists to transfer familiar concepts and familiar modes of thinking to the relatively new but rapidly emerging problems of the Third World. This does not of course mean that the thinkers and planners working in terms of GNP growth were necessarily unaware of poverty problems, or that they were necessarily insensitive to distributional problems. But it was assumed either that the 'trickle down' of GNP growth to the lower-income groups would be automatic, or that it could be taken care of through relatively orthodox policies, or that reduction of poverty could be tackled *after* a certain level of GNP had been reached – first the cake had to be produced and made bigger before it could be more equally distributed. A somewhat sharper version of this view was embodied in the Leibenstein–Galenson model, according to which a certain level of inequality is necessary to produce the amount of saving and investment that, according to the dominant Harrod–Domar model, was the necessary precondition for a reasonable growth of output.

With the benefit of hindsight it is not too difficult for us to see what is wrong with this doctrine. In the first place, automatic 'trickle down' is most unlikely since there is unequal access to the opportunities of producing, or obtaining the income from, incremental GNP. It is the richer groups that have privileged access and are likely to appropriate the increased GNP, producing even sharper inequalities in income distribution, at least up to medium-income levels. This was in fact established and described by the famous inverted U curve of Kuznets.

In the second place, it is not necessarily true that inequality of income distribution is needed to promote saving and productive investments. Neither side of the equation is necessarily true. It is quite possible that poorer people do save and invest productively. Where richer people do save and invest they may invest abroad or in the production of more luxury goods, which further solidify the production structure in the direction of greater inequality. Much of the additional investment in economies with unequal income distribution may be by foreign investors and multinational corporations, and the profits and surplus are drained away from the developing country.

In the third place, once a production structure geared to unequal income distribution and a domestic market largely reserved for the high-income groups have been established, it becomes extremely difficult, both economically and politically, to change them back at a later point in the direction of greater equality and a social welfare state. This process has taken place in the western industrialized countries after they had attained higher income levels, and as a result of specific political and social power shifts. For developing countries, however, it is not difficult to demonstrate from numerical models, given their high rates of population increase, increasingly capital-intensive technology, the technological monopoly of the industrialized countries, and their limited resources, that widespread 'trickle down', let alone the creation of social welfare states, is most unlikely in the normal context of purely economic growth. This is the weakness of the Leibenstein–Galenson model, which maps out a development path leading through inequality to greater equality of the turning point projection implied in the Kuznets' U curve, and also in the famous Arthur Lewis model.[2] At the time it was still possible to think of a 'turning point' or 'golden age' when the rural labour surplus would be exhausted and the actual rural population would begin to decline, when rural incomes as well as urban wages would rise at the expense of profits, and a more equal income distribution would result. Now, with the benefit of another thirty years or so of hindsight, we know that the empirical parameters in the development equation do not lend themselves to such a hopeful anticipation.

Instead, what we had as a result of the belief in GNP growth through saving and investment inevitably was what we now describe as 'dualism'. The GNP growth model did work but only in respect of a limited modern, typically urban, sector. The resources of the developing countries simply did not go far enough. The surpluses domestically retained were not large enough in the face of heavy population increases to extend the modern enclaves rapidly enough for there to be any chance of embracing the whole economy within reasonable periods. Moreover, neither the nature of modern technology nor the institutional character of foreign investment was designed to create the necessary linkages within the domestic economy. There are obvious exceptions: Korea, Taiwan, Hong Kong and Singapore represent one type of exception, a number of the OPEC countries another. But, by and large, the picture drawn above is true for the great majority of the Third World's population, including specifically India.

One aspect of this phenomenon of dualism, first noticed by some perceptive minds in the ILO and elsewhere, was in the form of insufficient employment opportunities. Because the scarce capital was pre-empted for capital-intensive investments in the modern sector, the rest of the population was deprived of the capital needed for job creation – hence the concern with high rates of unemployment in the developing countries, particularly by contrast with the full employment position that the western industrialized countries had generally achieved in the 1950s and the 1960s as a result of Keynesian management techniques. Unemployment was especially noted among school leavers and recent migrants to the city. An important explanatory element here was the Harris–Todaro model, which modified the Arthur Lewis model to take account of the new reality. Whereas Arthur Lewis originally had assumed that the process of urbanization and migration was in response to existing employment opportunities and at low wage levels (as long as there was a rural labour surplus), the Harris–Todaro model, more realistically, assumed that urban employment in the modern sector, where it could be obtained, provided incomes at a much higher level than the rural sector and that this, quite rationally, would induce migration heavily in excess of existing employment opportunities.

This model not only explained high urban unemployment rates, but it also threw doubt on the effectiveness of trying to cure unemployment simply by creating more urban jobs, since for every urban job created several migrants would move to the towns, attracted by the chance of such a job. This stage in development thinking was perhaps best exemplified by the earlier work of the ILO World Employment Programme and the terms of reference of the various ILO employment missions to Colombia, Sri Lanka, Kenya, the Philippines, etc.

The findings of these employment missions (as distinct from their original terms of reference), as well as other developments in thinking about employment problems, quickly made it clear that the *unemployment* concept, however suitable it might be for industrial countries – with their social security systems, well-established system of labour exchanges and widespread wage employment – was quite unsuited to the developing countries. For, in the absence of social security, with self-employment and family employment widespread, it was not possible for people to be unemployed in the strict western sense. They had to find some kind of work or perish. Paradoxically, in some of the developing countries those who could afford to be unemployed were often among the richer groups, especially secondary school leavers, university graduates, and professionals having received a university training, who could afford to refuse work other than the specific modern sector jobs for which they had been trained, while living on their own resources or being maintained by their families. The poorer people, on the other hand, had to find such part-time, seasonal, casual, or full-time work as they could.

Although initially this situation was analysed as 'disguised unemployment', or 'underemployment', or by similar terms, it became clear that this was not a satisfactory analysis. These people often worked extremely hard and extremely long hours and it seemed absurd to describe them as underemployed. Moreover, contrary to some earlier views, derived largely from Latin American theories of 'marginalization', it was found to be by no means true that the people involved were predominantly in marginal occupations – beggars, shoeshine boys, porters at airports and stations, etc. On the contrary, it was found that many of them were in fact rendering essential services to other poor people, as carpenters, blacksmiths, sandal-makers, builders, lamp-makers, etc. The problem with them was by no means lack of employment, or even lack of useful employment; their trouble was that within the context of an unequal income distribution their employment was not recognized as being productive in the sense that it was not considered to be worth an income that would put the employed person and his or her dependants above a minimum poverty line. Thus the problem came to be defined as one of the working poor,[3] or as a lack of productive employment, 'productive employment' being defined as employment yielding at least the minimum income required by the poverty line.

While it remains broadly true that employment is not a real objective of development, but rather a means to an end – the end being a decent minimum standard of living – yet employment, in some such sense as participation in national economic life or even as a basic human right, can also be said to have some aspects that render it a final objective.

Once the concept of the working poor, or productive employment, was introduced and once the idea of a poverty line entered into their thinking, development analysts were bound to become aware of further limitations of the employment concept. Two such limitations are particularly important here:

1 Although a high proportion, usually the majority, of those below the poverty line consists of people of working ages who should be capable of work, or their direct dependants, there are also other important poverty groups for which productive employment cannot be the main answer to poverty. Such groups include those too old to work and those without family support, people too ill or crippled to work, broken families, orphaned children, etc.
2 The concept of a poverty line and a minimum standard of living is by no means limited to those material goods that can be obtained from employment or through the income earned in employment. The concept also includes access to health, to education, to clean water, to sanitation, etc. – all services that relate to public action rather than to private employment.

At this stage, the question of income distribution obviously entered into the picture. Increased productive employment, particularly where it involves the use of more labour-intensive technologies, the encouragement of small-scale production and the encouragement of rural development, will help to make income distribution more equal. Although, as pointed out, this is not necessarily true of urban modern sector employment, where incomes may be above rather than below the national average, once we concentrate on the working poor, the rise in their living standards will almost by definition contribute to greater equality of income distribution. Here the analysts and planners must become concerned with the relationship between economic growth measured by GNP and more equal income distribution. Is there a dilemma here? Is there a trade-off? Or does fuller employment with concentration on labour-intensive technology, rural development and small-scale production actually increase the GNP by bringing previously unutilized or underutilized resources into full production?

The answer will largely depend on two factors: (1) the efficiency and impact of the institutional arrangements that accompany the spreading of productive employment among the working poor and more equal income distribution, and (2) the efficiency of the smaller and more labour-intensive units of production, especially the small farmer and the urban informal sector producer. As far as the latter point is concerned, such evidence as we have would tend to show that when expressed as output per unit of land – the relevant measure for land-short economies such as India – the small farmer, when properly supplied with land, water, fertilizers, credit, insecticides, marketing arrangements, etc., and given proper incentives, does not have to fear any comparison with larger units. The same can often be shown to be true of the small-scale urban producer in his use of the little capital that he has. Obviously, a great deal depends on whether or not it is possible to find or develop efficient labour-intensive technologies; here again, the scope is much wider than was often assumed.

Apart from the question of the impact of income distribution on growth, there is also the question of the reverse relationship of the impact of growth on income distribution, for example, whether or not growth will 'trickle down'. Obviously, in a growing economy it would be possible to reduce poverty largely through the creation of productive employment out of incremental income. Such a strategy of redistribution through growth has been developed for Kenya by the ILO Employment Mission[4] and, in a more generalized and systematic way, in the volume published jointly by the World Bank and the Sussex Institute of Development Studies.[5] The more rapid is economic growth, the more feasible such a policy becomes. Hence it is somewhat fallacious to describe the new trend in thinking as a 'dethronement of GNP'; it has been more accurately described as the 'enthronement of basic needs'.[6]

Apart from the macroeconomic possibility of reducing poverty by finding resources for employment creation out of the growing national income, there is a strong political factor. Incremental redistribution will encounter much less political resistance than would be the case if redistribution had to make the upper-income groups worse off in absolute terms. This is clear also from the experience of some of the western industrial countries, where the reduction or cessation of economic growth as a result of higher oil prices and other dislocations resulting from the breakdown of the Bretton Woods system have clearly had the effect of increasing social tensions and sharpening conflicts about income distribution. It is also a relevant matter in connection with the current debate on environmental issues and the New International Economic Order. If, for reasons of limitation of resources or of pollution, the rich countries will have to prepare for zero-growth economies in order to permit the poorer countries to improve their living standards, this will actually raise problems of social peace and distributional arrangements within the rich countries. The same is true under any actual redistribution of income away from the industrial countries to satisfy demands for a New International Economic Order.

For the developing countries, there remains the dilemma that, on the one hand, GNP growth is essential to provide the resources, and probably also the political preconditions, for a non-violent redistribution of incomes, while at the same time emphasis on GNP growth has inherent tendencies to solidify and accentuate existing inequalities. This dilemma is not insoluble but it ensures that development strategy clearly becomes a difficult tightrope operation. One cannot have confidence that all developing countries in all circumstances will be able to perform such a tightrope act.

Thus the concern for employment leads, via the concept of

productive employment and the working poor, to a concern with income distribution. Technically speaking, this could take the form of establishing a primary development objective of minimizing some inequality index such as the Gini coefficient. When expressed in those terms the difference between this and a poverty objective, such as is implied in terms like the 'working poor' or the notion of 'productive employment', becomes quite clear. The notion of the working poor requires the establishment of a poverty line usually in terms of minimum incomes, perhaps differentiated for rural and urban areas and increasing sequentially through time, as was done in the Kenya Employment Mission Report. Similarly, when we define productive employment we must define employment as productive in the sense of yielding an income above a certain minimum level. The notion of minimizing the Gini coefficient, on the other hand, does not require the establishment of a specific poverty line.

When we establish a poverty line, the objective is to concentrate development policy on those below the line until they are brought above the line. When we are merely concerned with reducing the Gini coefficient we want to increase welfare by distributing income from those at higher levels to those at lower levels regardless of where exactly the beneficiaries stand in relation to a specific poverty line. There is, however, a halfway house between a concern with income distribution and a concern with the reduction of poverty: the poverty group need not be defined with regard to some absolute poverty standard (whether expressed as physical indicators or as minimum incomes). Instead, it can be defined by way of *relative* poverty; for example, the objective may be to bring up the poorest 20 per cent of the population to the line that now separates them from the other 80 per cent. When expressed in such relative terms, the objective of reducing poverty seems closely linked to the objective of reducing income inequality.

Even then, however, there still remains one important difference. When we establish reduction of poverty as the objective, even if we define poverty as relative poverty, essentially we are not interested in what happens to incomes above the dividing line (except that, for reasons already mentioned, we would probably consider an increase in incomes above the poverty line as a good thing, other things being equal, and would also try, for welfare reasons, to concentrate such increases as much as possible on those only very little above the

298

poverty line). On the other hand, if we aim at greater equality of income distribution, we are interested in what happens to relative incomes all along the line. Thus, perhaps slightly paradoxically, the objective of reducing income inequality may in fact turn out to be a more radical social objective than the apparently more far-reaching objective of reducing or eliminating poverty. Perhaps this is the reason why the objective of reducing poverty has found relatively strong support in the industrial countries and in such international institutions as the World Bank, at least at the conceptual (and rhetorical) level.

The final step from an emphasis on reducing poverty to a basic needs strategy is a relatively easy one. It carries two distinct advantages:

1. It does away with the negative concept of reducing or eliminating poverty by substituting the more positive and operational concept of satisfying basic needs.
2. It moves away from a mere monetary definition of poverty in terms of incomes, which would not suit the conditions of many of the really poor in the developing countries, who may be subsistence farmers or other do-it-yourself producers, towards a definition in terms of physical needs, which can be defined in concrete terms such as calories or access to education, which are common to subsistence producers and income earners.

On the face of it, the move from poverty reduction to a basic needs strategy seems to get further away from income distribution by defining poverty in the absolute sense of lack of certain basic requirements rather than in the relative sense in relation to other income groups. In practice, however, much of this difference disappears when, in the evolution of the basic needs concept, increasing emphasis is given to the social character of basic needs standards and to the need to include in the very definition of basic needs such relative and social elements as participation in economic life or decision-making, or equal access with other population groups to schooling, or even other basic human rights. In fact, reasonable equality with other groups in the population could itself be defined as one of such basic human rights.[7]

The basic needs concept has a further advantage, compared with that of a reduction of poverty, in that it brings to our mind the fact that basic needs are not limited to goods and services either bought by an individual household out of income or produced by individual households for their own use. This is what the term *poverty* suggests. Basic needs also include such things as access to health, education, sanitation, transport, water – all areas in which private provision is the exception rather than the rule. This is clearly right, but there must be some question as to the extent to which it is useful to dilute this concept further by including participation, basic human rights, etc.

One final point may be emphasized. The original concept of GNP growth focuses our mind on macroeconomic planning, which indeed was developed in close parallel with implementing GNP targets. This is less true of employment targets. Clearly there is no single homogeneous employment problem: the problem of the unemployed school leaver, for example, is a rather different problem from that of the small farmer without access to water. So the employment emphasis paves the way for a less aggregated and more dispersed view of planning. This is even more true as we move to poverty and basic needs objectives. The character of the different poverty groups is even more diverse and heterogeneous than is the case for different employment problems. Moreover, the nature of poverty problems may differ even among neighbouring villages, or among urban households living close to each other in the same town.[8] Thus poverty-oriented planning and the provision of basic requirements for population groups now lacking them are by their very nature and almost by definition a highly decentralized affair. Local planning as well as local participation, particularly on the part of those directly affected by the lack of basic requirements, is naturally moving into the foreground of the picture. Community development rather than central planning seems the natural principal tool for a basic needs-oriented development strategy.

While the development thinkers' focus shifted from growth planning to employment to income distribution to basic needs, they none the less had in common a belief in the need for a separate 'development economics' – a belief that the policy requirements of developing countries required different doctrines and methods of analysis from the classical and neo-classical body of 'general economics' developed in and for industrial countries by Ricardo,

Mills and Alfred Marshall. This belief has been sharply questioned in recent years.

This questioning has been parallel – and closely related – to the questioning of the post-war Keynesian consensus by monetarist views. Just as the Keynesian assumption of the need for active policies to create full employment in view of the failure of market mechanisms to guarantee full-employment equilibrium was questioned in spite (or perhaps because of) its demonstrated success in the industrial countries during the twenty-five 'golden' years of 1946–1971, so the belief that the free market mechanism ('getting prices right') provided reliable and sufficient guidance for developing countries, in the same way as for industrial countries, was strongly and influentially put forward in criticism of the various schools of development economics.

The parallel between Keynesian 'duo-economics' (for economies in states of unemployment and full employment) and development economics (for developing and industrial countries) has been brilliantly described by Albert Hirschman. Similarly, the advocacy of 'mono-economics', on neo-classical foundations, questions both Keynesianism and the need for development econonics. Will the recent rise in unemployment in the industrial countries and the crisis in the developing countries swing the intellectual pendulum back to 'duo-economics' – to Keynesianism as well as to development economics?

Notes

1 This chapter draws on H. W. Singer's contribution to C. M. Hanumantha Rao and P. C. Joshi (eds), *Reflections on Economic Development and Social Change*, Essays in Honour of Professor V. K. R. V. Rao (Bombay: New Delhi Allied Publishers, for the Institute of Economic Growth, 1979), pp. 29–40.
2 'Economic development with unlimited supplies of labour', *Manchester School of Economic and Social Studies*, May 1954, pp. 139–92.
3 This was the term used in the Kenya Employment Mission Report, *Employment, Incomes and Equality: A Strategy for Increasing Productive Employment in Kenya* (Geneva: ILO, 1972).
4 ibid.
5 Hollis Chenery *et al.*, *Redistribution with Growth: An Approach to Policy* (London: Oxford University Press, 1973).

6 See A. R. Jolly, 'The World Employment Conference: the enthrone-ment of basic needs', *ODI Review*, No. 2, 1976.

7 Some such an evolution is visible in a rudimentary way in *Basic Needs, Growth and Employment: A One-World Problem*, prepared by the ILO World Employment Programme in 1976 as the basic document for the World Employment Conference. Discussions aiming at a clarification and methodology of basic needs have since tended towards a further broadening of the concept in the direction indicated above, thus bringing it closer to the earlier concern with income distribution, by emphasizing such aspects as absence of discrimination and harassment, and more equal access to various economic and social opportunities.

8 This has been shown for villages in India. See T. Scarlett Epstein, *Economic Development and Social Change in South India* (Manchester: Manchester University Press, 1962), p. 314.

Statistical Appendix

Table S.1 Trends in life expectancy, child mortality and literacy, 1960–83

	Life expectancy (years)			Child mortality (1–4 years) per '000			Literacy rate (%)		
	1960	1970	1983	1960	1970	1983	1960	1970	1983
Industrial market economies	69	71	74	2	1	0	96	98	99
All developing countries	44	51	59	25	17	9	37	45	59
low-income	42	49	58	27	19	9	27	36	55
middle-income	52	57	62	20	14	7	52	65	78
high-income oil exporters	44	50	59	42	25	11	10	20	32

Source: OECD, DAC Review Report 1985 (Paris: OECD, 1985), Table XII-2.

Table S.2 Network of world trade: share of world exports by origin, 1969–83 (%)

Destination		Developed market economy countries						Socialist countries		Developing countries		
Origin	World	Total	EEC	EFTA	Japan	USA	Other	Eastern Europe	Asia	Total	OPEC	Other
World												
1969–1971	100.0	100.0	100.0	100.0	100.0	100.0	100.0	100.0	100.0	100.0	100.0	100.0
1972–1974	100.0	100.0	100.0	100.0	100.0	100.0	100.0	100.0	100.0	100.0	100.0	100.0
1975–1977	100.0	100.0	100.0	100.0	100.0	100.0	100.0	100.0	100.0	100.0	100.0	100.0
1978–1980	100.0	100.0	100.0	100.0	100.0	100.0	100.0	100.0	100.0	100.0	100.0	100.0
1981–1983	100.0	100.0	100.0	100.0	100.0	100.0	100.0	100.0	100.0	100.0	100.0	100.0
Developed market economy countries												
1969–1971	71.7	78.1	79.0	86.8	53.4	73.6	85.3	24.6	46.4	72.3	81.6	70.4
1972–1974	68.2	72.9	75.4	85.6	44.7	66.4	79.7	30.5	61.0	68.0	80.2	64.9
1975–1977	65.2	69.2	74.4	83.3	37.9	56.6	75.9	32.8	58.3	67.4	82.9	60.7
1978–1980	65.0	68.8	75.6	83.2	35.9	53.5	75.2	32.1	63.5	65.1	79.5	59.3
1981–1983	63.4	68.6	75.6	81.9	34.6	58.3	74.1	28.6	57.3	61.0	75.2	55.0
EEC												
1969–1971	36.1	41.1	51.8	58.5	8.8	23.4	31.3	14.1	17.9	27.5	40.8	24.8
1972–1974	35.0	40.0	51.5	57.9	7.1	21.3	29.1	16.6	15.3	25.3	38.4	22.0
1975–1977	33.5	38.3	51.4	56.2	5.5	16.2	26.8	16.5	16.7	27.1	40.5	21.3
1978–1980	34.4	39.7	52.7	58.2	6.0	16.5	27.3	16.0	15.2	26.4	40.1	20.8
1981–1983	31.3	37.1	51.2	55.4	5.3	17.3	24.6	12.4	10.9	23.2	37.1	17.3
EFTA												
1969–1971	6.6	7.7	9.1	15.8	2.0	3.5	4.6	4.6	0.0	3.8	4.1	3.7
1972–1974	6.3	7.2	8.4	16.2	1.9	3.2	4.6	5.0	3.4	3.7	3.8	3.7
1975–1977	5.9	6.8	8.2	15.6	1.4	2.6	4.3	5.8	3.6	3.5	4.5	3.1
1978–1980	6.0	7.0	8.8	13.5	1.6	2.5	4.4	5.3	2.8	3.5	4.4	3.1
1981–1983	5.6	6.8	9.1	13.5	1.4	2.5	3.6	5.2	1.8	3.2	4.4	2.6

Table S.2 continued

Origin	Destination: Developed market economy countries							Socialist countries		Developing countries		
	World	Total	EEC	EFTA	Japan	USA	Other	Eastern Europe	Asia	Total	OPEC	Other
Japan												
1969–1971	6.4	4.9	1.7	2.6	—	15.5	6.1	1.4	17.9	13.9	11.2	14.5
1972–1974	6.6	4.8	2.2	2.9	—	14.2	6.9	2.2	23.7	14.6	14.3	14.7
1975–1977	6.8	4.7	2.2	3.1	—	13.2	6.7	2.9	26.2	14.1	14.5	13.9
1978–1980	6.7	4.7	2.4	2.5	—	13.6	6.2	2.7	24.7	13.3	14.2	12.9
1981–1983	7.8	6.1	3.1	3.4	—	16.2	8.3	2.8	22.3	13.3	14.9	12.6
United States												
1969–1971	13.2	13.1	9.7	6.8	27.0	—	38.7	1.4	0.0	21.0	21.4	20.9
1972–1974	11.8	11.1	7.8	5.4	21.5	—	34.2	2.6	8.5	18.6	18.6	18.6
1975–1977	11.3	10.5	7.4	5.4	17.5	—	34.2	3.4	2.4	17.5	18.1	17.2
1978–1980	10.7	9.4	7.1	5.2	17.4	—	33.5	3.5	11.8	16.6	14.9	17.2
1981–1983	11.2	10.1	7.7	6.1	18.0	—	34.1	2.5	13.2	15.6	13.1	16.7
All other developed market economy countries												
1969–1971	9.4	11.1	6.7	3.0	15.5	31.2	4.6	3.2	10.7	6.0	4.1	6.4
1972–1974	8.5	9.8	5.6	3.2	14.2	27.8	5.1	4.2	10.2	5.7	5.1	5.8
1975–1977	7.7	8.9	5.1	3.0	13.6	24.5	3.8	4.2	9.5	5.2	5.3	5.2
1978–1980	7.2	8.0	4.6	3.8	11.0	20.9	3.7	4.7	9.0	5.4	5.8	5.2
1981–1983	7.6	8.5	4.6	3.5	9.9	22.3	3.5	5.8	9.1	5.7	5.7	5.8
Socialist countries												
Eastern Europe												
1969–1971	9.8	3.2	3.6	6.0	3.4	0.5	3.4	64.4	39.3	6.4	7.1	6.2
1972–1974	8.6	3.3	3.6	6.5	2.7	0.7	3.3	58.0	27.1	5.8	5.1	5.9
1975–1977	8.7	3.5	3.8	7.4	2.3	0.8	4.2	54.7	27.4	5.2	4.2	5.7
1978–1980	8.2	3.5	3.9	7.1	1.7	0.7	4.6	55.5	20.8	5.3	4.3	5.6
1981–1983	8.8	4.0	4.9	8.6	1.2	0.5	4.9	57.4	20.0	5.9	5.5	6.0

306

Table S.2 continued

Destination Origin	World	Developed market economy countries						Socialist countries		Developing countries		
		Total	EEC	EFTA	Japan	USA	Other	Eastern Europe	Asia	Total	OPEC	Other
Asia												
1969–1971	0.8	0.4	0.4	0.0	2.0	0.0	0.3	1.8	—	2.1	1.0	2.1
1972–1974	0.8	0.5	0.3	0.2	2.7	0.1	0.2	1.8	—	1.8	1.3	1.9
1975–1977	0.8	0.5	0.3	0.1	2.6	0.2	0.3	1.7	—	1.5	0.9	1.8
1978–1980	1.0	0.6	0.3	0.2	3.2	0.3	0.4	1.9	—	1.9	1.1	2.2
1981–1983	1.3	0.8	0.4	0.2	4.1	0.7	0.4	1.4	—	2.4	0.8	3.0
Developing countries and territories												
1969–1971	17.7	18.4	17.1	6.8	41.2	25.9	11.3	9.2	14.3	19.4	11.2	21.1
1972–1974	22.4	23.4	20.7	7.7	49.9	33.4	15.8	9.7	13.6	24.4	13.5	27.1
1975–1977	25.3	26.8	21.6	9.2	57.3	42.5	19.5	11.0	15.5	25.9	12.1	31.8
1978–1980	25.9	27.1	20.2	9.4	59.2	45.4	19.9	10.5	15.7	27.6	15.2	32.6
1981–1983	26.5	26.6	19.1	9.3	60.0	40.5	20.6	12.6	21.8	30.7	18.5	35.9
OPEC												
1969–1971	6.0	6.6	7.5	1.7	17.6	4.7	4.6	1.1	0.0	6.0	1.0	7.0
1972–1974	10.7	11.8	12.2	2.9	28.3	10.5	8.3	2.0	0.0	10.8	1.7	13.1
1975–1977	13.4	14.9	13.2	4.2	36.5	17.9	11.5	2.6	1.2	13.0	1.6	17.9
1978–1980	13.6	15.3	12.2	5.2	37.7	21.2	11.3	2.6	1.1	13.1	2.6	17.3
1981–1983	12.4	13.3	10.9	4.7	38.3	12.8	10.2	2.6	0.5	14.0	3.6	18.5
All other developing countries and territories												
1969–1971	11.7	11.7	9.6	5.1	23.6	21.2	6.7	8.1	14.3	13.4	10.2	14.1
1972–1974	11.7	11.6	8.6	4.7	21.5	22.9	7.5	7.7	13.6	13.5	11.8	14.0
1975–1977	11.8	12.0	8.4	5.1	20.8	24.6	7.9	8.4	14.3	12.9	10.5	13.9
1978–1980	12.3	11.9	8.0	4.2	21.5	24.2	8.6	7.9	14.6	14.5	12.6	15.3
1981–1983	14.1	13.4	8.2	4.5	21.8	27.7	10.4	10.0	21.4	16.7	15.0	17.5

Source: UNCTAD, *Handbook of International Trade and Development Statistics 1985* (New York: UN, 1985), pp. 64–65.

307

Table S.3 *Import structure by origin and by major commodity groups, 1970–82*

Commodity groups	Year	World	Developed market economy countries	Developing countries and territories Total	OPEC	Other	Socialist countries of Eastern Europe Total	USSR	Socialist countries of Asia	Developed m Total	Europe EEC	EFT
Value (millions of dollars):												
All products	**1970**	**57,338**	**41,356**	**10,866**	**3,465**	**7,401**	**4,029**	**2,684**	**1,087**	**18,740**	**15,808**	**2,2**
	1975	200,407	137,978	49,083	24,291	24,792	10,231	6,165	3,115	65,067	55,383	6,8
	1982	477,687	291,224	144,961	65,300	79,661	29,557	18,323	11,945	138,014	113,440	15,4
Share by origin (%):												
All products	**1970**	**100.0**	**72.1**	**19.0**	**6.0**	**12.9**	**7.0**	**4.7**	**1.9**	**32.7**	**27.6**	3
	1975	**100.0**	**68.8**	**24.5**	**12.1**	**12.4**	**5.1**	**3.1**	**1.6**	**32.5**	**27.6**	3
	1982	**100.0**	**61.0**	**30.3**	**13.7**	**16.7**	**6.2**	**3.8**	**2.5**	**28.9**	**23.7**	3
All food items	1970	100.0	62.1	27.8	1.5	26.3	4.5	2.8	5.6	21.3	18.3	1
(SITC 0+1+22+4)	1975	100.0	61.4	28.9	1.4	27.5	4.4	2.3	5.3	21.0	18.9	1
	1982	100.0	60.4	30.5	2.1	28.4	4.6	1.5	4.5	24.8	22.1	1
Agricultural raw materials	1970	100.0	44.8	48.6	7.4	41.3	4.7	3.4	1.9	10.5	6.6	
(SITC −22−27−28)	1975	100.0	49.5	41.5	8.2	33.3	6.3	4.2	2.7	12.4	7.3	3
	1982	100.0	51.1	38.0	5.1	32.9	8.3	4.2	2.6	13.5	6.7	5
Ores and metals	1970	100.0	78.3	14.8	2.7	12.1	6.3	3.5	0.6	28.2	25.6	
(SITC 27+28+67+68)	1975	100.0	85.7	10.2	0.8	9.5	3.4	1.5	0.6	32.5	29.3	
	1982	100.0	73.9	19.4	2.0	17.4	4.6	1.7	2.2	27.5	22.1	
Fuels (SITC 3)	1970	100.0	13.4	82.4	64.2	18.3	4.0	3.3	0.2	5.2	4.8	(
	1975	100.0	6.8	89.7	76.8	13.0	3.3	2.8	0.2	3.2	3.0	(
	1982	100.0	9.3	84.7	63.6	21.0	4.5	4.0	1.5	4.2	3.9	(
Manufactured goods	1970	100.0	84.2	8.4	0.3	8.1	5.9	3.0	1.6	42.5	35.6	5
(SITC 5 to 8 less (67+68))	1975	100.0	85.0	9.6	0.7	8.9	4.2	1.7	1.2	44.1	37.1	5
	1982	100.0	79.3	14.0	1.5	12.6	4.1	1.6	2.5	39.4	32.1	4
Share by major commodity groups (%):												
All food items	1970	13.7	11.8	20.1	3.3	28.0	8.9	8.3	40.5	9.0	9.1	6
(SITC 0+1+22+4)	1975	12.9	11.5	15.2	1.5	28.6	11.2	9.8	43.9	8.4	8.8	5
	1982	11.1	11.0	11.1	1.7	18.8	8.2	4.2	19.9	9.5	10.3	4
Agricultural raw materials	1970	4.2	2.6	10.8	5.1	13.4	2.8	3.0	4.1	1.4	1.0	3
(SITC 2−22−27−28)	1975	2.7	1.9	4.5	1.8	7.2	3.3	3.7	4.7	1.0	0.7	3
	1982	2.5	2.1	3.1	0.9	4.9	3.3	2.7	2.6	1.2	0.7	4
Ores and metals	1970	8.1	8.8	6.4	3.7	7.6	7.3	6.1	2.6	7.0	7.6	3
(SITC 27+28+67+68)	1975	8.3	10.3	3.4	0.5	6.3	5.6	4.1	3.4	8.3	8.8	4
	1982	6.3	7.7	4.1	0.9	6.6	4.7	2.8	5.5	6.1	5.9	3
Fuels (SITC 3)	1970	8.0	1.5	34.6	84.5	11.3	4.5	5.6	0.7	1.3	1.4	0
	1975	14.6	1.4	53.5	92.4	15.3	9.4	13.4	1.8	1.5	1.6	0
	1982	19.3	3.0	53.9	90.0	24.4	14.1	20.2	11.5	2.8	3.2	0
Manufactured goods	1970	61.8	72.1	27.3	3.1	38.7	51.7	40.1	51.1	80.3	79.9	84
(SITC 5 to 8 (67+68))	1975	58.3	72.0	22.9	3.6	41.9	47.5	31.4	44.6	79.3	78.3	85
	1982	57.5	74.8	26.6	6.1	43.4	38.4	24.4	57.4	78.4	77.7	86
Annual average growth rates (%):												
All products	**70–82**	**19.3**	**17.7**	**24.1**	**27.7**	**21.9**	**18.1**	**17.4**	**22.1**	**18.1**	**17.8**	17
All food items	70–82	17.2	16.9	18.1	20.9	17.9	17.3	10.9	15.1	18.7	19.1	14
Agricultural raw materials	70–82	14.1	15.4	11.8	10.7	12.0	19.6	16.3	17.5	16.6	14.2	19
Ores and metals	70–82	16.9	16.3	19.5	13.9	20.5	13.7	9.9	30.1	16.6	15.4	17
Fuels	70–82	28.5	24.6	28.8	28.4	30.0	29.8	30.6	53.5	26.4	26.2	19
Manufactured goods	70–82	18.6	18.0	23.8	35.0	23.1	15.2	12.6	23.3	17.9	17.6	17

Source: UNCTAD, *Handbooks of International Trade and Development Statistics 1985* (New Yor
UN, 1985), pp. 94–95.

USA	Canada	Japan	Australia New Zealand	South Africa	Total	LAIA	Africa	West Asia	South and South-east Asia	Oceania	Year
		nomy countries by region					*Developing countries and territories by region*				
						America		*Asia*			
12,258	1,192	7,581	1,014	446	3,340	2,629	1,284	2,138	4,093	10	1970
37,758	2,895	27,458	3,478	921	11,576	8,912	4,964	18,512	13,966	67	1975
75,201	6,657	61,887	7,279	1,568	29,573	24,059	9,781	54,312	50,976	319	1982
21.4	2.1	13.2	1.8	0.8	5.8	4.6	2.2	3.7	7.1	0.0	1970
18.8	1.4	13.7	1.7	0.5	5.8	4.4	2.5	9.2	7.0	0.0	1975
15.7	1.4	13.0	1.5	0.3	6.2	5.0	2.0	11.4	10.7	0.1	1982
25.5	4.3	4.2	5.7	1.0	8.4	6.7	4.7	2.5	12.1	0.1	1970
27.2	3.4	1.4	7.4	0.9	10.9	8.1	3.8	1.8	12.4	0.1	1975
22.8	3.0	1.8	7.3	—	9.4	7.8	3.4	4.0	13.4	0.3	1982
20.7	2.2	6.5	4.3	0.6	10.1	9.0	7.2	2.0	29.4	0.0	1970
23.0	2.1	7.6	3.6	0.6	8.1	6.4	3.4	2.5	27.4	0.0	1975
23.0	3.4	6.6	3.9	—	5.7	4.6	3.2	2.0	26.9	0.2	1982
17.1	4.4	24.6	2.3	1.7	5.5	4.9	1.9	0.7	6.8	0.0	1970
14.1	2.2	33.7	2.4	0.8	3.7	3.3	1.5	1.1	3.8	0.2	1975
8.6	3.4	30.1	3.0	—	5.7	5.2	2.1	2.8	8.6	0.2	1982
6.2	0.1	0.8	0.8	0.4	31.7	26.6	6.3	35.6	8.7	0.0	1970
2.4	0.1	0.6	0.3	0.1	16.5	12.8	9.4	55.6	8.3	0.0	1975
3.6	0.2	0.2	0.9	—	16.4	13.1	6.2	49.0	13.1	0.0	1982
21.7	1.7	16.5	0.7	0.7	2.0	1.2	1.0	0.6	4.7	0.0	1970
20.6	1.3	17.7	0.7	0.4	2.4	1.9	0.7	1.2	5.3	0.0	1975
19.5	1.2	18.3	0.4	—	2.5	2.1	0.4	2.1	9.0	0.0	1982
16.4	28.3	4.4	44.5	16.8	19.9	20.1	28.9	9.1	23.3	40.0	1970
18.6	30.5	1.3	55.2	24.2	24.3	23.5	19.5	2.5	23.0	34.3	1975
16.1	23.6	1.5	52.8	—	16.7	17.1	18.5	3.9	13.9	55.2	1982
4.1	4.4	2.1	10.3	3.4	7.3	8.2	13.5	2.2	17.3	0.0	1970
3.3	3.9	1.5	5.6	3.6	3.8	3.9	3.7	0.7	10.6	3.0	1975
3.6	6.0	1.3	6.4	—	2.3	2.3	3.9	0.4	6.2	7.5	1982
6.5	17.3	15.1	10.7	17.5	7.7	8.7	6.8	1.4	7.7	0.0	1970
6.2	12.8	20.3	11.2	14.0	5.3	6.1	5.1	1.0	4.5	37.3	1975
3.5	15.5	14.8	12.4	—	5.9	6.6	6.5	1.5	5.1	21.9	1982
2.3	0.3	0.5	3.5	4.0	43.3	46.2	22.5	76.0	9.7	10.0	1970
1.9	0.9	0.6	2.8	4.0	41.6	41.9	55.4	87.8	17.3	6.0	1975
4.5	3.1	0.4	11.7	—	51.3	50.5	58.3	83.3	23.7	2.2	1982
62.8	49.3	77.3	25.7	58.5	21.3	16.2	27.9	10.4	41.0	30.0	1970
63.6	51.5	75.4	22.1	53.4	24.5	24.3	16.1	7.8	44.1	17.9	1975
71.3	51.4	81.4	15.1	—	23.5	23.5	10.9	10.8	48.5	10.0	1982
16.3	15.4	19.1	17.9	11.0	19.9	20.3	18.4	30.9	23.4	33.4	70–82
16.1	13.7	8.9	19.5	—	18.2	18.7	14.1	22.0	18.2	37.1	70–82
15.1	18.5	14.3	13.3	—	8.9	8.1	6.8	14.1	13.3	—	70–82
10.3	14.4	18.9	19.4	—	17.3	17.5	18.0	31.6	19.2	—	70–82
22.8	42.3	15.8	30.5	—	21.6	21.1	28.2	31.9	32.8	17.6	70–82
17.6	15.8	19.6	12.7	—	20.9	24.0	9.5	31.3	25.1	21.8	70–82

309

Table S.4 *Sources of financing of current account deficits: developing countries and territories, excluding major petroleum exporters, 1970–83 (millions of dollars)*

	1970	1973	1975	1979	1980	1981	1982	1983
1. Current account deficit	**−9,531**	**−9,351**	**−34,035**	**−47,069**	**−71,422**	**−81,794**	**−70,906**	**−53,146**
2. Long-term financing	**9,317**	**16,869**	**34,638**	**64,761**	**62,799**	**72,720**	**64,108**	**52,107**
Bilateral	*8,137*	*14,308*	*30,094*	*57,059*	*52,947*	*62,941*	*53,372*	*40,152*
Official development								
assistance (ODA)	3,202	5,415	11,446	14,495	17,539	17,250	14,963	13,855
DAC member countries	3,202	3,605	5,546	9,501	10,669	11,145	10,731	10,011
OPEC member countries	—	1,810	5,900	4,994	6,870	6,105	4,232	3,844
Other official	542	1,779	2,567	2,446	3,675	3,208	3,289	5,037
DAC member countries	542	1,700	1,301	2,410	3,651	3,214	3,258	3,206
OPEC member countries	—	79	1,266	36	24	−6	31	1,831
Private flows from DAC								
member countries	4,393	7,114	16,081	40,118	31,733	42,484	35,120	21,260
Overseas direct								
investment	2,243	3,168	7,045	12,403	8,001	12,243	11,465	8,093
Export credits	1,650	593	1,097	5,909	8,879	7,893	5,385	2,501
Bilateral portfolio								
investment	380	2,931	7,971	21,218	14,281	22,631	17,976	11,453
International bond								
lending	120	422	−32	588	572	−284	294	−787
Multilateral	*1,076*	*2,143*	*4,154*	*7,100*	*8,871*	*9,046*	*10,037*	*11,097*
Official development								
assistance (ODA)	543	1,187	2,328	4,251	5,625	4,880	5,125	5,192
DAC member countries	543	1,187	2,306	4,026	5,365	4,531	4,786	4,891
OPEC member countries	—	—	22	225	260	349	339	301
Other official	533	956	1,826	2,849	3,246	4,166	4,912	5,905
DAC member countries	533	956	1,826	2,811	3,243	4,057	4,972	5,855
OPEC member countries	—	—	—	38	3	109	−60	50
Socialist countries	*104*	*418*	*390*	*552*	*981*	*733*	*699*	*858*
3. Short-term financing and								
errors and omissions	**3,033**	**−288**	**−4,606**	**−13,660**	**6,073**	**1,061**	**−11,636**	**−13,618**
4. Reserves and related								
items	**−2,819**	**−7,230**	**4,003**	**−4,032**	**2,550**	**8,013**	**18,434**	**14,657**
of which:								
Use of IMF credit	−430	72	1,815	598	1,684	5,147	4,961	8,996

Source: UNCTAD, *Handbooks of International Trade and Development Statistics 1985* (New York: UN, 1985), p. 330.

Table S.5 Structure of financial flows from DAC member countries, OPEC member countries and multilateral agencies to developing countries and territories, (1970–83) (%)

Region and economic grouping	Total flows	ODA Total	ODA Bilateral Total	ODA Bilateral DAC	ODA Bilateral OPEC	ODA Multilateral Total	ODA Multilateral DAC	ODA Multilateral OPEC	Non-concessional Total	NC Bilateral Total	NC Bilateral DAC Total	NC Bilateral DAC Other official flows	NC Bilateral Private	NC Multilateral Total	NC Multilateral DAC	NC Multilateral OPEC	DAC official and private export credits
Total																	
1970	100.0	46.8	38.9	38.9	—	7.9	7.9	—	53.2	48.3	48.3	5.2	43.1	4.9	4.9	—	17.9
1973	100.0	47.8	38.7	29.3	9.4	9.1	9.1	—	52.2	46.6	45.9	8.8	37.1	5.7	5.7	—	9.7
1975	100.0	41.0	33.4	18.8	14.5	7.7	7.6	0.1	59.0	54.1	51.2	3.6	47.6	4.9	4.9	0.0	10.5
1979	100.0	36.9	28.9	19.7	9.2	8.1	7.7	0.3	63.1	58.0	57.9	3.5	54.3	5.1	4.7	0.3	12.1
1980	100.0	43.7	33.7	22.1	11.6	10.0	9.6	0.4	56.3	50.5	50.3	5.8	44.5	5.8	5.7	0.1	16.9
1981	100.0	35.4	27.4	18.8	8.7	8.0	7.6	0.4	64.6	58.5	58.5	4.5	54.0	6.1	5.7	0.4	11.8
1982	100.0	36.8	27.7	20.9	6.8	9.1	8.6	0.4	63.2	55.6	55.6	6.4	49.2	7.6	7.6	0.0	11.4
1983	100.0	40.3	30.0	23.2	6.8	10.3	9.9	0.4	59.7	49.9	46.7	4.9	41.9	9.8	9.6	0.2	13.6
America																	
1970	100.0	27.7	20.0	20.0	—	7.6	7.6	—	72.3	63.8	63.8	1.9	61.9	8.5	8.5	—	19.1
1973	100.0	17.1	11.8	11.8	0.0	5.3	5.3	—	82.9	75.0	75.0	5.2	69.8	7.9	7.9	—	5.8
1975	100.0	16.9	11.4	11.4	0.0	5.4	5.4	—	83.1	75.3	72.9	6.1	66.9	7.9	7.9	—	7.6
1979	100.0	11.4	8.4	8.2	0.1	3.0	2.9	0.1	88.6	82.7	82.7	1.7	81.0	5.9	5.9	0.1	8.8
1980	100.0	12.6	8.8	8.7	0.0	3.9	3.7	0.1	87.4	79.2	79.2	4.7	74.5	8.2	8.2	0.1	18.8
1981	100.0	10.2	7.3	7.0	0.3	2.9	2.7	0.1	89.8	82.7	82.7	2.7	80.0	7.1	7.0	0.1	10.9
1982	100.0	10.8	8.2	8.2	—	2.6	2.5	0.1	89.2	81.7	81.4	5.8	75.6	7.6	7.6	0.0	5.6
1983	100.0	16.3	12.3	12.3	0.0	4.0	3.9	0.1	83.7	71.0	70.9	2.1	68.8	12.7	12.7	0.0	11.0
Africa																	
1970	100.0	53.7	41.4	41.4	—	12.3	12.3	—	46.3	44.3	44.3	1.8	42.5	2.0	2.0	—	16.5
1973	100.0	63.6	50.5	37.8	12.7	13.1	13.1	—	36.4	32.6	29.7	8.5	21.3	3.7	3.7	—	13.9
1975	100.0	53.2	44.5	22.8	21.7	8.7	8.5	0.2	46.8	43.3	36.3	2.2	34.1	3.5	3.5	0.0	23.1
1979	100.0	51.8	38.5	31.8	6.8	13.3	12.5	0.8	48.2	43.4	43.2	3.7	39.5	4.8	3.9	0.9	24.5
1980	100.0	53.4	39.8	33.6	6.2	13.6	12.7	0.8	46.6	42.5	42.4	5.5	36.9	4.1	3.6	0.5	22.9
1981	100.0	53.4	39.2	34.8	4.4	14.2	13.4	0.9	46.6	41.9	42.0	6.7	35.3	4.7	3.8	0.8	18.5
1982	100.0	49.5	36.8	32.9	3.9	12.7	11.8	0.9	50.5	46.4	46.4	7.3	39.1	4.1	4.3	-0.3	15.4
1983	100.0	49.7	36.4	33.2	3.1	13.4	12.5	0.9	50.3	44.5	37.4	6.1	31.3	5.8	5.6	0.2	18.8

Table S.5 *continued*

Region and economic grouping	Total flows	ODA Total	ODA Bilateral Total	ODA Bilateral DAC	ODA Bilateral OPEC	ODA Multilateral Total	ODA Multilateral DAC	ODA Multilateral OPEC	Non-concessional Total	Non-concessional Bilateral Total	Non-concessional Bilateral DAC Total	Non-concessional Bilateral DAC Other official flows	Non-concessional Bilateral DAC Private flows	Non-concessional Bilateral OPEC	Non-concessional Multilateral Total	Non-concessional Multilateral DAC	Non-concessional Multilateral OPEC	DAC official and private export credits
Asia																		
1970	100.0	56.5	50.2	50.2	—	6.3	6.3	—	43.5	38.9	38.9	10.2	28.7	—	4.6	4.6	—	21.3
1973	100.0	58.3	46.2	41.3	4.9	12.1	12.1	—	41.7	35.1	35.1	6.3	28.8	—	6.6	6.6	—	18.1
1975	100.0	47.7	36.9	23.4	13.5	10.8	10.7	0.1	52.3	45.6	44.5	3.7	40.8	—	6.7	6.7	0.5	9.2
1979	100.0	50.6	39.3	22.1	17.2	11.3	10.9	0.4	49.4	42.0	41.7	4.4	37.2	—	7.4	7.0	0.1	16.6
1980	100.0	76.4	55.5	30.0	25.5	20.9	20.4	0.5	23.6	14.2	13.6	8.8	4.9	—	9.4	9.3	0.6	27.3
1981	100.0	48.4	36.7	21.2	15.5	11.7	11.1	0.6	51.6	42.5	42.4	4.9	38.5	—	9.2	8.6	0.6	14.3
1982	100.0	52.7	36.9	22.8	14.1	15.8	15.1	0.6	47.3	33.5	33.3	4.9	28.6	—	14.0	13.8	0.3	19.1
1983	100.0	46.9	32.5	21.9	10.7	14.4	13.8	0.6	53.1	38.1	34.1	5.5	28.6	—	15.0	14.6	0.4	16.6
West Asia																		
1970	100.0	45.0	29.2	29.2	—	15.8	15.8	—	55.0	47.4	47.4	12.4	34.9	—	7.6	7.6	—	33.8
1973	100.0	192.2	161.3	64.9	96.4	30.9	30.9	—	-92.2	-147.9	-148.5	35.9	-184.4	—	55.7	55.7	—	131.9
1975	100.0	33.7	30.1	4.2	25.8	3.7	3.4	0.2	66.3	60.8	58.8	3.5	55.3	—	5.5	5.5	0.0	9.7
1979	100.0	50.5	44.7	8.7	36.1	5.7	5.0	0.7	49.5	45.8	45.1	2.4	42.8	—	3.8	3.3	0.5	15.1
1980	100.0	111.7	102.1	23.0	79.1	9.7	8.2	1.5	-11.7	-20.2	-22.2	13.6	-35.8	—	8.4	8.1	0.4	36.3
1981	100.0	78.3	70.4	14.7	55.6	7.9	6.5	1.4	21.7	13.1	13.1	10.0	3.3	—	8.5	7.2	1.3	9.1
1982	100.0	58.6	50.8	13.3	37.5	7.8	7.3	0.5	41.4	34.4	34.9	4.5	30.4	—	7.0	6.1	0.9	21.4
1983	100.0	49.1	43.6	12.0	31.6	5.5	4.8	0.7	50.9	43.8	35.0	1.4	33.5	—	7.1	6.5	0.6	30.9
South and South-east Asia																		
1970	100.0	61.7	57.1	57.1	—	4.6	4.6	—	38.3	33.9	33.9	10.3	23.6	—	4.3	4.3	—	20.1
1973	100.0	56.6	44.4	44.1	0.3	12.2	12.2	—	43.4	38.8	38.8	5.3	33.5	—	4.6	4.6	—	13.7
1975	100.0	58.0	42.4	36.1	6.3	15.6	15.6	—	42.0	34.3	33.4	4.1	29.3	—	7.7	7.7	—	9.4
1979	100.0	52.2	35.6	34.6	1.1	16.6	16.3	0.2	47.8	36.6	36.6	5.7	31.0	—	11.2	10.6	0.5	18.6
1980	100.0	56.1	33.2	29.8	3.5	22.8	22.7	0.1	43.9	34.9	34.9	6.0	28.8	—	9.1	9.1	0.0	21.8
1981	100.0	37.2	24.3	23.6	0.7	12.9	12.5	0.3	62.8	53.1	53.1	2.0	51.1	—	9.6	9.3	0.3	16.3
1982	100.0	42.1	24.9	24.0	1.0	17.1	16.5	0.6	57.9	42.4	42.4	4.5	37.9	—	15.5	15.5	0.0	16.1
1983	100.0	40.8	24.6	23.4	1.2	16.2	15.7	0.5	59.2	42.3	40.5	6.5	34.0	—	16.9	16.5	0.3	9.6

Table S.5 *continued*

Region and economic grouping	Total flows	ODA							Non-concessional								DAC official and private export credits
		Total	Bilateral			Multilateral			Total	Bilateral				Multilateral			
			Total	DAC	OPEC	Total	DAC	OPEC		Total	DAC Other official flows	Private flows	OPEC	Total	DAC	OPEC	
Oceania																	
1970	100.0	59.5	58.2	58.2	—	1.3	1.3	—	40.5	40.4	4.1	36.3	—	0.2	0.2	—	6.5
1973	100.0	70.6	69.3	69.3	—	1.3	1.3	—	29.4	27.2	3.1	24.1	—	2.2	2.2	—	0.8
1975	100.0	94.5	91.8	91.8	—	2.7	2.7	—	5.5	2.6	5.2	-2.6	—	3.0	3.0	—	-4.3
1979	100.0	89.0	85.3	85.1	0.2	3.7	3.6	0.1	11.0	9.1	4.8	4.4	—	1.9	1.9	—	0.5
1980	100.0	89.1	82.5	82.5	0.0	6.6	6.5	0.1	10.9	8.3	2.9	5.4	—	2.6	2.6	—	1.0
1981	100.0	94.0	86.6	86.6	0.0	7.4	7.2	0.2	6.0	3.6	7.6	-3.9	—	2.4	2.4	—	3.2
1982	100.0	73.7	68.9	68.9	—	4.8	4.7	0.1	26.3	24.0	11.1	12.8	—	2.3	2.3	—	9.8
1983	100.0	74.1	66.6	66.6	—	7.5	7.5	—	25.9	23.0	11.0	12.0	—	2.9	2.9	—	14.5
By major category																	
Major petroleum exporters																	
1970	100.0	36.4	29.3	29.3	—	7.1	7.1	—	63.6	58.6	5.9	52.7	—	5.0	5.0	—	20.4
1973	100.0	36.5	28.1	21.8	6.3	8.4	8.4	—	63.5	55.8	5.4	48.5	1.9	7.7	7.7	—	21.5
1975	100.0	24.7	20.5	9.1	11.3	4.3	4.1	0.2	75.3	69.9	4.7	64.2	1.0	5.4	5.4	0.3	28.6
1979	100.0	27.4	25.0	9.0	16.0	2.4	2.2	0.2	72.6	66.0	2.0	63.5	0.5	6.6	6.3	0.3	33.5
1980	100.0	24.1	22.3	8.9	13.4	1.8	1.7	0.1	75.9	68.4	5.1	62.7	0.6	7.5	7.5	0.0	26.7
1981	100.0	19.6	17.5	7.4	10.1	2.1	2.0	0.1	80.4	73.1	4.9	68.2	—	7.3	6.7	0.6	19.9
1982	100.0	19.8	17.7	9.1	8.7	2.1	2.0	0.0	80.2	72.8	13.0	59.8	—	7.4	7.8	-0.4	19.5
1983	100.0	18.6	16.4	9.1	7.3	2.2	2.1	0.1	81.4	73.8	1.9	68.5	3.4	7.6	7.2	0.4	45.9

Source: UNCTAD, *Handbook of International Trade and Development Statistics 1985* (New York: UN, 1985), pp. 334–5.

313

Table S.6 Total financial flows (net) from DAC member countries, OPEC mem[ber] countries and from multilateral agencies to developing countries and territories, 1970–[...] (millions of dollars)

Type of flow / Region, economic grouping, country or area	Total financial flows[1]								Concessional			
	1970	1973	1975	1979	1980	1981	1982	1983	1970	1973	1975	
Unspecified world	593.3	2,080.9	8,504.1	12,047.7	13,494.5	13,053.8	7,166.3	7,747.3	345.3	1,707.5	3,130.8	3,
Developing countries and territories	13,362.1	21,469.9	47,913.9	75,212.2	76,571.8	91,479.1	81,094.0	69,125.3	6,252.8	10,261.9	19,666.8	27,
By major category												
Major petroleum exporters	2,521.0	3,351.9	9,396.9	11,940.4	15,147.1	17,868.9	15,067.3	13,437.0	917.9	1,224.1	2,323.8	3,
Other developing countries and territories	8,656.9	14,869.8	25,378.7	42,714.3	47,515.1	54,629.9	53,999.5	43,165.6	4,712.8	6,956.7	13,776.4	19,
of which:												
Major exporters of manufactures	2,064.0	4,650.2	4,831.3	10,655.1	9,999.2	15,639.0	13,173.4	8,997.9	512.7	442.4	430.4	
Least developed countries	664.5	1,744.2	3,917.6	6,184.3	7,620.6	6,716.2	7,294.1	6,706.5	589.1	1,449.1	3,364.8	5,
Remaining countries	5,915.7	8,443.7	16,577.1	25,830.1	29,868.0	32,228.7	33,493.5	27,404.8	3,602.0	5,047.4	9,944.0	13,
By income group (per capita GDP in 1980)												
Over 1,500 dollars	4,906.7	8,776.4	13,486.0	24,588.4	26,045.8	32,355.7	29,552.7	21,172.6	1,326.6	1,536.1	2,361.5	2,
500–1,500 dollars	3,062.4	3,639.1	7,900.7	16,774.1	18,064.7	20,299.0	20,321.8	17,540.5	1,581.7	2,229.8	3,989.6	8,
Under 500 dollars	3,151.2	5,727.8	13,384.0	13,265.5	18,457.8	19,828.0	19,170.5	17,829.7	2,689.9	4,373.5	9,737.4	11,
Memo item												
China	—	—	—	129.0	323.6	1,888.3	678.1	833.7	—	—	—	
Gibraltar	2.9	8.6	6.1	14.6	17.4	35.3	29.4	13.4	2.6	6.3	3.0	
Greece	90.0	148.3	328.6	275.6	770.9	131.7	78.7	19.8	-2.9	-11.4	9.4	
Israel	249.9	735.1	861.6	1,686.8	1,275.1	1,060.5	1,551.0	2,204.1	63.3	186.0	467.5	1,
Portugal	-37.0	21.0	197.0	818.2	425.4	963.5	1,053.4	545.7	-4.0	17.0	-3.7	
Spain	374.0	551.7	1,145.8	1,541.1	1,347.5	1,904.7	658.4	—	13.7	-7.8	-11.4	
Vietnam	441.4	467.6	315.1	446.2	201.7	302.5	137.6	91.1	436.6	478.1	310.3	3
Yugoslavia	149.5	413.7	468.3	1,531.9	1,175.7	461.3	189.1	431.8	-39.0	121.6	25.6	
Unspecified Europe	200.8	22.1	110.0	1,279.2	1,715.9	1,171.0	864.0	1,253.5	7.6	3.0	7.0	

Note:
[1] Including flows from multilateral agencies largely financed by OPEC member countries.

Source: UNCTAD, *Handbook of International Trade and Development Statistics 1985* (New Yo[rk]: UN, 1985), pp. 344–5.

				Non-concessional							
1980	*1981*	*1982*	*1983*	*1970*	*1973*	*1975*	*1979*	*1980*	*1981*	*1982*	*1983*
5,191.7	**5,023.4**	**3,967.9**	**4,317.4**	**248.0**	**373.4**	**5,373.3**	**8,065.1**	**8,302.8**	**8,030.4**	**3,198.4**	**3,429.9**
33,447.6	**32,404.1**	**29,831.9**	**28,763.0**	**7,109.3**	**11,207.9**	**28,247.0**	**47,437.3**	**43,124.2**	**59,075.0**	**51,262.1**	**40,362.3**
3,656.6	3,506.4	2,984.1	2,583.7	1,603.0	2,127.8	7,073.1	8,669.8	11,490.5	14,362.6	12,083.2	10,853.3
23,455.9	22,730.5	21,579.8	20,788.8	3,944.0	7,913.2	11,602.3	23,363.6	24,059.2	31,899.4	32,419.7	22,376.8
256.1	648.5	294.0	194.7	1,551.3	4,207.8	4,400.8	10,350.7	9,743.1	14,990.4	12,879.4	8,803.2
6,373.2	6,061.2	6,490.2	6,186.8	75.4	295.1	552.8	882.1	1,247.4	655.0	803.9	519.7
16,803.8	15,997.7	14,763.6	14,370.8	2,313.7	3,396.4	6,633.1	12,127.7	13,064.2	16,231.0	18,729.9	13,034.3
3,245.1	3,562.1	2,883.2	2,978.9	3,580.1	7,240.3	11,124.6	21,856.2	22,800.7	28,793.6	26,669.5	18,193.7
9,860.6	9,736.6	8,504.2	7,614.7	1,480.7	1,409.2	3,911.1	8,147.4	8,204.1	10,562.4	11,817.6	9,925.8
13,982.4	12,915.6	13,147.2	12,744.0	461.3	1,354.3	3,646.6	2,016.4	4,475.4	6,912.5	6,023.3	5,085.7
66.1	476.9	524.0	627.5	—	—	—	112.1	257.5	1,411.4	154.1	206.2
11.1	7.4	3.1	3.4	0.3	2.3	3.1	8.0	6.2	27.9	26.3	10.0
40.1	13.9	12.1	12.7	92.9	159.6	319.2	245.7	730.8	117.8	66.6	7.1
892.2	772.4	857.4	1,344.9	186.5	549.1	394.0	502.1	382.9	288.1	693.6	859.2
113.0	82.3	49.2	45.3	-33.0	4.0	200.7	682.0	312.4	881.1	1,004.2	500.4
23.3	2.2	21.9	—	360.4	559.5	1,157.3	1,547.2	1,324.1	1,902.4	636.5	—
228.5	242.2	135.3	107.0	4.9	-10.4	4.8	109.8	-26.8	60.2	2.3	-15.9
-16.9	-14.8	-7.6	2.4	188.6	292.1	442.7	1,561.1	1,192.6	476.1	196.7	429.4
6.6	17.5	21.1	41.9	193.2	19.1	103.0	1,266.5	1,709.3	1,153.5	842.9	1,211.6

Table S.7   *Developing countries: Annual changes in terms of trade, 1968–86[1] (%)*

	Average 1968–77[2]	1978	1979	1980	1981	1982	1983	1984	1985	1986
Developing countries	**5.0**	**–6.8**	**10.9**	**16.7**	**3.0**	**–1.2**	**–3.9**	**1.2**	**–2.2**	**–11.7**
By region:										
Africa	3.8	–9.7	8.7	15.2	2.3	–4.8	–3.3	2.4	–3.0	–15.8
Asia	0.3	–2.5	2.5	–1.8	–4.7	–0.8	–0.6	1.1	–1.2	–2.3
Europe	–1.8	–0.2	–1.4	–3.9	0.3	–0.3	–1.2	–1.6	–1.0	7.5
Middle East	12.5	–10.0	24.8	41.3	14.0	2.2	–8.8	—	–3.5	–37.9
Western hemisphere	4.6	–9.4	6.6	7.0	–4.4	–5.8	–2.8	4.0	–3.0	–5.1
By predominant export:										
Fuel exporters	13.2	–10.3	26.8	43.8	11.8	0.1	–8.8	1.1	–4.2	–37.4
Non-fuel exporters	–0.3	–3.9	–1.2	–5.9	–5.3	–2.6	0.2	1.5	–1.2	3.6
Primary product exporters	0.6	–6.9	0.4	–7.9	–10.4	–6.2	0.9	3.5	–3.2	7.3
Agricultural exporters	1.6	–8.0	–0.3	–10.0	–10.9	–5.6	1.0	5.2	–3.3	7.9
Mineral exporters	–1.5	–4.4	1.3	–3.8	–8.1	–7.7	0.6	—	–2.6	5.7
Exporters of manufactures	–1.4	–1.3	–2.3	–5.8	–1.8	0.3	–0.8	—	0.1	2.2
Service and remittance countries	–0.9	–1.7	–4.1	2.2	0.6	–2.6	0.1	–0.3	0.6	–2.3
By financial criteria:										
Capital-exporting countries	14.8	–11.1	28.6	48.7	16.4	1.9	–9.4	—	–4.5	–42.7
Capital-importing countries	2.0	–5.3	4.1	3.9	–2.3	–2.6	–1.7	1.7	1.7	–4.4
Market borrowers	2.8	–5.7	6.2	8.0	–2.2	–3.0	–2.6	1.6	–1.6	–6.0
Official borrowers	1.5	–6.0	0.5	–7.4	–4.0	–2.2	2.2	4.7	–1.9	5.1
Diversified borrowers	–0.2	–3.3	–1.5	–5.1	–2.4	–1.7	–0.1	0.7	–1.9	–1.4
Countries with recent debt servicing problems	2.8	–7.1	6.5	6.3	–2.8	–4.8	–2.8	2.7	–2.5	–5.8
Countries without debt servicing problems	1.2	–3.7	2.1	1.7	–1.9	–0.8	–1.0	1.1	–1.0	–3.3
By miscellaneous criteria										
Capital-importing fuel exporters	11.0	–9.8	24.0	36.2	5.6	–2.5	–7.7	2.5	–3.8	–31.8
Fifteen heavily indebted countries	5.2	–8.1	9.8	13.3	–2.9	–4.5	–3.6	2.8	–3.1	–8.5
Small low-income countries	1.1	–5.7	–1.8	–11.6	–8.7	–4.4	6.3	6.8	–4.5	8.3
Sub-Saharan Africa[3]	1.6	–9.3	0.8	–5.4	–7.3	–6.5	1.2	5.0	–2.0	–1.9
By alternative analytical categories:										
Oil-exporting countries	14.8	–11.2	27.8	47.7	14.7	1.4	–9.4	0.8	–4.4	–40.7
Non-oil developing countries	—	–3.9	0.4	–3.8	–4.9	–3.1	–0.3	1.5	–1.4	0.9
Net oil exporters	2.2	–4.1	20.1	12.1	–4.6	–6.9	–2.9	2.9	–4.3	–21.2
Net oil importers	–0.4	–3.8	–2.6	–6.6	–5.0	–2.3	0.2	1.3	–0.8	5.4

Notes:
[1] Excluding China prior to 1978.   [3] Excluding Nigeria and South Africa.
[2] Compound annual rates of change.

Source: IMF, *World Economic Outlook*, April 1986, p. 209.

Index

global prosperity. It would also indicate that the choice between the two strategies is much more a matter of what is ultimately a *political* judgement about the state and future of the world economy, rather than a matter of firm *economic* analysis as it has usually been debated in the past.

Empirical evidence exists to support this view. Kavoussi has reported the results of an analysis of export performance during 1967–77, dividing it into a period of favourable market conditions (1967–73) and a period of unfavourable market conditions (1973–7). He found that, when a sample of some fifty developing countries was divided by certain criteria into free-trade–outward-oriented or trade-restrictive–inward-oriented, the correlation between export orientation and growth performance in the favourable period showed superior performance by the export-oriented countries; but in the less favourable, relatively restrictionist period there was no evidence of any such correlation. Thus he concludes:

> Free trade appears to enhance growth only when external demand is favourable. When foreign markets are slack, the association of the economy's growth with export-orientation tends to be quite weak. This result seems to imply that when free trade produces a moderate expansion of export earnings (when external demand is weak), the gains from openness are likely to be cancelled by its negative effects. On the other hand, when export-orientation leads to an exceptionally rapid expansion of export earnings (when external demand is strong), the benefits of openness clearly outweigh its costs.[19]

The ISI strategy may well appear to national decision-makers safer and more appealing on grounds other than growth rate arguments. ISI increases a country's national control over its own destiny and holds out the prospect that the growth could well be more stable from year to year, being less dependent on external conditions. On the other hand, one can also see that to an internationalist bureaucracy, such as the IMF, EOI may be preferable even in the absence of a superior growth performance since international integration is treated as a 'good thing' in itself. This difference may well explain a good deal of the controversy between the IMF and many LDC governments on the question of the right way of adjusting to debt-induced balance-of-payments pressure.

Another reason why unfavourable external conditions have led to a revival of ISI strategy is the strong emphasis, recently fortified by the African drought and famine, on the need for developing countries to reverse the heavy shift from net food exports to net food imports during the post-war period. This near unanimous emphasis on higher priority for domestic food production and restoration of food security and food sufficiency in fact amounts to a recommendation of import substitution – if not of ISI. Some of the sharpest critics of ISI are also among the keenest advocates of higher priority for domestic food production. There is nothing logically inconsistent in this: one can stress the advantages of ISI in agriculture and its disadvantages in industrialization. However, it does throw a certain onus on the critics of ISI to explain what exactly are the differences between the two sectors that account for advocacy of such different strategies for them.

The critics of ISI also often overestimate the freedom of LDCs to choose their industrialization strategy and underestimate the significance of external pressure in influencing the pattern and direction of resource allocation. Several problems that face the industrialization process of LDCs may be largely a result of the pressures exerted on LDCs by the imperfect markets of the advanced industrialized world. Donors and foreign investors might represent interests that could conflict with the national interest of a developing country. Donors, whether international agencies or governments, might attach tying and other types of conditionality on utilization of aid/loans; also inappropriate (e.g. too capital-intensive) design and selection of their projects might substantially contribute to inefficiency of investible resources. Similarly, foreign investors might pressurize the recipient government to implement policies, including prolongation of a high level of protective duties, to ensure a high level of profit. In such conditions, debates on optimal industrialization strategies may be beside the point, and strategies of coping with such external pressures may be more relevant.

Economic policy-makers in the West and in international economic organizations dominated by the West have however remained concerned with promoting the adoption of freer trade policies by the LDCs. This concern has manifested itself in policies aimed at the stabilization of export earnings and stimulating the growth of North–South trade. Some of these policies are reviewed below.